Germany were setting on a firm base the system of decipherment of Egyptian hieroglyphs which was begun by Young and finished by Champollion. The author is anonymous, but the contents of the book show that he was in touch with the early decipherers, and owed much of his information to them. Then we have two excellent little volumes on *Jerusalem*, by Dr. J. Kitto, whose articles in the *Bible Cyclopaedia* are still valuable. The decipherment of the Persian Cuneiform Inscriptions at Bahistûn and Persepolis aroused great interest throughout the learned world, and Dr. Kitto's two little volumes on *Persia, Ancient and Modern*, supplied the general reader with all he required to know about the country. The volume *Babylon and the Banks of the Euphrates*, published anonymously, was a truly admirable work. It included the results of Rich's researches at Babylon, and of Chesney's Expedition to the Euphrates, and a good account of Botta's work on the palace of Sargon II at Khorsabad, and Layard's excavations at Nineveh. The writer, who was probably W. S. W. Vaux or J. Bonomi, derived much of his information at first hand from Sir Henry Rawlinson. The amount of knowledge condensed in the 192 pages of this sixpenny book is, considering that it was published as far back as 1851, truly wonderful.

The transport of "Cleopatra's Needle" to London and its erection on the Thames Embankment in 1878, and the occupation of Egypt by the British in 1883, stirred up public interest in Egypt and the Near East to a remarkable degree, and the Committee of the Religious Tract Society decided that the time had come for the issue of a new series of volumes on the Archaeology and History of Egypt and Palestine and of Western Asia generally. More than thirty years had passed since any work on these subjects had appeared in their Sixpenny Monthly Library, and during this interval the progress of Egyptology and Assyriology had advanced by leaps and bounds. The excavations in Egypt had yielded large numbers of historical inscriptions, papyri, etc.; from the mounds of Nineveh and Babylon and Lower Babylonia innumerable inscribed tablets had been dug up, the Babylonian Accounts of the Flood and the Creation had been discovered and translated by George Smith, and the Holy Land and the Peninsula of Sinai had been surveyed and mapped. The long series of works entitled *By-Paths of Bible Knowledge,* which the Society published in 1884 and the following years, was warmly received and each volume was reprinted several times. During the Great War the stereotype plates of them were requisitioned by the Government for military purposes, and the publication of a set of entirely new works was decided upon. The two volumes which I had the honour of contributing to the By-Paths Series have been entirely re-written and enlarged throughout, and at the request of the Rev. C. H. Irwin, D.D., General Editor of the Religious Tract Society, I have prepared the present work, which is intended to take the place of *Cleopatra's Needle,* by the late Rev. J. King.

Mr. James King was born at Jedburgh in October, 1839. He gained a Foundation Scholarship at Durham in 1863; he took the degrees of B.A. in 1866, M.A. in 1869, and Bachelor of Divinity in 1894. Between 1868 and 1872 he held two curacies in London, and during this period he became acquainted with Mr. (later Sir) Walter Besant, the Honorary Secretary of the Palestine Exploration Fund, and he was brought into close contact with Colonel Conder, Professor Palmer and many other scholars and travellers who were specially interested in the languages and history of the Near East. Fired by Besant's learned enthusiasm, King began to study the history and antiquities of Palestine, and especially of Jerusalem, and for many years he lectured extensively on behalf of the Palestine Exploration Fund. In 1878 he visited Egypt and Palestine, and a few years later published the results of his studies, his works on the discoveries in the Temple Hill in Jerusalem, and on the Stele of Mesha, king of Moab, about 900 B.C., and on "Cleopatra's Needle." On his return from Egypt he made the acquaintance of Dr. S. Birch, keeper of Oriental Antiquities in the British Museum, and at his suggestion began to prepare a popular work on "Cleopatra's Needle." Birch had made the official translation of the inscriptions on the "Needle," which was written on parchment and placed in the hollow of the pedestal, and in the Introduction to his book King says that "he feels much indebted to Dr. Samuel Birch, the leading English Egyptologist, for his kind assistance in rendering some obscure passages on the Obelisk." In 1883 King pointed out to the Religious Tract Society the need which existed for a new series of books on the discoveries which had been made in Bible Lands, and suggested the publication of the volumes which for many years led the student into "By-Paths of Bible Knowledge." The Rev. James King died December 28, 1913. A full account of his numerous writings and activities will be found in *The Berwick Journal*, January 1, 1914.

In his work *Cleopatra's Needle* King contents himself with giving the texts with translations of the inscriptions on the obelisk, and some short chapters in which he set out some of the facts connected with the history of the period of the XVIIIth and XIXth Dynasties, and tentative explanations of the meaning of the hieroglyphs. But the copies of the texts which were available in 1883 were faulty and incomplete, and the meanings of many of the words in them were not known. Now the student has accurate texts to work from, and the labours of Egyptologists during the last forty years have removed the difficulties which stood in the way of understanding them. It has been shown too that the Egyptian obelisks are historical as well as religious monuments, and that the series of royal obelisks which began in the XIIth Dynasty and ended in the Ptolemaïc Period, in Egypt, must be treated as a whole and studied as a whole. Like the small funerary stone obelisks which are found in the mastabah tombs of the Vth and VIth Dynasties, the great obelisks set up before the pylons of temples were erected in pairs, or multiple pairs. The pair of obelisks in a tomb, placed one each side of the "false door," seem to have represented the two pillars of the entrance to the Underworld, from which the beatified soul emerged from time to time, and the pair of mighty obelisks which stood one on each side of the gateway of a pylon symbolized the two pillars of the double doors of the eastern heaven, from which the sun appeared when he left his night abode and rose on this world. This view is supported by the words of Queen Hatshepsut, who says in the inscription on the base of one of her obelisks, "The Two Lands (*i.e.* Egypt) are bathed in light when the solar Disk rolleth up between them (*i.e.* her two obelisks) as he riseth up on the horizon of heaven" (*see* page 113). Both the funerary and the royal temple obelisks were believed to be the abodes, or at least resting places, of beatified or deified souls, and even of gods, and therefore offerings were made to them on stone tablets or specially constructed altars. The great temple obelisks were erected to the glory of the Sun-god, by whatever name called, but they were made monuments of the triumphs of the Pharaohs, who were the sons of Rā, by the inscriptions cut upon them. They represented the fusion of many religious beliefs, some of which were very ancient, and the setting up of a pair of obelisks was regarded as an act of worship and thanksgiving in return for which Rā the Sun-god was expected to prolong the life of the king and make his name to flourish for ever.

The piety and religious enthusiasm and devotion which were associated with the making and erection of a pair of royal temple obelisks are well illustrated by the inscription of Queen Hatshepsut, which is printed in full, with a translation, on pages 111–124. In this she says, "I went to meet him (*i.e.* Father Amen) on the first day. I acquired knowledge from his wise spirits. I hesitated not on any occasion when he commanded. My Majesty understandeth his divine power and behold I worked under his direction: he was my leader. I was unable to think out a plan for work without his prompting; he was the giver of the instructions. I was unable to sleep because of his temple. I never turned aside from any order which he gave. My heart was like Sia (*i.e.* wisdom personified) in respect of my father Amen. I entered into the plans of his heart . . . . . I remembered him that created me . . . . . I made them for him in rectitude of heart."

The first scholar in modern times who attempted to interpret the inscription on an obelisk was the Jesuit Athanasius Kircher. In 1650 he published a large volume of about 600 pages on the Pamphylian Obelisk in Rome, and professed to translate the inscriptions upon it, but his decipherment and renderings were worthless. In 1797 G. Zoega published his work, *De origine et usu obeliscorum,* which contained the statements of ancient writers about obelisks and a great mass of learned commentary, but he was unable to translate the hieroglyphic inscriptions. To him belongs the credit of suggesting that the cartouches contain royal names and titles. Copies of the texts on several of the great temple obelisks were published by Champollion, Rosellini and Lepsius, but without translation. Another attempt to read the inscriptions on the obelisks in Rome was made by L. M. Ungarelli in his *Interpretatis Obeliscorum urbis*, Rome, 1842, fol., but his translations displayed more learned imagination than accuracy. The Latin inscriptions on the obelisks in Rome were published by Parker in his *Archaeology of Rome* (Part IV), Oxford, 1876, but his views on Egyptian history and his identifications of the kings' names were erroneous. The first really useful work on obelisks was that by W. R. Cooper, entitled *A Short History of Egyptian Obelisks*, London, 1877. He was guided in making his translations by the Egyptologists Birch and Chabas, and there was very little guesswork in them. The publication of the large, well-illustrated and stately volume, *Egyptian Obelisks*, London, 1885, by Lieutenant-Commander H. H. Gorringe, of the United States Navy, marked a great advance in the study of Egyptian obelisks. Gorringe had transported with great success and re-erected the second of "Cleopatra's Needles" in New York, and the primary object of his book is to describe this work from a scientific and engineering point of view. But in Chapters III–VI he described the obelisks in Thebes, Constantinople, Rome, Paris and elsewhere, and added much archaeological information which was derived from the best sources then available. It contains no hieroglyphic texts, but it will probably continue to be a standard authority on all matters relating to the quarrying, transport and re-erection of obelisks. For some unknown reason no authoritative account of the transport and re-erection of "Cleopatra's Needle" on the Thames Embankment by Mr. John Dixon, C.E., other than that given in *Engineering*, was published. The accounts given by Sir Erasmus Wilson in his book on Egypt, and by Mr. James King in his *Cleopatra's Needle*, are incomplete. Finally, mention must be made of Marucchi's *Gli Obelischi Egiziani di Roma*, Rome, 1898. In this work Signor Marucchi describes the obelisks in Rome, and translates many of the inscriptions, and gives two valuable photographic copies of the texts on the Lateran and Del Popolo obelisks.

The present work consists of two parts: Part I deals with the obelisk as a historical and religious monument, and describes the transport and re-erection of "Cleopatra's Needle" on the Thames Embankment; Part II gives the hieroglyphic and other texts of all the important Egyptian obelisks, with English translations, arranged generally in such a way that text and translation are on the same page. The obelisks in Rome which are inscribed with texts written during the Roman Period represent ideas of a non-Egyptian character, and form a very small and uninteresting class by themselves. A short Chapter has been added on the monoliths at Aksûm, the most modern of which possess many of the characteristics of the Egyptian obelisk. They were set up in honour of the Sabaean Sun-god, and offerings were made to them on altars

LIST OF PLATES

LIST OF ILLUSTRATIONS IN THE TEXT

In this city of Thebes, among many works of art and different structures recording the tales relating to the Egyptian deities, we saw several obelisks in their places, and others which had been thrown down and broken; which the ancient kings, when elated at some victory or at the general prosperity of their affairs, had caused to be hewn out of mountains in distant parts of the world, and erected in honour of the gods, to whom they solemnly consecrated them. Now an obelisk is a rough stone, rising to a great height, shaped like a pillar in the stadium; and it tapers upwards in imitation of a sunbeam, keeping its quadrilateral shape, till it rises almost to a point, being made smooth by the hand of a sculptor. On these obelisks the ancient authority of elementary wisdom has caused innumerable marks of strange forms to be cut all over them, which are called hieroglyphics.—Ammianus Marcellinus, Bk. xvii, §§ 6–8.

PART I

CHAPTER I

THE EGYPTIAN OBELISK

THE CULT OF STONES IN GENERAL

THERE seems to be no reason to doubt that, in all periods and in every country of the world, man has always included stones among the objects of his various cults. He has always associated stone mountains and hills, isolated rocks, and rocky formations of unusual shapes and forms, with gods and spirits, who were sometimes good and sometimes bad, and has regarded them as the temporary or permanent dwelling-places of supernatural beings. When Nature has failed to provide him with suitable abodes for his gods or spirits he has constructed them for himself, and made standing stones, set up with great ceremony by himself, to take their places. The rock or boulder that was of unusual shape, or form, or colour, or had any curious mark upon it, or any indentation, or any perforation in it, assumed special importance in his eyes, and soon became a sacred object.

A standing stone was often reverenced because it was supposed to form the abode of a tribal ancestor, or because it was considered to have been a witness of some important event connected with the tribe, or because it was believed to have exercised some friendly influence on behalf of those who lived near it. It will be remembered that when M. Clermont Ganneau wanted to carry off the Stele of Mesha, King of Moab (the Moabite Stone), all the tribes resisted violently, and they lighted a fire around it and, when the Stele was very hot, they poured vinegar upon it and so split it in pieces. This was done to prevent the Frank from enjoying the protection which the good spirit that dwelt in the Stone had always given to the tribes near it. The good spirit left the Stone and went elsewhere.

When the stone happened to be a meteorite, or a part of one, special sanctity was attached to it, and virtues of every kind were attributed to it. A good example of such a sacred stone is the famous Black Stone, which has been set in silver and built into the south-east corner of the Ka'abah at Mekka. This Stone is quite small, measuring only 8 inches by 6 inches, and is of a reddish-brown colour ; it was probably a most sacred object to the Arabs for many centuries before they accepted Islâm. The original reason why it was sacred had been forgotten, and the Muhammadan priests invented the story that it descended from heaven in the days of Adam, that it was preserved miraculously during the Flood, and that the Archangel Gabriel, who had been deputed by God to watch over the

Stone, gave it to Abraham to build into the Ka'abah. For a drawing of the Black Stone, *see* Muir, *Life of Mohammad*, page 28. When once a standing stone was supposed to be the abode, temporary or permanent, of a god, offerings were brought and laid at its foot, and prayers and requests for help were made to it. Similarly, when a standing stone was held to be the abode of an ancestor of the tribe, offerings were brought to it regularly, and prayers made to it, and frantic appeals were addressed to it by the tribe in times of calamity. In the Southern and Eastern Sûdân attempts were frequently made to give to the standing stone somewhat of the form of the ancestor the abode of whose spirit it was. The offerings to such stones were intended to maintain the life of the spirits that resided in them, whether they were the spirits of gods or men, and the stones themselves were frequently bathed with the blood of the victims, which were sometimes human, that were slaughtered before them.

THE CULT OF STONES IN EGYPT

The cult of stones was as common in Egypt and the Egyptian Sûdân as in other countries of the world. The predynastic peoples made beads of various kinds of coloured stones, to which they ascribed beneficial and protective qualities, and they seem to have attached great value to rock-crystal. Both they and their successors made extensive use of flint, diorite, haematite, black-and-white and red-and-white breccia, black-and-green basalt, carnelian, lapis-lazuli, malachite, etc., and each of these was supposed to possess peculiar and individual properties. Flint was the commonest material of which, before metal was known, tools and weapons were made, and in the performance of ritual ceremonies and solemn social customs the implements used were always of flint and stone. Thus in a tomb of the VIth Dynasty at Sakkârah, when the Egyptians had a good knowledge of working in metals, we see in a painting on the wall the act of circumcision being performed on a youth by an operator who uses a flint knife. (*See* Müller, *Egypt. Researches*, 1908, pl. 106, and Montet, *Tombeaux Égyptiens*, p. 165.) The Hebrews in like manner used knives made of stone, *i.e.* flint, long after they were acquainted with metal knives, as we see from Exod. iv. 25 and Josh. v. 2. In the former passage we read that Zipporah circumcised her son with a stone knife, and in the latter it is stated that Joshua made flint knives to circumcise the people a second time.

The earliest axe-heads, whether single or double, were made of flint or stone, and it is a significant fact that the hieroglyph for "god," 𓊹, represents a stone axe-head tied to a short handle. The spirit in the stone aided the efforts of the man wielding the axe, and, presumably, absorbed the blood of the man whom it slew. The small calcareous stone tablets which are found in graves of the Predynastic and Archaïc Periods afforded resting-places for the spirits of the dead when they came to the graves to partake of the spiritual portion of the offerings laid on them, or wished to abide in them. On the painted wooden sepulchral stelae of the New Kingdom wooden figures of a human-headed hawk,  , are often found, a fact showing that the standing stone and tomb stele, of whatever material made, was in all periods regarded as a house for the spirit of the deceased. Before the Egyptians acquired the art of writing, the standing stones, or memorial stelae, bore no mark to show whom they commemorated, but when once that had been introduced the names of the deceased were cut upon them in hieroglyphs. Good examples of the standing stones or monoliths which, being inscribed on one face, served as memorial stelae in the tombs of the kings of the Ist and IInd Dynasties at Abydos, are those of King Tcha,  , and Per-ab-sen. The former is in the Egyptian Museum in Cairo, and the latter in the British Museum (No. 35597).

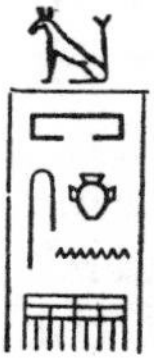

THE OBELISK AS A FUNERARY MONUMENT

The stelae found in the tombs of the Ist and IInd Dynasties at Abydos were often rough slabs of grey granite, of which only one face had been wholly or partially dressed to receive the inscription and a representation of the so-called "banner" frame. So little is known of the tombs of the IIIrd Dynasty that nothing definite can be said about the funerary stelae that were probably in them. Under the IVth Dynasty it became customary to place a pair of small stone obelisks, one on each side of the "false door," in the mastabah tomb, but with exactly what object it is hard to see. Lepsius, in his *Letters from Egypt*, London, 1853, page 64, says that he found a small obelisk erect, in its original position, in a tomb made in the beginning of the VIth Dynasty, but later he corrected his dating and ascribed the object to the IVth Dynasty (*see* his *Denkmäler*, Abt. ii, Bl. 88). This obelisk is in the Royal Museum in Berlin, where it is numbered 1146; it is about 4 feet in height and is inscribed with the name of Ahi, a high official. A similar obelisk, only about 5 inches less in height, bears the name of the priestly official Ati; it also is in the Berlin Museum. A photograph of the obelisks in the tomb of Sabna (VIth Dynasty) is given by Baumgärtel, *Dolmen und Mastaba*, Leipzig, 1926, Taf. v.

There are two smaller inscribed sandstone obelisks of the same period in the British Museum, and they stand one on each side of the main doorway at the northern end of the Egyptian Gallery. The red sandstone obelisk on the west side (No. 202) was set up to the memory of an official or soldier stationed at the copper mines of Sarābît al-Khâdam in the Peninsula of Sinai; his name is illegible. On two of its sides are the names of his sons Aqen, , and Ahnem, , who were soldiers. The obelisk is 20 inches high, and dates from the XIIth Dynasty; it was found at Sarābît al-Khâdam. The other obelisk, of a lighter-coloured sandstone (No. 495), commemorates the high priest [of Memphis] called Ara, . Each face of the shaft contains a column of hieroglyphs, which read (?) , and show that he was also a director of one of the Departments of Agriculture in Egypt. The pyramidion of each obelisk is uninscribed. The obelisk of Nub-kheper-Rā Antef described on pages 268–70 is clearly a sepulchral monument, because the deceased calls himself "beloved" by both Osiris and Anubis. Yet another example of the funerary obelisk is B.M. No. 780. This commemorates Ptahertana, , captain of the military guard of the temple of Ptah of Memphis, and is inscribed with prayers to Osiris, Upuatu and Ptah-aneb-resu for sepulchral offerings. As an example of a funerary monument which is part obelisk and part stele may be mentioned B.M. No. 694. This monument has sides which taper upwards and a rounded top, and before it was a rectangular slab with hollows, indicating that it was an altar or slab on which offerings to the dead were placed. In connection with this it may be mentioned that Thothmes III endowed some of his obelisks with offerings. The monument commemorates Sebek-her-heb, an officer of certain royal apartments, Kemtt, a deputy keeper of the seal; and Hathor, lady of the copper and malachite mines, is entreated to give the deceased persons a "king's gift,"

Both stele and altar were found at Sarābît al-Khâdam, and an inscription on the rounded portion of the front of the stele gives the date of the 44th year of Amenemhat (?) III.

THE SUN STONE AND THE OBELISK

At a period which is so remote that no date can be assigned to it, the people of Anu (the On of the Hebrews and the Heliopolis of the Greeks) had as the object of their cult a stone, which was thick at the base and tapered to a point at the top, and much resembled in shape the funerary stelae found in the tombs of Tcha, or Tchat, and other early kings at Abydos. This stone was called BEN, and in the texts of the VIth Dynasty its determinative resembles a small obelisk, , *i.e.* a short, thick shaft surmounted by a little pyramid, △. (*See* the Pyramid-Text N, line 663.) Why this Ben Stone was sacred, or how it acquired its sanctity, is not known, and it is very probable that the ancient Egyptians themselves never had any clear ideas on the subject. In early dynastic times they thought that it was the abode of the spirit of the sun, which made itself visible at the Creation by emerging from the top of the stone in the form of a bird something like this  . This bird was called the "Benu," and in the texts of the later period was given the form of  in its name  . It was regarded as the incarnation of the soul of Rā and the heart of Osiris. It was self-produced and, according to some texts, appeared each morning at dawn on the sacred Persea tree of Anu. A temple called He-t Benu,  , was dedicated to it in very early times. The Greeks identified the Benu with the Phoenix, a bird which resembled an eagle and had parti-coloured feathers, red and golden. The home of this bird was somewhere in Arabia, and a phoenix visited Heliopolis at the close of every period of 500 years. Towards the end of his life he built a nest in Arabia to which he imparted the power of generation, so when he died another phoenix arose out of it. When the new phoenix had grown up he went to Heliopolis and burned his father, whose ashes he buried in the temple of the Sun-god there (*see* Herodotus ii. 73; Tacitus, Annals, vi. 23). Another view was that only one phoenix lived at a time, and that the successor was developed from a worm that crawled out of the dead bird under the influence of the heat of the sun (Pliny, *Hist. Nat.* x. 2; Tzetses, *Chil.* v. 397). Other opinions were that the phoenix burned himself to death after a life of 500, or 1461, or 7006 years.

The cult of the Ben Stone was far older than the belief in the Benu bird, which belonged to the time when the Egyptians assigned to their gods the forms of birds, animals, reptiles, etc.; and it persisted, though perhaps in a modified form, even after human forms had been assigned to the gods and goddesses. In the temples built at Abusîr by some of the kings of the Vth Dynasty in connection with their pyramid tombs, the Ben Stone, or, as we may call it, the "Sun Stone," was the principal symbol of the Sun-god Rā, who was then represented in human form. It preserved the form of the Ben Stone, and was a short, thick obelisk which stood upon a base in the form of a truncated pyramid. On the east side of this sacred "standing stone" was an altar on which victims were sacrificed, and on the north side were channels by which the blood was conducted into alabaster bowls placed in position to receive it (*see* Borchardt and Schäfer in *Aegyptische Zeitschrift*, 1899, page 1). From the pyramidal top of the obelisk the spirit or soul of the Sun-god witnessed the slaughter of the victims and enjoyed the spirit entities of the

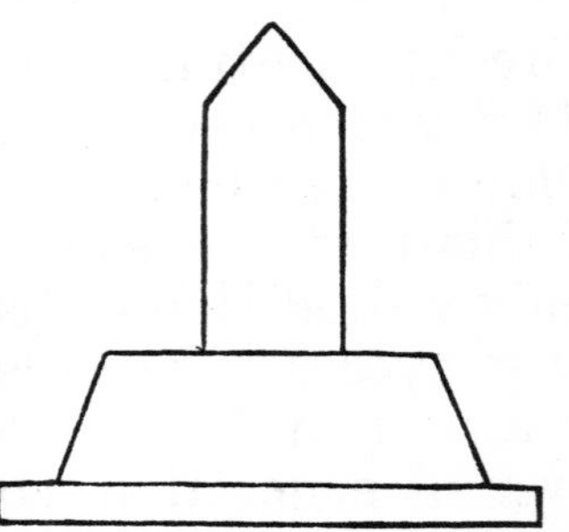

various offerings made to him. It is nowhere in the texts so stated, but it is clear that the pyramidal part of the obelisk was believed to be the abode of the spirit of the Sun-god, and therefore the most important part of the monument. It was called " Ben Ben," , *i.e.* the " Ben of the Ben," and the shrine in which the Sun Stone was kept was called " Ben-ben-t," .

The Ben Ben, which may be regarded as a small pyramid, was probably intended to represent the heaven, wherein the gods dwelt, above the sky, which, as Maspero pointed out long ago, was supposed to be formed of a rectangular layer of some indeterminate material supported on four columns, one at each angle. If this be so it is easy to understand why tombs were made in the form of pyramids. The substructure of the pyramid represented the shaft of the Ben Stone, and the superstructure the pyramid, or, as it is commonly called, pyramidion, on top of it. It is not known whether any part of the Ben Stone was inscribed, but the sides of pyramid tombs were covered with inscriptions, and the apex was probably formed of a single pyramidal stone bearing special inscriptions, or perhaps Vignettes in which the occupant of the tomb was represented worshipping the Sun-god. Under the New Kingdom funerary stelae were often made in the form of pyramids, and even of the Ben Stone ; compare the pyramid of the priestly official on which are cut figures of the eyes of the sun, 𓂀, and moon, 𓂀, and of the deceased adoring them (B.M. No. 558); the pyramid of Amenemheb, on which are cut figures of Rā in his boat (B.M. No. 560); and the monument of Ani, 𓇋𓈖𓏭, which is inscribed with prayers to Rā and Osiris (B.M. No. 561); and the pyramid of Her-nefer (B.M. No. 699).

There is little doubt that the Ben Stone, which was associated with the cult of the Sun-god at a very early period, cannot be grouped with the monolithic pillars which were so often used by ancient peoples in their worship, *e.g.* the Semites and the Cyprians and the early Abyssinians, and that it had a special character and significance of its own. It may have been a stone of volcanic or meteoric origin, like the Black Stone of Mekka. It has been thought that the Egyptian obelisk was developed out of the Ben Stone by adding to it a long shaft, and that is often stated in books, but the Pyramid Texts show that this can hardly be the case. The oldest of the large obelisks we have is that which still stands at Heliopolis, and the king who set up it and its fellow, the remains of which were found by Petrie, simply says that he did what he did, without specifying exactly what, on the occasion of the first celebration of the Set Festival by him. The kings of the XVIIIth Dynasty, when they set up obelisks, stated definitely in the inscriptions upon them that they had set up their obelisks in honour of the god Rā, or Amen-Rā, or Tem, in order to obtain from them the gift of eternal life. Thus Thothmes III says that he "set up obelisks, great, large," ; Rameses II "set up two great obelisks," , and Hatshepsut set up two great obelisks, , *tekhenui urui*, to obtain life everlasting. From this and from many other passages we see that the obelisk was called TEKHEN or *tekhenu*, , , and not BEN, even though the determinative of this word is usually an obelisk. Now *tekhen*, obelisk, is a very old word, and we find it in the dual in the Pyramid Texts, which were written before the close of the VIth Dynasty. Thus in Pepi, line 391, we read of the two *tekhenui*, , belonging to Rā, and we have the variants and , in two variant versions of the passage. These *tekhenu*, or obelisks, had pyramidal tops like the Ben Stone, but they were undoubtedly only pillars which men in Egypt and other countries set up before the doors of their temples or shrines for ceremonial purposes, or perhaps as architectural adornments. At all events there seems to be no reason for saying that Usertsen (Sen-Usrit) I lengthened the shaft of the Ben Stone, or Sun Stone, but it is quite likely that he set up at Heliopolis obelisks that were larger than any that had stood before the old House of Rā of the Vth and VIth Dynasties. And it is quite clear that the obelisk did not take the place of the Ben Stone at Thebes under the XVIIIth Dynasty. For, though obelisks set up by Thothmes I, Hatshepsut and Thothmes III, were standing at Thebes when Amenhetep IV came to the throne, he insisted on building a shrine for a Ben Stone between the Temple of Karnak and the Temple of Luxor, and it was the presence of this shrine in the city which, in the end, made it necessary for him to abandon Thebes.

The fact is that the Ben Stone and the obelisk, though both might be described as "Sun Stones," represented different forms of religious thought. 'Abd al-Latîf, the famous Arab physician who visited Egypt in the later years of the XIIth century, says that he saw many obelisks at Heliopolis, and that several of them were quite small; it is probable that many of them were set up as funerary monuments, and were intended to indicate regeneration, new life, stability, and perhaps resurrection. Many uninscribed obelisks, varying in height from 3 to 5 feet, have been found in tombs of the New Kingdom in the neighbourhood of Memphis and of Heliopolis, a fact that seems to suggest that they represented to the Egyptians what the memorial pillars did to the Semites, *i.e.* they marked the place where the offerings to the dead were to be placed. The obelisk is frequently seen on scarabs, where it is often the symbol of the god Amen, and at one time the hieroglyph 𓉾 had the phonetic value of "Amen"; compare the inscriptions on two scarabs published by Newberry (*Scarabs*, pl. xxxix, Nos. 7 and 8). And the large sanctuary obelisks are sometimes referred to or cut upon the bases of scarabs, *e.g.* the scarab of Amenhetep II (B.M. No. 41875), where we read  , "stable are the two obelisks in the House of Amen" (Hall, *Catalogue*, page 161). The obelisks here referred to must be the pair that this king set up in the temple at Madamûd (*see* page 177). A statement similar to that of Amenhetep II is found on a scarab at Berlin; see *Ausführliches Verzeichniss*, Berlin, 1899, page 417, No. 3530. In his great inscription at Karnak Thothmes III enumerates the offerings of incense, myrrh, and various kinds of cakes, which he gave in hundreds for the four obelisks. During the reign of Hatshepsut green glazed steatite plaques were made in Thebes on which the Queen's prenomen was inscribed between obelisks, thus:—

See the example in the British Museum (Hall, *Catalogue*, page 53, No. 41977).

The dedication of a pair of obelisks was accompanied by an endowment of offerings, and according to the Book of the Dead offerings were made to a pair of obelisks on behalf of the deceased. Thus in the Turin Papyrus (Lepsius, *Todtenbuch*, Bl. v) we see two obelisks in front of a great heap of offerings of cakes, geese, fruit, flowers, joints of meat, etc. A priest stands before an altar-coffer, on which are laid [hieroglyph], a censer (?), [hieroglyph], [hieroglyph] and [hieroglyph], and presents incense; he

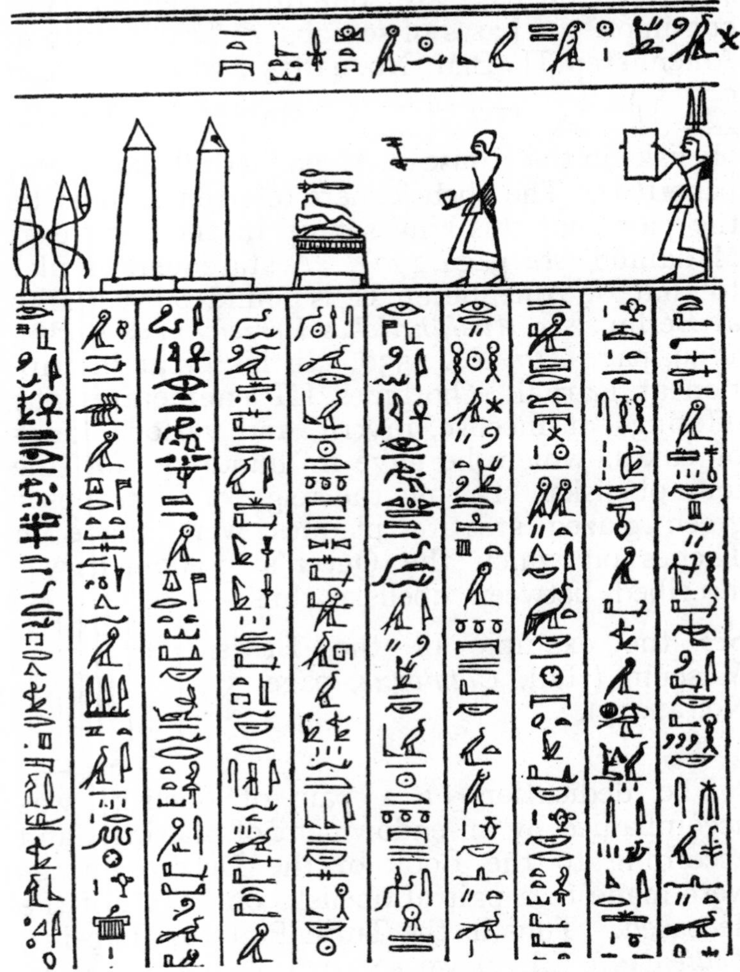

Vignette of Chap. xv of the Book of the Dead illustrating the presentation of offerings to obelisks. The foremost priest is performing the ceremonies of the Book of Opening the Mouth, and the Kher-heb behind him is reciting the Liturgy of Funerary Offerings.

grasps in his right hand the ram-headed staff or magician's rod. Behind him stands another priest, wearing plumes, 𓆄𓆄, on his head, and reading the service of offerings from a sheet of papyrus. This copy of the Book of the Dead was written late in the Saïte period, and the Vignette described above shows that the views held by the Egyptians under the Old Kingdom about obelisks and offerings were current two thousand years later, under the New Kingdom.

THE NAME AND SYMBOLISM OF THE SANCTUARY OBELISK

Our common word for the monument which the Egyptians called "Tekhen," 𓏏𓐍𓈖𓉶, is "obelisk"; this is derived from the Greek ὀβελίσκος = ὀβελός, meaning "spit," "dagger," "spear," "sword point," etc. The exact meaning of "Tekhen" is unknown to us, and it is probable that the Egyptians had forgotten it at a very early period. As we have seen, it occurs in inscriptions of the VIth Dynasty, and was, no doubt, at that time an old word. There was another monument that had an obelisk as a determinative, viz. "Manu," 𓅓𓏌𓉶, but it is followed by 𓊖, the sign for "city" or "district," and it may have indicated a private cemetery with one or more obelisks in it. It is used in connection with some funerary monument of Khufu (IVth Dynasty), but is never found on the great obelisks of Thebes or Heliopolis. Strabo (xvii. 1, 27) speaks of the " obelisks " of Heliopolis, and many other classical writers do the same, but give no clue to the native Egyptian word for them in their days, or its meaning.

The early Arab writers who describe Egypt and her principal towns naturally mention 'Ain ash-Shems, *i.e.* the Fountain of the Sun (Heliopolis), and usually refer to the two obelisks of Usertsen I with their copper caps as " pillars," *e.g.* Ibn Khurdâdhbah (ed. De Goeje, page 161), who calls them "Astuântân." Here the question arises, How came the two obelisks of Thothmes III which had been transported to Alexandria by Augustus to be called " Cleopatra's Needles " ? Cleopatra, as is well known, visited Upper Egypt and built a small temple near Thebes, but nowhere is it stated that she expressed any special admiration for the obelisks of Thebes or Heliopolis, or that she wished to transport any of them to Alexandria, or that she had two quarried in Syene and set them up in her city. The Arab physician 'Abd al-Latîf, who wrote at the close of the XIIth century, calls them " *misallatî Fir'ûn*," i.e. " Pharaoh's big needles," and Yâḳût, the geographer, says that the natives generally call them *masâlla Fir'ûn* (Wüstenfeld's text, vol. iii, page 762, at the bottom), with the same meaning. So, then, the Arab writers associated the obelisks with a Pharaoh, which was right and proper. Another Arab writer, Hasan ibn Ibrâhîm, says they were in the " temple of the Sun where Zulêkhâ tore Joseph's shirt in pieces " (quoted

PLATE I.

Cleopatra wearing the headdress of the Mother-goddess Mut, surmounted by the horns of the Cow-goddess Hathor and the disk of the Moon. Above this is the symbol of the goddess Isis. From a bas-relief at Denderah.

by Yâḳût), but she is the only woman whom the Arabs associate with the building. Now the word *misallah,* مسلّة, means a " big needle " of the kind which is used by packers in sewing up bales, and in the written Arabic never means anything else. The word is in all the good dictionaries, and it will be found in the excellent work of the Rev. J. B. Belot, S.J. (3rd ed. Beyrouth, 1893, page 333), where the meaning " obelisk " is also given to it, but the mark prefixed to it indicates that this meaning is only given to it in the vulgar tongue, and more especially in Syria. This explains well enough how in modern times the obelisks at Alexandria came to be called needles, but not why they were named " Cleopatra's Needles " instead of " Pharaoh's Needles." It can only be surmised that the vulgar were unable to associate the idea of big needles with a Pharaoh, thinking that they ought to be the property of a queen rather than of a king. And as they were at Alexandria, and as the name of Cleopatra, **Plate I,** is imperishably connected with that city, they assigned them to her, with perhaps an obscene suggestion that they resembled phalli lurking in their minds. One thing is quite certain : that the obelisks of Thothmes III formerly at Alexandria were not in any way connected historically with Cleopatra.

The obelisk practically consists of two parts—the shaft and the pyramidion on the top of it. The shaft may be considered as an offering of a standing stone or pillar in honour of the Sun-god, and the pyramidion as the symbol of the rays of the sun spreading out as they descend to embrace the earth. Both shaft and pyramidion were sacred to the Sun-god (by whatever name he was called), whose visible emblem (and perhaps abode) was the sun that "rolled up" into the sky daily to light and warm the earth. The Egyptians were fond of making puns, and there is a play on the word *ben*, "sunshine," and *uben*, "to shoot up in the sky" (of the Sun). The obelisk was under the Middle and New Kingdoms the Sun Stone *par excellence*, and Amenhetep III, in his great inscription at Karnak, tells us that he placed two large obelisks in the great sacred barge made of cedar-wood plated with gold and silver, which he had made in honour of Amen-Rā, king of the gods at Thebes. The inscriptions on the shafts of obelisks contain the various "strong names" and titles of the kings who set them up, and only in the case of the obelisks of Hatshepsut do we find Vignettes cut upon them. On the pyramidions were often cut Vignettes in which the king is seen worshiping the god Rā, or Amen-Rā, or forms of him, and making offerings of incense and wine to him. The inscriptions accompanying these give the name of the god worshipped, and make it clear that the king kneeling before him owes to him his life, health, strength, stability, well-being, wealth and victories. In the accompanying illustrations we see (No. 1) Thothmes III, in the form of a bearded, man-headed sphinx, offering two vases of wine to the god Rā Her-aakhuti. The god holds a sceptre from which proceed "life," ☥.

and " eternity," , towards the king's face. In No. 2 the king, in the form of a bearded, man-headed sphinx, is offering two vases of holy water to Tem, the lord of Heliopolis, who promises to give him life, stability and content.

As Rā was eternal, the obelisk symbolized stability and permanence, and all the powers of rebirth, and virility, and fertility and creative force which he possessed. The pyramidion

1 2

was, as we have seen, called " Ben Ben," and in the tomb of Seti I the god Benbeniti, , is said to be one of the 75 forms of Rā. Now the word *ben*, , or *benen*, , and forms of it all indicate " virility " and " reproduction," and there seems to be no doubt that both the Ben Stone and the Ben Ben of the obelisk symbolized the active creative power of the Sun-god. This being so, it may be that the cult of the Sun Stone at Heliopolis was of a phallic character, and that the Heliopolitans were, as some ancient writers affirmed, phallic worshippers. And as the obelisk symbolized rebirth its use as a funerary monument is explained, for it was believed to bring into the tomb the power of the revivifying rays of the Sun-god, which would effect the resurrection of the deceased.

CLASSICAL WRITERS ON OBELISKS

The principal ancient writers on Egyptian obelisks are Pliny and Ammianus Marcellinus, but they tell us little about the history of them; the former says that in shape they resembled the rays of the sun (xxxvi. 14), and the latter that they were erected in honour of the gods by kings who were elated by some victory or by the general prosperity of their affairs (xvii. 4, § 6). Pliny says that the first king of Egypt to erect an obelisk was Mesphres. At a later period Sesosthes (Usertsen I ?) set up four at Heliopolis, each being 48 cubits (*i.e.* between 72 and 80 feet) in height. Rhamsesis (Rameses II) set up one which was 148 cubits in height, and another which was 128 cubits in height and 11 cubits in breadth; 120,000 men were employed in making the latter. While this was being erected the king, thinking that the machinery might not be able to support the weight, had his son fastened to the top so that the safety of the prince might ensure that of the obelisk. Cambyses admired this obelisk so much that when the city was being destroyed by fire at his command he ordered the fire to be extinguished. Pliny goes on to say that Zmarres and Phius each erected an obelisk 48 cubits in height, and that Ptolemy II erected at Alexandria an obelisk 80 cubits in height, which had been made by Necthebis (Nekht-Her-Heb ?). A canal was dug under this last obelisk as it lay, presumably in the quarry, and two broad boats loaded with stones were floated in under it ; the stones being removed, these boats rose and supported the obelisk. When brought to Alexandria it was erected upon a basis of six square blocks, of the same kind of stone, in the Arsinoeum. Later the Prefect Maximus had it removed to the Forum in Alexandria, intending to remove the pyramidion and to replace it by a gilded point.

Pliny also mentions two other obelisks, which were in Caesar's temple in Alexandria ; each was 42 cubits in height and was made by King Mesphres (Thothmes III ?). One was transported to Rome by Augustus, and the other by Caligula. The obelisk that Augustus set up in the Circus Maximus was made by Semenperteus, during the lifetime of Pythagoras ; it was 85¾ (or 82¾) feet in height, exclusive of the base. Another obelisk erected by Augustus in the Campus Martius was 9 feet less in height, and was made by King Sesothis. They were both covered with inscriptions, which interpret the operations of Nature according to the philosophy of the Egyptians. The obelisk in the Campus Martius was used as a sundial. Another obelisk, 100 cubits in height, was made by Nuncoreus, the son of Sesoses, and, in obedience to an oracle, was dedicated by him to the sun, after having lost and recovered his sight.

The paragraphs of Ammianus Marcellinus on obelisks deal chiefly with the famous obelisk that Constantine took from Heliopolis, intending to set it up in Rome; for the account of how it was transported to Rome by Constantius *see* page 163. About its erection Ammianus says: "Vast beams having been raised on end in a most dangerous manner, so that they looked like a grove of machines, long ropes of huge size were fastened to them, darkening the very sky with their density, as they formed a web of innumerable threads; and into them the great stone itself, covered over as it was with elements of writing, was bound, and gradually raised into the empty air, and for a long time suspended, many thousands of men turning it round and round like a millstone, till it was at last placed in the middle of the square; and on it was placed a brazen sphere, made brighter with plates of gold; and as that was immediately afterwards struck by lightning and destroyed, a brazen figure like a torch was placed on it, also plated with gold—to look as if the torch were fully alight." Both Pliny and Ammianus regarded obelisks as monuments erected by the Pharaohs to commemorate their victories, and failed to grasp their **religious symbolism and character.**

THE QUARRYING OF THE OBELISK

The greater number of the Egyptian obelisks known to us are made of granite, the red or "rose granite" which the Egyptians called *mat*, , or *maut*, ; the living granite rock was *mat rutt*, . The obelisks dedicated by Nekht-Her-Heb to "Thoth the Twice-great," and now in the British Museum, were made of a greenish-black basalt, , *bekhen*; and a few small obelisks were made of sandstone, which was an obviously unfit material for the large obelisks intended to be placed in temples. The great **granite quarry** of Egypt lay at the foot of the First Cataract, on the east bank of the Nile, near the ancient town of Suwan (the Sewêneh of the Hebrews, Syene of the Greeks, and the modern Aswân); a common name for its granite is "Syenite." But though the quarry whence came the obelisks has been well known for centuries, the exact methods which the Egyptians followed in quarrying these mighty blocks of stone and transporting them from the quarry to the Nile are still largely matters difficult to understand. Many travellers have called attention to the unfinished obelisk that lies in the Aswân quarry, but until quite recently nothing was done to collect the information which an adequate examination of the block would supply. In 1922 the Egyptian Service of Antiquities instructed one of their officers, Mr. R. Engelbach, to clear out that portion of the quarry in which the obelisk lies, and now, for the first time, the immense size of the monument can be realized. Its length is 137 feet, its base 13 feet 9 inches, and the height of its pyramidion 14 feet 9 inches; had it been extracted its weight would have been about 1,168 tons (*see* Engelbach's Report, *The Aswân Obelisk*, Cairo, 1922). When the quarrying of this obelisk began cannot be said, but it cannot have been before the reign of Thothmes I, and it may have been as late as the time of Rameses II. The completion of the obelisk was abandoned because of the flaws and cracks which were discovered to exist in some parts of it, and the frequency and persistence of them made the craftsmen give up the plan of cutting the block down and extracting from it a smaller obelisk.

The blocks of granite intended for obelisks, or colossal statues of kings, or monolithic shrines such as Herodotus (ii. 175) describes,[1] were detached from their beds by the use of fire or by **wedges** made of wood or iron. Several of the earlier European writers on the method of quarrying thought that the wedges were of wood, well-driven home, which when flooded with water would swell and burst the block from its bed. But some modern investigators think that the wedges were made of metal, and

[1] This granite shrine at Saïs was 21 cubits ($31\frac{1}{2}$ feet) high, 14 cubits (22 feet) broad, and 8 cubits (12 feet) thick; to drag it from Aswân to Saïs occupied 2,000 men for three years.

that they were driven into the slots in the rock between thin plates of metal. The method by which the block was separated from its bed is not known. Wilkinson, and following him Gorringe, thought that in cutting under this lower surface supports of the native rock were at first left at regular intervals. The spaces between these supports were filled with beams of wood, and then the supports were cut away, leaving the block standing upon the beams. The holes or slots into which the wedges were driven were probably cut with chisels made of copper hardened with some alloy. The flattening of the surface of the block was, according to Mr. Engelbach, done by bruising it with a ball of "dolorite," which was probably held in the hand. Balls were from 5 to 22 inches in diameter, and had an average weight of 12 lb.

THE REMOVAL OF THE OBELISK FROM THE QUARRY

How this was done is not certain. It was at one time supposed that a canal was dug from the Nile into the quarry, and that at the time of the Inundation the rising waters would float the obelisk out on the huge raft which had been built under it during low Nile. But there are no traces of any canals at Aswân, and it would have been impossible to cut a canal through the granite mountain in which the quarry lies. It is far more likely that the obelisk was raised by means of levers and ropes to a height sufficient to enable it to clear the sides of the quarry, and that it was then dragged down over a bed of sand by ropes to the level by the side of the river. In the absence of any ancient information on the subject we may assume that the obelisk was then raised along its length by levers in some form, and a sledge built under it. We know from a wall-painting at Al-Barshah that colossal statues were tied to sledges, and at Dêr al-Baharî there is a relief in which we see one of Hatshepsut's obelisks lying on a sledge. Whether the sledge and its burden were rolled over the ground to the river on rollers, which is very probable, or moved along by levers worked by a row of men on each side of it, cannot be said.

TRANSPORT OF THE OBELISK BY RIVER

We know from the Palermo Stone that in the reign of Seneferu the Egyptians were able to build sea-going boats of great length and beam, and of great carrying capacity, and it is not surprising that at a later period they found no difficulty in building barges or lighters that were able to transport blocks of stone weighing 900[1] or 1,000 tons from the quarry to the temple. An inscription of Anna (*see* Sethe, *Urkunden*, i. 56), who flourished in the first half of the XVIIIth Dynasty, throws much light on the style of boat, or more probably raft, that was used in the transport of obelisks. He says :—

[1] The colossal statue of Rameses II at the Ramesseum weighed nearly 900 tons.

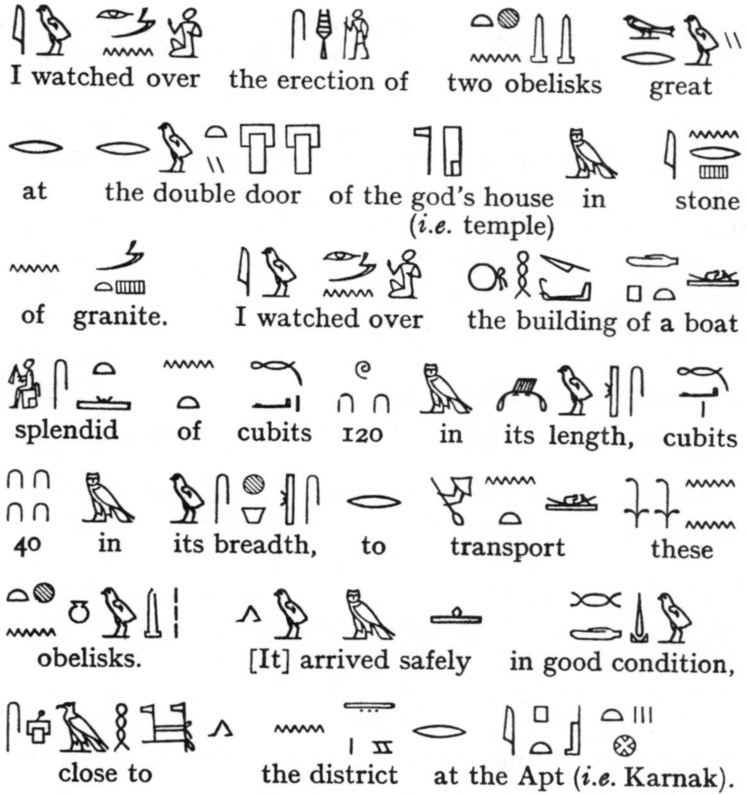

I watched over the erection of two obelisks great
at the double door of the god's house (i.e. temple) in stone
of granite. I watched over the building of a boat
splendid of cubits 120 in its length, cubits
40 in its breadth, to transport these
obelisks. [It] arrived safely in good condition,
close to the district at the Apt (i.e. Karnak).

According to Pliny (xxxvi. 14), the ships that brought the obelisks for Augustus from Egypt to Rome excited the greatest admiration. The Emperor ordered the one that brought over the first obelisk to be preserved as a lasting memorial of the undertaking in the docks at Puteoli, but it was destroyed by fire. The ship that brought over the obelisk for Caligula was preserved for many years, and was regarded as the most wonderful craft that had ever sailed the seas. But eventually it was taken to Ostia by the command of Claudius and was sunk to form the foundation of a part of the harbour which he was building there. Each of the boats mentioned by Pliny was, of course, built in Egypt, a fact which proves that the native boat-builders had inherited the skill in boat-building of their ancestors. The boat, or raft, built under the superintendence of Anna, was 120 cubits long and 40 cubits broad ; if we reckon the cubit at 20 inches, we obtain 200 feet and 60 feet as the dimensions of the *tept*, [hieroglyphs]. When the obelisks on their sledge arrived at about 200 feet from the river, a halt was made until a special arrangement could be prepared for getting both on to the lighter or raft. It was impossible to roll the two obelisks, or even one, on to the lighter—for each of them weighed over 300 tons—therefore it was necessary to get the lighter under the obelisks and to lower them down into or upon it. A portion of the bank was cut away and a sort of channel made, into which the lighter was backed. The channel was then filled in, probably with sand, and when this was on the same level as the ground on which the sledge with its obelisks rested, it was rolled to the place immediately above the lighter. The filling of the channel was then removed and the sledge came down by degrees until it rested on the raft. All this was probably done when the Nile was low, and when the river rose during the Inundation its waters would lift the raft and its load, so that it would be easy to drag them out into the stream. They would then be taken in tow by a large number of well-manned river boats, and floated down to Thebes. Or it may be that the whole process of transporting the obelisks to the temple was conducted during the time of high Nile, *i.e.* between the beginning of July and the middle of October. It must be remembered that no one knows exactly how the obelisk was got on to the lighter, and that whether the Egyptians dug a channel to receive the lighter, or whether they built an embankment round it and over it, is alike uncertain. The late Sir Benjamin Baker, who gave much thought to the question, believed that a channel was dug into the bank to receive the lighter. One thing is quite certain, viz. that whatever method was followed by the Egyptians, it was a very simple one. When the lighter had to be unloaded it was towed head on to the river bank, and as soon as firm ground had been reached the obelisk was worked on to it by levers, and then the rolling of it to the temple began.

From what has been said above it is quite clear that in the days of the Ptolemies and Roman Emperors the Egyptians were as able to transport obelisks from Heliopolis to Alexandria as from Syene to Heliopolis. It may be assumed that the craftsmen and raftsmen were Egyptians, who were thoroughly accustomed to the work, and that the Roman Prefects in Egypt would employ native labour. The lighters, or barges, that bore the obelisks across the sea were probably of the same kind as those that the

Egyptians employed to transport the cedars of Lebanon, which were intended to be used in the construction of the great sacred boats of the gods, from the Syrian coast, probably to the Damietta mouth of the Nile. But on one point Herodotus, Diodorus, Pliny and Ammianus Marcellinus are silent, viz. the taking down of the obelisks which were to be transported to Rome or Constantinople from their bases. We cannot assume that all those that were removed from Egypt had fallen down, and therefore it is certain that the Egyptians had some means of lowering safely to the ground the obelisks chosen by the Emperors for transportation. I believe that they used ropes and even pulleys, and were well acquainted with the importance of wedges and levers, but there is no evidence to show that they employed cranes, either in erecting or lowering obelisks. It has been suggested by engineering authorities that when the Egyptians had to lower an obelisk to the ground they built a huge mound of earth and sand on one side of it, and that the obelisk was pulled over on to it by means of ropes, then the sand and earth were removed from beneath it, and at length the obelisk lay unbroken on the ground. This appears to have been the method employed, although on such a matter the opinion of the archaeologist is of no value. But it is quite certain that the Egyptians could and did take obelisks off their bases and lower them unbroken to the ground, and it is equally certain that the method they followed in doing this work was a simple one.

THE ERECTION OF OBELISKS

We know no more how the Egyptians erected obelisks than how they lowered them. Some writers, who were neither engineers nor archaeologists, have definitely stated that the Egyptians must have known of and used machines, such as cranes and winches and pulleys, but no evidence to support this view is to be found in the Egyptian inscriptions. It is true that Pliny (xxxvi. 14) tells us that the King "Rhamsesis" (Rameses II ?) erected an obelisk 120 cubits in height by means of "machines" (machinae), but he gives no details of the way in which they were used, and the statement that Rhamsesis had his son tied to the top of the obelisk suggests that Pliny is quoting what was merely a legend. The various opinions of Sharpe, Letronne, Cooper, Canon Rawlinson and others are all summarized by Gorringe (*Egyptian Obelisks*, page 156), but are rejected by him. The Romans used balks of timber in large numbers, and innumerable ropes, as we learn from Ammianus Marcellinus (xvii. 4), but he supplies no details. It is, however, tolerably clear that the engineers built a huge framework round the site of the obelisk and hauled the obelisk upright by ropes and pulleys, and then fitted it on to its base.

Sharpe pointed out that a groove was cut on one side of the surface of the pedestal on which the obelisk was to stand, and that the obelisk, when lying on the ground, was moved in such a way that one edge of its base lay close alongside of it. When the obelisk was raised at one end this edge of the base would drop into the groove and keep it in position during the further raising of the obelisk. As the raising continued the space between the obelisk and the ground was packed with earth and sand, and the raising of the obelisk continued until it lay on the steeply sloping mound, ready to be hauled upright by ropes. This method would serve admirably if the obelisk had to be erected in an open space, but as Wilkinson and, later, Engelbach have shown, it was impossible to apply it when the obelisk had to be set up in the court of a temple without pulling down the walls; and the obelisks of Hatshepsut were set up in the court of Thothmes I without disturbing the colonnade. There are other objections to this method, which only the engineer can discuss usefully. The theory that now finds favour is that a huge embankment with a sloping side was made, and that the obelisk was dragged up this until the balancing-point was reached. The part of the mound under the base of the obelisk was then cleared away and the end of the monolith dropped down until it rested with one edge in the groove in the pedestal. The obelisk would still be lying against the slope of the mound, but it would be easy to pull it upright with ropes. This view was, substantially, that of the late Sir Benjamin Baker.

Against this view Mr. R. Engelbach urges certain objections (*Problem of the Obelisks*, London [no date], page 69), and sets forth the following suggestion. The obelisk was not let down over the edge of an embankment or mound, " but down a funnel-shaped pit *in* the end of it, the lowering being done by removing sand, with which the pit had been filled, from galleries leading into the bottom of it, and so allowing the obelisk to settle slowly down. Taking this as the basis of the method, the form of the pit resolves itself into a tapering square-sectioned funnel—rather like a petrol funnel—fairly wide at the top, but very little larger than the base of the obelisk at the bottom. The obelisk is introduced into the funnel on a curved way leading gradually from the surface of the embankment until it engages smoothly with the hither wall of the funnel. The sand is removed by men with baskets through galleries leading from the bottom of the funnel to convenient places outside the embankment." Mr. Engelbach gives in his book a series of plates illustrating his theory, which is undoubtedly very ingenious. As to its value the archaeologist dare not pass an opinion, but he may be permitted to say that it seems to be too elaborate for the Egyptians to have employed. I am convinced that all their methods of quarrying and working stone, and the building of pyramids and the setting-up of obelisks, were extremely simple, and that the tools they used in their greatest works were few and simple. But whatever were their methods they have left us no description of them, and in spite of all the thought that has been devoted to them by engineers, master-masons and archaeologists, we are still ignorant of the exact means that the Egyptians employed in the quarrying and erecting of obelisks.

When the roughly hewn monolith which was to be " dressed " into a stately obelisk had been set up, the operations of smoothing and polishing the faces began ; but here again nothing is known of the processes employed. It is possible that dolorite balls were used in smoothing the faces, and that the polishing of them was done with emery powder. The inscriptions were " set out " on the faces in red-ochre paint, and the figures and hieroglyphs were probably cut with chisels made of copper with an alloy in it, and polished with emery in some form.

But even when the obelisk was set up and polished and inscribed the work in connection with it was not finished, for the pyramidion had to be supplied with a metal casing, or cap. The obelisks which 'Abd al-Latîf saw at Heliopolis had copper casings on their pyramidions, and he describes how the rain-water, running off these on to the stone, had stained the shafts of the obelisks nearly down to their bases. This disfigurement of the monoliths set up in honour of the Sun-god was displeasing both to the Pharaohs and their people, and so we find that when Thothmes I, several centuries later, set up his two great obelisks before the double door of the house of the god, he covered their pyramidions with casings made of a metal which the Egyptians called *tchām*, . This word has been translated by " gold," " electrum," " white gold," " gilded copper," but no one knows what the exact constituents of the metal were. It can hardly have been gold, for the common word for gold is *nub*, [hieroglyphs]; on the other hand, *tchām* may be an old, and perhaps foreign, word for gold. Much of the gold ore found contains silver, and when the proportion of silver was one-fifth the ore was called "electrum" (Pliny, *N.H.* xxxiii. 23); an artificial electrum was made by mixing silver with gold. It is probable that *tchām* was a kind of natural gold which was found in the Sûdân and was called "green gold." In any case it was capable of a very high polish and reflected the light almost as brightly as quicksilver. It was used for the casings of the tops of obelisks throughout the XVIIIth and XIXth and following Dynasties; but we may note that Nekht-Her-Heb states distinctly that he covered the pyramidions of his two basalt obelisks with "black copper." Seeing that the pyramidion was usually decorated with vignettes and inscriptions, it is difficult to understand why it was covered with a metal casing.

Of the style and thickness of such a casing we know nothing, but a great deal of metal must have been needed for its construction, for Queen Hatshepsut says about her obelisks, "I allotted for them refined *tchām* [which] I weighed out by the *heket* measure, like sack[ful]s of grain." [hieroglyphs], in other words, she used the precious *tchām* not by the pound but by the hundredweight. These words suggest that the casings of the pyramidions of her obelisks were made of thick plates of *tchām*;

that they were of considerable value is proved by the fact that no trace of them has ever been found. It is probable that they were removed or stolen during the early years of the reign of the " heretic " king Amenhetep IV. Some have thought that the queen covered the shafts of the obelisks with gold, but there is no proof that any large temple obelisk was plated with gold. But it is very probable that the small obelisks standing in front of or by the sides of shrines were wholly covered with plates of gold, I mean the small obelisks like those that Amenhetep II made for the temple of Madamûd, or the small one made by this king recently found at Aswân. Some reason for this view is given in the Annals of the Assyrian king Ashurbanipal, 668–626 B.C. When he had conquered the Delta and punished the Egyptians who had murdered or expelled the governors whom his father Esarhaddon had appointed, he set out for Upper Egypt in order to capture and slay the Nubian King Tanutamen, who had seized Egypt. Ashurbanipal says, " I took the road in pursuit of Tandamanie (Tanutamen in Egyptian). I came to his fortified city Ni' (Thebes). He saw the approach of my mighty army and abandoned Ni'. He fled to the city Kipkip. I captured that city, the whole of it, by the aid of Ashur and Ishtar. Gold, silver, precious stones, his palace furniture, whatsoever there was, cloaks of many colours, linen shirts, great horses, people male and female, two tall pillars made out of bright *zaḫalu*-metal, which weighed 2,500 talents ; the fixtures in the temple gateway I tore up from their fittings and took to Assyria. A heavy booty past counting I carried away from Ni'." This took place in the year 663 B.C. It is now generally believed that the "two tall pillars" were two small obelisks that stood in front of some shrine, for obelisks were frequently described as "pillars" by Semitic writers. The metal of which they were made was "bright *zaḫalu*," and Sidney Smith, of the British Museum, translates the word by ὀρείχαλκος, copper ore, or aurichalcum, *i.e.* a metal formed by mixing silver and copper, the Ψευδάργυρον of Strabo, which the Assyrians used for inlay in their chariots. But whether the metal was composed of silver and copper or silver and gold, it is certain that Ashurbanipal would never have taken the trouble to carry off these two bright pillars unless they were of very considerable value. He says that they weighed 2,500 talents, *i.e.* about 49 cwt. 1 qr., or about 5,000 lbs. troy. One ounce of gold (22 carat) troy is worth £4 4*s*. 11½*d*.; if the two objects were of solid gold their present-day value would be well over £300,000 sterling.

THE RE-ERECTION OF OBELISKS IN THE ROMAN PERIOD AND IN MODERN TIMES

Reference has already been made to the re-erection of the obelisk from Heliopolis in the Circus Maximus in Rome, as described by Ammianus Marcellinus (*see* page 24), and the reader's attention may now be drawn to the bas-reliefs on the pedestal of the obelisk of

Thothmes III at Constantinople which commemorate its re-erection by the Emperor Theodosius. The bas-reliefs are on the north and south sides of the pedestal, and outline drawings of them are here reproduced. These are taken from the description of certain travels undertaken by Jacob Spon and George Wheeler, which they published under the title

The re-erection of an obelisk of Thothmes III in Constantinople.

Voyage d'Italie, de Dalmatie, de Grece, et du Levant, fait ès années 1675 & 1676, tomm. 4, Lyon, 1678. The upper and middle registers, which are taken from the north side of the pedestal, deal with the erection of the obelisk. In the top right-hand corner of the upper register is a construction with five arched openings, which has been supposed to represent the barrier by which spectators were kept away from the immediate scene of operations. In front of it lies the obelisk, which is supposed to be lying on a sledge, one of the large wheels of which is shown by the square end of the obelisk. The monolith is being hauled along by ropes attached to four capstans, each of which is worked by four men. The directions as to the hauling are being given by a man with his right hand raised, and the man standing on a block appears to be watching the progress of the work. The actual setting up of the obelisk on its plinth is not represented, but in the second register we see it standing upright. On one side of it is a man apparently carrying someone who has been injured, and on the other are three men, one cleaning the obelisk, one holding aloft a hammer in his left hand, and a third who is probably giving directions. In the lower register, which is taken from the south side of the pedestal, are two obelisks, and a pillar, two mounted horsemen, two men presenting torches (?) to sacred pillars, or perhaps goals, and a victor in the games who is about to be crowned. This relief probably represents the performance of games in the Circus at Constantinople after the erection of the obelisk.

About the transport, lowering and re-erection of obelisks in comparatively modern times we possess a considerable amount of information, which may now be summarized. Pope Sixtus V was very anxious to remove to the Piazza before the Vatican the obelisk that Caligula had brought from Alexandria and set up in the Circus of Caligula. At his direction this obelisk was carefully examined by the architect Domenico Fontana, who reported that its foundations were unsafe, and that the pyramidion was 17 inches out of the perpendicular. Sixtus V decided to move the obelisk and, in order to do away with its pagan character, he intended, when it was re-erected, to set up on it the Christian Cross. He discussed his project with dignitaries of all kinds, and as nothing practical emerged from his discussions he called a general meeting and offered a prize for the best plan for carrying it out. A very large number of engineers and others attended the meeting, and many plans were described and discussed. The propositions put forward were: to remove it, with its pedestal, in an upright position; to take it down and re-erect it by means of a huge wheel; to incline it in a cradle to an angle of 45 degrees and then move it; to take it down and raise it by means of a huge lever; to lower and raise it by means of endless screws worked vertically and horizontally, and so on. Plans of these various machines were submitted to the Pope, and drawings of several of them are given by Fontana in one of the plates of his work *Della Trasportazione dell' Obelisco Vaticano*, Rome, 1590. Comments on them will be found in *Egyptian Obelisks*, by Lieut.-Commander H. H. Gorringe, pages 111 ff.

The plan suggested by Fontana was to lower the obelisk, lay it flat, haul it on rollers to the new site, and then raise it by ropes worked by capstans. The Pope accepted his plan and,

Scaffold built by Fontana for the removal of the obelisk from the Circus Maximus to the Piazza of St. Peter, Rome. Above are the drawings of the mechanical instruments to be used in its removal, and below is a capstan with men in position for working it.

"Fontana's Castle," in which the obelisk is lying flat between the uprights, with its pyramidion visible. Underneath it are a capstan and the horses used in working it.

brushing aside all opposition, entrusted the whole responsibility for the performance of the work to him. Fontana began to dig the trench for the new site in September, 1585. The Pope ordered all buildings that were likely to hinder the work to be removed, and gave him authority to take everything he required from the Papal stores. And everyone was called upon to help Fontana in carrying out his plans. Wood was collected, ropes were made, capstans were built on a special plan, and every care was taken in choosing the materials to be used in lowering and re-erecting the obelisk, which was estimated to weigh about 325 tons. Forty capstans, each with four bars and the necessary sets of tackle, were made, and these were worked by 800 men and 75 horses, and 5 great levers worked by 106 men. A huge scaffolding, 90 feet high, and of immense strength, was built to provide fixed points for the pulleys. Fontana's drawing of it is reproduced on **Plate II.** Each upright, made of oak and walnut, was four beams thick, and these were kept in position by key-bolts, iron bands and ropes, fixed at regular intervals. The uprights and their struts were secured by tie-beams, iron bands, etc., and the former were connected by trusses, to which the tackle blocks were attached. The whole scaffolding was built on a heavy timber platform, and was commonly known as "Fontana's Castle." In the illustration on **Plate III** we see the arrangement of the tackles, the capstans worked by men and horses, and the obelisk in the course of lowering.

The obelisk was then covered on all sides with a layer of matting and planks of wood, which were kept in position by thick iron bars ; these in turn were secured with iron bands, which served as points for the attachment of the lower blocks of the tackle. The obelisk was to be raised 2 feet above its pedestal on four bronze blocks, and so the iron bars could be passed under the base of the obelisk without injuring the pedestal. The casing of rope, wood, and iron was estimated to weigh about 23 tons. The brass globe which had been fixed on the top of the obelisk when Caligula set it up was removed ; it was empty, though many believed that it would be found to contain valuable objects. Meanwhile the houses that would have interfered with the working of the tackles and the capstans were pulled down, and the pit, which was to contain the foundations of the obelisk in the new site in the Piazza of St. Peter, was dug. When the latter was finished, two stone boxes, containing several medals commemorative of the great work of Sixtus V and others bearing his effigy, were placed in it. Towards the end of April, 1586, everything was ready for the lowering of the obelisk. On the night of the 29th, Fontana and his colleagues attended Mass and received the Pope's benediction, and two special Masses were celebrated, during which the help and guidance of the Holy Spirit were invoked. When the news spread abroad that the work was to begin on the 30th, people flocked to Rome in large numbers, and these, together with the dwellers in the city, formed very large crowds. No unauthorized person was allowed to pass the barriers that were set up, and absolute silence was ordered. Fontana took up his position in a prominent place, and addressing the people he called upon them to entreat God to help them in this great undertaking, the object of which was to exalt the Cross ; when he had ceased to speak, everyone, gentle and simple, rich and poor, clergy and laity, fell upon their knees and recited a Paternoster and an Ave Maria.

At a blast of a trumpet the capstans began to turn, wedges were driven under the obelisk, and the tackles began to raise it into an upright position ; a few hours later the obelisk had been lifted 2 feet above the pedestal, and all the machinery had stood the strain. The next day the cradle on which the obelisk was to roll was inserted under it, and a week later the monolith had been taken off its pedestal and laid safely upon the cradle. Its position is well illustrated by the reproduction of Fontana's drawing on **Plate IV**. The general rejoicing was great and Fontana was carried home escorted by a band with drums and trumpets. The next step was to roll the obelisk on its cradle to its new site, about 300 yards distant, and as that was on a lower level an embankment of earth had to be made ; the sides of it were supported by strutted wood revetments with transverse and diagonal braces. The height of this embankment or roadway increased from zero at the old site to 27 feet at the new ; its width at the base was 73 feet and at the top 36½ feet. The illustration on page 46 shows a portion of this roadway with the obelisk lying upon its cradle on top of it. When the obelisk had been dragged away from the pedestal,

A portion of the roadway which had been specially constructed, with the obelisk lying upon its cradle on top of it.

the masonry was removed and rebuilt on the foundations at the new site, which, with the oak and chestnut piles, descended into the ground to a depth of about 40 feet.

PLATE IV.

The obelisk lying on its cradle ready for re-erection.

PLATE V.

The obelisk in course of erection.

By September 10 everything was ready for the re-erection of the obelisk. The scaffolding had been rebuilt, and the obelisk had been dragged by means of the capstans and tackles from the old site to the new, and it lay immediately over the centre of the pedestal. The work of raising (*see* **Plate V**) began at daylight on the 10th, and after 13 hours' toil, with only one short interval for refreshment, the obelisk stood in a vertical position over the pedestal, but separated from it by the cradle. This was removed on the following day, when the obelisk was again lifted and made to rest on the wedges; one week later the bronze "crabs," or blocks, which were under the obelisk when it stood on its old site, were replaced, and the obelisk stood firmly on the new site, where it now is.

The first European in modern times to transport an obelisk from Egypt and re-erect it in his native land was the French engineer **Le Bas.** It will be remembered that early in the XIXth century the Pâshâ of Egypt presented the obelisk that was still standing at Alexandria and was known as "Cleopatra's Needle" to Louis XVIII, but the French took no steps to remove the gift to France. About 1829 Champollion le Jeune was travelling in Egypt on behalf of the French Government. When he was at Luxor he was struck by the magnificence of the pair of obelisks which Rameses II set up in the temple there, and he advised the home authorities to demand them as a gift from Muhammad 'Alî. After much negotiation the French diplomatic representatives in Cairo were told that they could have one of them. Thereupon the French built a special barge, called the **Luxor,** and sent it out to Egypt to bring home the obelisk, and in 1836 Le Bas was deputed to go out and dismount the obelisk chosen by Champollion and bring it back and re-erect it in Paris. Now the pair of obelisks at Luxor were the only pair left standing in all Egypt, and to remove one of them was, as many writers have justly said, a gross

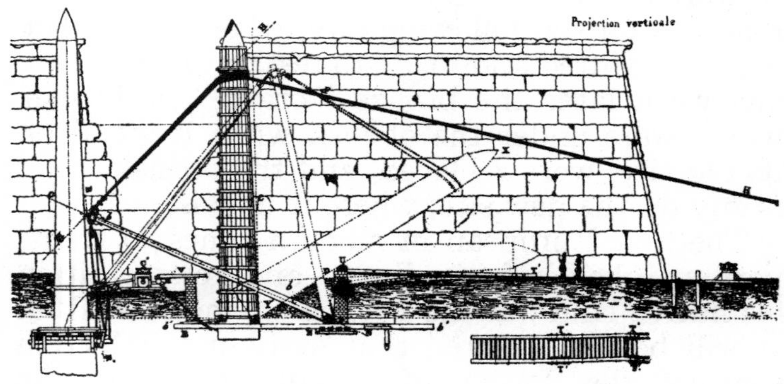

The lowering of an obelisk of Rameses II at Luxor for removal to Paris by Le Bas.

act of vandalism. How the French Government could have sanctioned such a proposition as the removal of one of these, and supplied funds lavishly for giving effect to the suggestion, is a thing not easily understood. Le Bas went to Luxor, uprooted the obelisk, and did an immense amount of damage to the ancient Egyptian buildings clustering around it. He did not build a scaffold like Fontana, but used multiple sheers, with the necessary pulleys and tackle. After much delay and vast expenditure he took

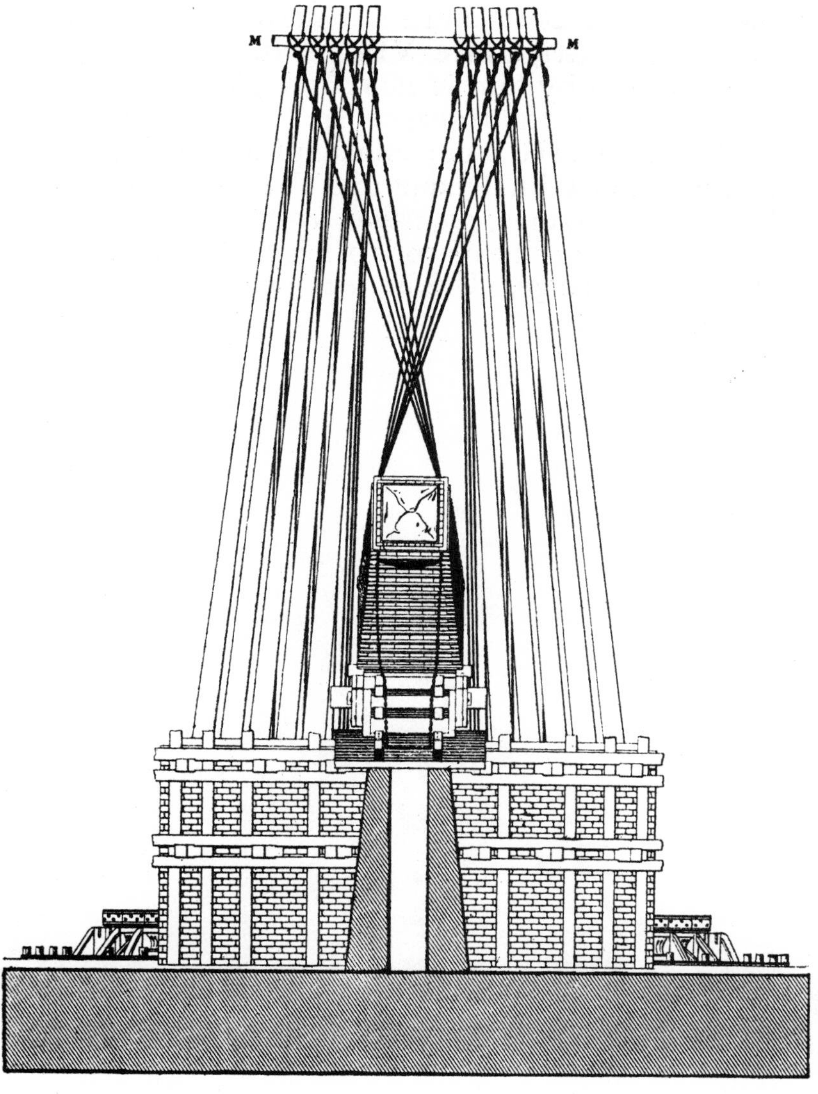

Scaffold used by Le Bas in re-erecting an obelisk of Rameses II in Paris.

the obelisk to Paris and set it up in the Place de a Concorde (*see* **Plate VI**). A drawing of the scaffold used by him is given on page 49. For descriptions of the transport of the two obelisks of Thothmes III from Alexandria, the one to London, by John Dixon, and the other to New York, by Gorringe, *see* pages 67–75 of this little book and the masterly work of Lieut.-Commander H. H. Gorringe, U.S.N., *Egyptian Obelisks*, London, 1885.

PLATE VI.

Obelisk of Rameses II re-erected by Le Bas in the Place de la Concorde, Paris.

CHAPTER II

HOW CLEOPATRA'S NEEDLE CAME TO LONDON

WHEN the military operations which the British carried out in Egypt in 1798–1802 came to an end, the British officers in command at Alexandria determined to put on record the principal facts about the work that they had done in the country. The British Army, under Sir Ralph Abercromby, and the British Navy, under Lord Nelson, restored both Egypt and Syria to the Turks, and were proud of their victories over the French, which had, however, cost them dear, for at the moment of the great victory gained on March 21, 1801, Abercromby fell mortally wounded. To erect a suitable monument to the memory of this great soldier was out of the question, for the British knew that it would be pulled down as soon as they left the country and the stones used for other purposes. They therefore decided to cut a brief account of their victories upon a slab of stone, which they intended to deposit in a safe and secret hiding-place. The inscription,[1]

[1] A copy of the complete text was published in the *Bombay Courier* of June 9, 1802, and another copy is given in my *Handbook for Egypt and the Sûdân,* page 132.

drawn up by the Earl of Cavan (1763–1836), stated that in 1798 the Republic of France landed in Egypt an army of 40,000 men under the command of General Bonaparte, and occupied the country. The French fleet was destroyed in Abukîr Bay by Admiral Lord Nelson, and the attempt of Napoleon to seize Syria was frustrated by Commodore Sidney Smith. A decisive action fought near Alexandria in March, 1801, left the British Army masters of the country, which they made haste to evacuate, the work for which they had come being accomplished. Lord Cavan concludes with a mention of the loss sustained by the death of Sir Ralph Abercromby, and states that the inscription has been drawn up to " record to future ages these events." When the inscription had been cut upon a slab of stone, the soldiers looked for a suitable hiding-place in which to bury it, and this they found in the pedestal of Cleopatra's Needle, which was then lying on the ground close to the pedestal. According to the *Bombay Courier*, " the pedestal of the fallen Needle of Cleopatra having been heeled to starboard," a cavity, sufficiently deep to receive the inscribed tablet, was then cut in the block of stone on which the pedestal had rested, and when the inscribed tablet had been laid in the cavity the pedestal was worked back into its former position. Some who have written about this matter appear to have thought that the inscribed tablet was inserted in the pedestal of the obelisk, but the actual words of the writer in the *Bombay Courier* are : " The pedestal of the fallen Needle of Cleopatra having been heeled to starboard, and a proper (*i.e.* suitable ?) excavation made in the centre of the base stone, this inscription on a slab of marble was inserted, and the pedestal restored to its former situation." It seems to me that the " base stone " was not the pedestal itself, but the block of stone on which it rested. I can find no evidence to show that either the pedestal or the block containing the tablet on which it was replaced has been discovered by those who have examined or excavated the site. The inscribed slab was undoubtedly buried in the masonry on which the obelisk once stood, and it is to be hoped that it may one day be brought to light and find a resting-place in some museum, though, considering all the stone buildings that have been built in Alexandria during the last 50 years, it seems to be hardly possible.

It is well known that the members of the scientific Mission which followed Napoleon to Egypt were instructed by him to collect important monuments in Upper and Lower Egypt to form the nucleus of a collection of Egyptian Antiquities which he intended to house in Cairo. These *savants* obeyed his instructions with thoroughness, and a considerable number of inscribed objects of all kinds were sent to Cairo in 1799 and 1800. The French officers in Alexandria also collected many monuments, including the Rosetta Stone, and the more portable of these were sent to Cairo. The Battle of Alexandria on March 21, 1801, compelled the French to capitulate,[1] and the

[1] Alexandria surrendered on September 2, 1801.

labours of the French *savants* came abruptly to an end, and all the antiquities which they had collected passed under certain clauses of the Capitulations into the hands of the British.

The Earl of Cavan and all the soldiers who were serving under him wished to send the fallen obelisk to England as a trophy which would commemorate Nelson's victory at the Battle of Abukîr (August 1, 1798) and Abercromby's victory at the Battle of Alexandria. Looking back at the events of that time, and the splendid services that the British had rendered to Muhammad 'Alî, it is difficult to understand why Cleopatra's Needle was not brought to this country forthwith. But there was no one in the Government who was interested in the matter, and as Lord Cavan was instructed by his official superiors to cease from his exertions, the obelisk was allowed to remain where it lay for some 70 years more. Both Ministers and high officials, in truly British fashion, seemed to be ashamed of the victories that British soldiers had won in Egypt, or at any rate were unwilling to allow any really great monument to be set up that would commemorate them. Much light was thrown upon this matter by the publication in the *Athenæum* for September 22, 1877 (No. 2604),[1] of a memorandum preserved in the British Museum. From this we learn that " At the termination of the Campaign in 1801, in Egypt, General the Earl of Cavan was left in command of the portion of the British forces

[1] Extracts from it were reprinted by W. R. Cooper in his book, *On Obelisks*, London, 1877.

"Matters being thus arranged, the necessary Working Parties were allotted daily, in the general orders issued by M.-Genl. the Earl of Cavan, and the undertaking proceeded most prosperously. To compensate the soldiery for the tear and wear of their Necessaries, Working Pay was issued to the Working Parties from the Funds to which they themselves had contributed. Considerable progress was made with the Jetty, and the Superior Officers of the Royal Navy then at Alexandria, viz. Captains Larcom and Donelly, embarked most zealously and cordially in our project, which must have been therefore perfectly successful, had it not been abandoned, in consequence of orders received from Lord Keith and General Fox, who at that time held the chief Command of the Fleet and of the Troops serving in the Mediterranean, . . .[1] The Working Parties were of course discontinued: the bargain with the Prize Agents for the Ship was dissolved, and the Funds remaining undisbursed were returned to the Subscribers. The project of conveying the fallen Needle to England being no longer practicable, it was resolved that another expedient should be adopted, in order to establish some lasting Record of the results of so glorious an expedition; accordingly, the uppermost Block of the Pedestal of the fallen Needle was raised upon one side sufficiently high, by means of levers, to admit of a space of about Eighteen Inches square being chiselled out of the middle of the lowest

[1] The dots represent the criticism of the writer of the memorandum on the causes that led to the abandonment of the work.

Block of the Pedestal. In that space a brass[1] plate was laid, on which was engraved a short detail of the principal Events of the Campaign."

The text of the Inscription was as follows :—

In the Year of the Christian Era 1798,
The Republic of France
Landed on the Shores of Egypt an Army of 40000 Men,
Commanded by their most able and successful Commander Bonaparte,
The Conduct of the General and the Valour of the Troops,
Effected the entire subjection of that Country;
But under Divine Providence
It was reserved for the British Nation
To annihilate their ambitious Designs.
Their Fleet was attacked, defeated and destroyed, in Aboukir Bay,
By a British Fleet of equal Force,
Commanded by Admiral Lord Nelson,
Their intended conquest of Syria was counteracted at Acre
By a most gallant Resistance under Commodore Sir Sidney Smith;
And Egypt was rescued from their dominion
By a British Army, inferior in Numbers, but
Commanded by General Sir Ralph Abercrombie,
Who landed at Aboukir on the 8th of March, 1801,
Defeated the French on several Occasions,
Particularly in a most decisive Action near Alexandria,
On the 21st of that month, when they
Were driven from the Field, and forced to shelter themselves
In their Garrisons of Cairo and Alexandria,
Which places subsequently surrendered by Capitulation.
To record to Future Ages these Events;
And to commemorate the Loss sustained by the Death of
Sir Ralph Abercrombie,
Who was mortally wounded on that memorable Day,
Is the design of this Inscription.
Which was deposited here in the year of Christ 1802
By the British Army on their evacuating this country,
And restoring it to the Turkish Empire.

[1] The *Bombay Courier* says: "this inscription on a slab of marble was inserted." If the plate or tablet was made of brass it would rapidly oxidize and perish, and it is probably due to this fact that no trace of the tablet has been found.

The reasons which induced Lord Keith and Lord Hutchinson to direct the Earl of Cavan to abandon the obelisk have often been discussed and commented on; some authorities have thought that they did so because they were not satisfied that Muhammad ‘Alî had given the formal permission for its removal, and this may well have been the case. At all events, nothing further was said in high quarters about the removal of Cleopatra's Needle to England until 1820, when the question was raised by Samuel Briggs, sometime British Consul at Alexandria. In April of that year he addressed a letter on the subject to Sir Benjamin Bloomfield, one of the Ministers of King George IV, in which he wrote:—

"Having, on my late visit to Egypt, witnessed the stupendous labours of the celebrated Mr. Belzoni, and received from him the assurance that he could confidently undertake the removal to England of one of the granite obelisks at Alexandria, I was encouraged to submit to His Highness [the Viceroy] my opinion that one of the obelisks known in Europe under the appellation of Cleopatra's Needles, might possibly be acceptable to His Majesty, as unique of its kind in England, and which might, therefore, be considered a valuable addition to the embellishments designed for the British metropolis. His Highness promised to take the subject into consideration; and, since my return to England, I have received a letter from his Minister, authorising me, if I deemed it acceptable, to make, in his master's name, a tender of one of these obelisks to His Majesty, as a mark of his personal respect and gratitude . . . After the glorious termination of the conjoint expedition to Egypt in 1801, it was proposed by some officers of high rank to convey to England this identical obelisk as an appropriate trophy. Representations were actually made, and subscriptions entered into, among the officers of both army and navy ; but being found inadequate, the design was reluctantly relinquished ; and it was generally understood to have been a subject of regret with the administration of that period, that government had been apprised of it too late to afford the necessary means towards its accomplishment."

To lend weight to his application Briggs then gives the names of several distinguished officials and others who thought the obelisk well worth removal, among them being Lord Cavan, Lord Beresford, Sir R. Rickerston, Sir D. Baird, Sir H. Oakes, Admiral Donelly, etc. He describes the obelisk as a—

"single block of red granite (weighing 183 tons, exclusive of the pedestal and steps), originally brought from the quarries in Upper Egypt, near the cataracts. It is now close to the sea-shore at Alexandria, suspended horizontally on its pedestal, in the manner in which it was placed by our officers in the year 1802, near to the site where the other obelisk is erected. It is about 68 feet in height from the base to the apex, and about 7 feet square at the base. On the four sides it is richly sculptured with hieroglyphics in a superior style, more than an inch deep ; and though in the lapse of ages it has partially suffered on two sides from the desert winds, the other two are in good preservation. The pedestal is a plain block of the same granite, about 8½ feet square, and 6½ feet high. All travellers mention it with encomiums. Clarke, Walsh, and Sir R. Wilson, lament in their works, it was not secured to England ; and Denon contemplated the feasibility of one day transporting it to France . . . . In the present state of the arts and sciences in England, it may reasonably be presumed no obstacle can exist but what the munificence of the Sovereign can readily surmount. What Belzoni has already done, with only common local means, in conveying to Alexandria, from ancient Thebes, the colossal head which now ornaments the British Museum, together with the success of his other labours, is an earnest of what he is capable of performing; whilst, at the same time, the unprecedented extent of the excavations attests the liberal character of the present ruler of Egypt, no less than the various improvements he has of late years introduced into the country.

"Eminently brilliant as the Government of His Majesty has been, during the Regency, in arms and politics, it will, in future times, be no less distinguished for the liberal encouragement given to the arts and sciences, and for the splendid embellishments conferred on the metropolis. Rome and Constantinople are the only cities in Europe which can boast of Egyptian monuments of this description. They, however, still attest the power and grandeur of the ancient masters of the world; and if the bronze column erected at Paris in modern times serves to ornament that city, and perpetuates the trophies of the French arms, this Egyptian obelisk, in the capital of England, would equally remain a permanent memorial of British achievements, and would be admired by posterity, as well as by the present age, for the boldness of the undertaking as much as for its intrinsic merits. I respectfully submit to you, Sir, in the first instance, this offer of the Viceroy of Egypt, as being in its nature more personal than official, and therefore more complimentary to His Majesty. Should you deem it proper to take His Majesty's pleasure thereon, I shall be happy to convey to His Highness the Viceroy, the acceptance of his offer, if approved. But should you consider it more correct that I should make this communication to His Majesty's Ministers, I shall immediately comply with your suggestion."[1]

This eloquent appeal had no effect from a practical point of view, and no attempt was made to bring Cleopatra's Needle to England. Antiquaries and the public generally rejoiced to hear that the obelisk had been formally presented to H.M. George IV, and assumed that the Government would find both the means for

[1] *See* Wilson, E., *Cleopatra's Needle*, page 186.

transport and the men for bringing this splendid gift to England. It would have been easy to raise the necessary funds for its transport by private subscription, but the suppression of the activities of Lord Cavan in 1802 by Lord Keith and Lord Hutchinson had not been forgotten by the nation, and men hesitated to propose a public subscription, fearing that once again moneys subscribed might have to be returned to the givers.

In 1831, Muhammad 'Alî, thinking, it is said, that the British Government did not realize that he had already given the obelisk to the British Nation, offered it again to the King, and proposed to defray all expenses that might be incurred in removing it from the place where it lay on the sea-shore to the ship to be provided by the British for conveying it to England. In spite of the interest of the public generally, and the constant urging which the principal Ministers received, nothing was done, and the offer of the obelisk would have been allowed to lapse but for the exertions of Joseph Hume (1775–1855), the famous politician and leader of the Radical Party. As the result of his questions in Parliament the Government had enquiries made as to the proposed method and the cost of transport, which was said to be about £15,000, and though Hume and his supporters were given to understand that the money would be provided by the Government, and that the work of removing the obelisk would be put in hand forthwith, nothing was done, and the obelisk was apparently forgotten. Time after time a question about the removal of it was asked in Parliament, and at length in 1849 the Government declared on April 15 that they intended to bring one of the two obelisks at Alexandria to London. Another estimate of the cost was prepared, and a lively discussion ensued as to the site most suitable for the obelisk when it arrived, but still the Government did nothing, and Hume was informed that they intended to do nothing because a little band of enthusiasts for classical antiquities, headed by Sir Gardner Wilkinson, had made it clear to them that the obelisk was too much defaced to be worth removal. When Wilkinson heard of the decision of the Government, he said: "The project has been wisely abandoned; and cooler deliberation has pronounced that, from its mutilated state, and the obliteration of many of the hieroglyphics by exposure to the sea air, it is unworthy the expense of removal."[1] Two years later a proposal was made by Hume to bring the obelisk to London and set it up in Hyde Park as a memorial of the great work which had been done by the Prince Consort in connection with the Great Exhibition of 1851; but even this suggestion produced no result.

In 1853, whilst Joseph Bonomi was building the Egyptian Court at Sydenham for the Crystal Palace Company, it was suggested that Cleopatra's Needle should be brought to England and set up in the transept near the Egyptian Court. The expense was estimated at £7,000.

[1] Cooper (*On Obelisks,* page 130) quotes from Murray's *Egypt,* page 91.

The Directors of the Crystal Palace Company discussed the matter and decided to adopt the suggestion. They applied to the Government for permission to remove the obelisk to England, and this was granted. The Company assumed that if they paid for the transport of the obelisk the object would become their property, and so the shareholders understood. They had no intention of doing for the Government what it was the duty of the Government to do for themselves. And when those in authority informed the Company that the obelisk was the property of the nation, and that it could only be *lent* to them, the Directors decided that they could not afford to spend £7,000 of the money of their shareholders on the loan of the obelisk, and so once again the public, who on this occasion were very excited and hopeful, were disappointed.

About 15 years later His Highness the Khedive of Egypt (Sa'îd Pâshâ) brought the question of the removal of the obelisk to England before the British Government. He had let the land on which the monument lay to a certain Greek called Dimitri, who wished to develop the property he had rented, and the obelisk made it impossible for him to carry out his plans for building. He therefore applied to the Khedive either to remove the obelisk or to have it buried, and the Khedive politely asked the British Government to remove the obelisk which Muhammad 'Alî had given to England more than once.[1] Nothing was done until General Sir James E. Alexander interested himself in

[1] See *The Times* for February 12, 1877 (quoted by Cooper).

the matter. This enthusiastic soldier spent much time in clearing the obelisk from the *débris* in which, during the course of centuries, it had become almost buried, and for seven years he never ceased, in season and out of season, to urge the British Government to act and move the obelisk. It is said that his interest in the obelisk dated from the year 1867, when he was in Paris and had an opportunity of observing the fine effect produced on the landscape of Paris by the great granite obelisk which the French had brought from Thebes and set up in the Place de la Concorde. He was urged on to redouble his efforts by the rumours which reached him from Alexandria to the effect that a certain French engineer resident in that city had offered to break up the obelisk for Dimitri, so that he might use the pieces for building purposes. Towards the close of 1876, when General Alexander had lost all hope of ever seeing the obelisk in England, he found it necessary to write to Dr. (later Sir) **William James Erasmus Wilson**[1] (1809–1884), F.R.S., F.R.C.S.,

[1] He was the son of William Wilson, a native of Aberdeen, who, after serving as a surgeon in the Navy, practised at Dartford in Kent. In 1840 he became sub-editor of the *Lancet*. He was elected a Fellow of the College of Surgeons in 1843, and a Fellow of the Royal Society in 1845. He was the first authority of his day on skin diseases, and founded a professorship of Dermatology, which in 1869 he endowed with a sum of £5,000. He built a new wing and chapel at the sea-bathing Infirmary at Margate at a cost of £30,000, and was a generous benefactor to many other charities. After the death of his wife, the bulk of his property, amounting to upwards of £200,000, reverted to the Royal College of Surgeons of England.

on certain professional matters, and went on to describe his difficulties connected with Cleopatra's Needle, and to say that he hoped to collect by private subscriptions enough money to bring it to England. A few days later Erasmus Wilson had an interview with General Alexander, who told him that the Government had again refused to give him any pecuniary assistance, though they were quite ready to instruct their diplomatic and consular officials to give him every help possible when he had collected the necessary funds for the removal of the obelisk. Without any hesitation Erasmus Wilson offered to defray the whole cost of the transport of the obelisk to England, and then asked how it was to be done. During General Alexander's stay in Egypt he had met Mr. **John Dixon,** a civil engineer who had specially studied this problem, because he hoped that one day, when he was sufficiently rich, he would be able to bring the obelisk to England at his own expense. In November, 1876, Erasmus Wilson called on Mr. J. Dixon, who in answer to his questions described the method of transport he proposed to use if commissioned to undertake it.[1] He would enclose the monolith in a cylinder made of boiler plates, and roll it into the sea. He would steady the cylinder by means of bilge plates, ballast it, fix a rudder and a cabin and a spar deck, and then tow the cylinder to England. He thought it might be done for

[1] The various plans suggested by Admiral Smyth, Mr. J. L. Haddan and others, are described at length in Gorringe, *Egyptian Obelisks,* pages 98 ff.

£5,000, but was willing to contract to do it for £7,000. Erasmus Wilson asked if he would undertake to set the obelisk up safely on the bank of the Thames, and he said, "Willingly." A week later Erasmus Wilson, Gen. Alexander, Mr. Dixon and another engineer, Mr. H. P. Stephenson, met at a solicitor's office in Bedford Row and agreed to the terms of a contract which was duly signed on January 30, 1877.

Mr. Dixon then set to work on his plans for the cylindrical ship, which was built at the works of the Thames Iron Works Company. The **Cleopatra,** as she was called, was 93 feet long and 15 feet in diameter, and she was divided into ten compartments by nine watertight bulkheads; her Captain was Henry Carter of the P. & O. Steam Navigation Company. Whilst this ship was being built application was made to Lord Derby for permission to bring the obelisk to England, but he referred the applicants to the Khedive, saying that England had refused the gift. Gen. Alexander went to Cairo and had an audience of His Highness, who not only gave the obelisk to England once more, but told him that he had his permission to remove it. Then a new difficulty presented itself. Dimitri, the Greek who had leased from the Khedive the land on which the obelisk lay, and had claimed damages in the Courts against him, on the ground that it obstructed his building operations, now declared that the Khedive had no right to give anyone permission to trespass on his land. When Mr. Dixon and Captain Carter went to make preparations for removing the obelisk, Dimitri stopped them and complained bitterly of the high-handed action of the Khedive.

At length Mr. Dixon found a way to soothe his susceptibilities, and they were allowed to begin work early in June. Stout balks of timber were placed under the obelisk, which was then turned round so that it lay parallel with the sea. As soon as the plates arrived the building of the case around it was begun, and by the middle of August the obelisk in its iron case was ready for launching. The launch began on August 28, and fair progress was made, but on the 29th the fore part of the Cleopatra struck a huge boulder, which pierced the iron casing and allowed the ship to become half-full of water. Several days were spent in removing the boulder, which weighed at least half a ton, and had made a hole in the casing 18 inches wide. The ship was rolled over and the hole patched up, and on September 7 the obelisk was afloat. She was then towed into the great floating dock of the Egyptian Government, bilge keels, 40 feet long, were riveted on, the cabin and bridge were fitted, the rudder hung, the mast stepped, and 20 tons of iron ballast were stored in her. She was christened **Cleopatra** by Miss MacKillop on September 21, and, in tow of the S.S. Olga, she started on her voyage. (*See* **Plate VII.**) Captain Carter stopped at Algiers and Gibraltar, and all was well, but as soon as he had passed Cape St. Vincent the weather became " dirty," and a heavy gale from the S.S.W. burst on the ships. As Captain Carter decided to bring his ship head to wind, he signalled to Captain

PLATE VII.

The Cleopatra at sea carrying "Cleopatra's Needle" to London.

PLATE VIII.

The Cleopatra cut adrift and on her beam ends.

—From the *Illustrated London News*.

Booth of the Olga to cast off, but before this could be done a tremendous sea broke over the Cleopatra with such violence that she lurched heavily, and as the iron ballast, which had, unfortunately, not been securely fastened, shifted the ship went over on her "beam ends." (*See* **Plate VIII.**) It was impossible to secure the rails of the ballast, and Captain Carter decided to abandon the Cleopatra; the life-boat was cleared and lowered, but was dashed to pieces against the rudder-yoke. Captain Booth of the Olga guessed what had happened, and called for volunteers to go aboard the Cleopatra and secure the ballast. Six gallant sailors answered his call and lowered and manned their boat, and succeeded in getting away from their ship; but as they were nearing the Cleopatra a mighty sea fell upon them, their boat was engulfed and those brave men were drowned. Captain Booth, after many attempts, succeeded in throwing a line over the Cleopatra, and by means of this a boat was hauled alongside, and Captain Carter and his crew were able to reach the Olga. Captain Booth, having cast off the tow-line, searched for the boat that had been swamped, but could find neither that nor the Cleopatra; and concluding that both had gone to the bottom he steered his course for Falmouth, which he reached on October 17. But the Cleopatra had not foundered, and soon after she was abandoned by the Olga she was sighted when about 70 miles from Ferrol by the captain of the Fitzmaurice, who towed her into that port and demanded £5,000 for his salvage. The Admiralty Court awarded him £2,000. Finally, the Cleopatra was taken in tow by the tug Anglia, and she reached London on January 20, 1878.

Meanwhile a heated discussion had been going on in the Press about the site on which the obelisk was to be erected. The site in the gardens on the Thames Embankment, which had been granted to General Alexander in 1872 by the Metropolitan Board of Works, was generally considered to be unsuitable. The best site for it would have been the centre of the courtyard of the British Museum, Bloomsbury, but it was feared that the great weight of the obelisk would, in passing through the streets, crush the water-pipes and gas-pipes laid under them and damage the sewers. Mr. Dixon wanted to set it up in the garden plot opposite Westminster Abbey, but the Directors of the Underground Railway proved that there would always be a risk of its breaking through into the tunnel, and the idea of this site was abandoned. Finally, the Metropolitan Board of Works offered a site for the obelisk at the foot of the Adelphi steps on the Victoria Embankment, between the Waterloo and Charing Cross bridges. A concrete base, reaching down to the London clay beneath the mud bed of the river, having been made, the Cleopatra was towed up from the East India Docks and brought alongside, and when she was taken to pieces the obelisk was raised by hydraulic jacks and slid on to the Embankment. An iron jacket 20 feet long, with two projecting pivots on opposite sides, was placed

PLATE IX.

" Cleopatra's Needle " being raised by hydraulic jacks preparatory to being swung into position on its pedestal.

round the obelisk, with a stirrup strap to prevent its slipping when being swung into a vertical position. It was then raised in a horizontal position by hydraulic jacks (*see* **Plate IX**), and supported on timbers as the raising proceeded. Three steps and a pedestal were then built up under it to a total height of 18 feet 8 inches. The pedestal is of masonry, is 10 feet 5 inches high, and tapers from 10 feet square at the base to 9 feet 3 inches; the gradual diminution of diameter, or "batter," produces an admirable effect. The three lower courses have a core of brickwork and cement, but the fourth and fifth are of granite throughout.

A curious, but interesting, collection of objects was placed in the pedestal before the obelisk was set up on it; these include:—A scale model of the obelisk 2 feet 10 inches high, in bronze, a piece of granite from the obelisk itself, a complete set of British moneys and a rupee, a standard foot and standard pound, a two-foot rule, a standard gauge to the $\frac{1}{1000}$ part of an inch, a portrait of Queen Victoria, a history of the transport of the obelisk from Alexandria to London, with plans, printed on vellum, Dr. Birch's translation on parchment of the inscriptions on the obelisk, copies of the Bible in several languages, a translation of St. John's Gospel, chapter iii, verse 16, printed in 215 languages, the Pentateuch in Hebrew, the Book of Genesis in Arabic, a copy of the *London Directory*, a copy of Whitaker's *Almanack*, a copy of Bradshaw's *Railway Guide*, a map of London, copies of the current daily and weekly illustrated papers, a Tangye hydraulic jack and specimens of wire ropes and cables used in raising the obelisk, a shilling razor made by Mappin, a box of cigars, a number of tobacco pipes, an Alexandra feeding-bottle, a collection of toys, a box of hairpins and other articles used by women when making their toilette, photographs of 12 pretty Englishwomen, etc.

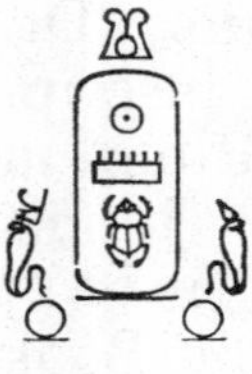

Early in September it was found that the obelisk had been raised to a height sufficient to enable it to be turned preparatory to being lowered in an upright position on the pedestal, and controlling tackles were fixed to each end of it. The actual turning of the obelisk from a horizontal to a vertical position took place on September 12 at 3 p.m., and in half an hour it was in a vertical position above its pedestal. The British and Turkish flags were run up, and as they flew free a roar from the great crowd filled the air. The obelisk was lowered into its position on the pedestal, and the great monolith of red granite, 68 feet long and weighing 180 tons, stood securely where it stands to-day. Castings in bronze of a pair of wings intended to represent the wings of the Winged Disk of Horus of Edfu were fixed at each corner, and between each pair is a bronze casting bearing the prenomen of Thothmes III, which reads Men-kheper-Rā. Above the cartouche are the disk and plumes of the Sun-god ; on the right is a uraeus, *i.e.* cobra, wearing the crown of the South, and on the left is another uraeus wearing the crown of the North. From the body of each uraeus hangs the sign for "eternity," Ω, *shen*. The obelisk is flanked by two bronze sphinxes which are enlarged copies of a sphinx of Thothmes III preserved in the Egyptian Collection of the Duke of Northumberland at Alnwick Castle (No. 379 in Birch's *Catalogue*, London, 1880, page 42); each is 19 feet long, 6 feet wide, and 9 feet high, and weighs about 7 tons. The models and the castings were made under the direction of Mr. G. Vulliamy, Architect to the Metropolitan Board of Works, and the sphinxes were placed in position in September, 1881. On the breast of each is the inscription, "Beneficent god, Men-kheper-Rā, giver of life." The original from which these enlargements were made is of black basalt and is 11 inches long and 8 inches high. On the pedestal are four inscriptions, which read :—

NORTH FACE.

THROUGH THE PATRIOTIC ZEAL OF
ERASMUS WILSON F.R.S.
THIS OBELISK
WAS BROUGHT FROM ALEXANDRIA
ENCASED IN AN IRON CYLINDER
IT WAS ABANDONED DURING A STORM
IN THE BAY OF BISCAY
RECOVERED AND ERECTED
ON THIS SPOT BY
JOHN DIXON C.E.
IN THE 42ND YEAR OF THE REIGN OF
QUEEN VICTORIA
1878

EAST FACE.

THIS OBELISK QUARRIED AT SYENE
WAS ERECTED AT ON (HELIOPOLIS)
BY THE PHARAOH
THOTHMES III ABOUT 1500 B.C.
LATERAL INSCRIPTIONS WERE ADDED
NEARLY TWO CENTURIES LATER
BY RAMESES THE GREAT
REMOVED DURING THE GREEK DYNASTY
TO ALEXANDRIA
THE ROYAL CITY OF CLEOPATRA
IT WAS THERE ERECTED IN THE
18TH YEAR OF AUGUSTUS CÆSAR B.C. 12.

WEST FACE.

THIS OBELISK
PROSTRATE FOR CENTURIES
ON THE SANDS OF ALEXANDRIA
WAS PRESENTED TO THE
BRITISH NATION A.D. 1819 BY
MAHOMMED ALI VICEROY OF EGYPT
A WORTHY MEMORIAL OF
OUR DISTINGUISHED COUNTRYMEN
NELSON AND ABERCROMBY

SOUTH FACE.

WILLIAM ASKIN	MICHAEL BURNS
JAMES GARDINER	WILLIAM DONALD
JOSEPH BENBOW	WILLIAM PATAN

PERISHED IN A BOLD ATTEMPT
TO SUCCOUR THE CREW OF THE
OBELISK SHIP "CLEOPATRA" DURING
THE STORM OCTOBER 14TH 1877

The inscription on the south face was added, it is said, at the suggestion of Queen Victoria. The actual cost of the removal of the obelisk from Alexandria to London is stated by Lieut.-Commander H. H. Gorringe (*Egyptian Obelisks*, London, 1885, page 107) to have been about £11,500, and the salving expenses were about £2,000. The concrete foundations, the sphinxes, and the ornamental bronze work were paid for by the Metropolitan Board of Works. The timber and other materials were supplied by Mr. Dixon; the cost of these has not been disclosed.

Full details concerning the transport and erection of Cleopatra's Packing Needle will be found in *The Builder*, vol. ix, pages 478, 558, 798; vol. xxxvi, pages 55, 410; in "The Cleopatra Needle," reprinted from *Engineering*, London, 1877–78; and in Gorringe's book mentioned above. The steps and pedestal of the obelisk were damaged by a bomb during the air raid which took place on September 4, 1917, and the marks made by the pieces of metal are visible to this day.

As the obelisk was made by Thothmes III, the text and translation of the inscriptions upon it are given in the section of this book in which the obelisks of Thothmes III are enumerated and described.

PART II

DESCRIPTIONS OF EGYPTIAN OBELISKS, WITH HIEROGLYPHIC TEXTS, TRANSLATIONS, ETC.

I

THE OBELISKS OF USERTSEN (SEN-USRIT) I AT HELIOPOLIS

Usertsen I, who is called Sesonchôsis by Manetho,[1] was the son of Amenemhat I [cartouche], the founder of the XIIth Dynasty, which lasted about 200 years, *i.e.* from about 2300 B.C. to 2100 B.C. Amenemhat I reigned about 30 years, but in the 20th year of his reign he associated Usertsen I with him in the rule of the kingdom. Usertsen I reigned about 45 years, but in the 32nd year of his independent reign associated his son Amenemhat II with him in the rule of the kingdom. Though the kings of the XIIth Dynasty made Thebes their capital, each of them took care to repair and rebuild and found temples in other parts of their kingdom, especially at Abydos,

[1] An Egyptian priest of Sebennytus in Lower Egypt, who flourished in the reign of Ptolemy II Philadelphus, and wrote a History of Egypt, of which all is lost except the List of the Kings of Egypt compiled by him from native sources.

Memphis and Tanis (*i.e.* Zoan), and in the Fayyûm. Vast quantities of stone were brought from the quarries in the Wâdî Hammâmât, and copper was obtained from the mines at Wâdî Ma'ârah and Sarābît al-Khâdam in Sinai. Usertsen I followed his father's example and raided Lower Nubia, and established an Egyptian colony in the plain at the head of the Third Cataract; the modern town of Karmah marks the site of the town ruled by the Egyptian governor of that time, who was called Hep-tchefa. From the Egyptian Sûdân Usertsen obtained gold, ebony, precious stones, etc., which were devoted to the decorations of his temples, and served as offerings to his gods and goddesses. The remains of the pyramid that he built for his tomb are to be seen to this day at Al-Lisht, on the west bank of the Nile, about 40 miles south of Cairo. His father's pyramid-tomb lies to the north of it.

One of the most important temples rebuilt, or more probably founded, by Amenemhat I, was the great temple that he dedicated to the Sun-god of Heliopolis, in his forms of **Her-em-aakhu,** , *i.e.* Horus on the eastern or morning horizon, and **Atem,** , *i.e.* the Sun-god on the western or evening horizon. The city of **Heliopolis,** called in Egyptian *Anu Meht,* , *i.e.* the "Northern Anu," to distinguish it from *Anu rest,* , the "Southern Anu," or

Hermonthis, which lies a few miles to the south of Thebes, was one of the oldest cities in Egypt. From time immemorial Heliopolis formed the terminus of the caravan roads from the north, west and south, and was in consequence a flourishing trade centre. It is probable that it was the capital of the "kings of the North," *i.e.* Lower Egypt, in predynastic times. It was the home of many cults, first and foremost among which was the cult of the Sun-god, whose various forms were, in early times, called Khepera, Atem, etc.

The Hebrews called the city "On" or "Aven" (Gen. xli. 45, 50; Ezek. xxx. 17), and "Bêth Shemesh" (Jer. xliii. 13), or "House of the Sun," and it will be remembered that Joseph married a daughter of Potipherah (in Egyptian, , or *Pa-ta-pa-Rā*, "The gift of Rā"), a priest of On (Gen. xli. 45, 50; xlvi. 20). There was a famous **well** or **fountain** at Heliopolis in which, according to tradition, the Sun-god Rā bathed his face when he rose for the first time on the world. This well is still to be seen at Matarîyah, which the Arabs call "'Ain ash-Shems," *i.e.* "Fountain of the Sun." It is stated in the Apocryphal Books that the Virgin Mary rested by this well, and drew from it the water with which she washed the clothes of her Child, and that wherever the water fell balsam-bearing plants sprang up; drops of the oil made from them were always mixed with the water used in baptizing Christians. Tradition also says that when the Virgin and Child approached Heliopolis during the flight from Palestine all the idols in the city fell down on their faces and did homage to them.

The priests of Heliopolis were famed for their learning, and they were a very powerful body at all times. Little is known of them or of their god **Rā,** [hieroglyphs], under Dynasties I–III, but the name of their god forms part of the prenomen of Neb-ka-Rā, a king of the IIIrd Dynasty, and it also appears in the names Khāf-Rā and Men-kau-Rā, kings of the IVth Dynasty. The first three kings of the Vth Dynasty were sons of a high priest of Rā, and from this time onwards each Pharaoh bore a special name as the " son of Rā." Several of the kings of the Vth Dynasty built great " sun-temples " on the west bank of the Nile at Abu Gurâb and Abusîr, and the object of the cult was a monolith, probably of sandstone, in the form of a short obelisk resting on a plinth or pedestal in the form of a truncated pyramid. That the priests of Rā were able to seize the throne of Egypt and to set, first, members of their corporation and, next, their nominees upon it in succession makes it clear that they were predominant among the priesthoods of that country. Their god Rā, with whose worship **human sacrifices** were associated, became little by little the chief god of the country, and the religious texts compiled by his priests form the foundation of much of the theological literature of Egypt. Rā was the god of day and of this world, and his power was believed to be supreme and absolute ; all the other great gods were regarded as forms of him. But when his priesthood attempted to force his cult upon all the Egyptians in the South as well as upon those in the North, they found it most difficult to accomplish, because the people generally worshipped the ancient, and perhaps indigenous, god Osiris, [hieroglyphs], *Asar*, or *Asari*, the god of night, the Underworld and death. A great struggle took place between the priesthood of Rā and the priesthood of Osiris, and in the end the supposed powers of Rā and the extent of his dominion were curtailed. The King and his Court and the upper classes were followers of Rā, but Osiris, the god of the resurrection and the judge of the dead, was the principal object of the worship of the bulk of the nation.

We may reasonably assume that there was a great Temple of Rā at Heliopolis during the rule of the last three Dynasties (IV–VI) of the Old Kingdom, but of it no remains have been found. It is probable that all the temples at Heliopolis, Memphis, Tanis, etc., were plundered and demolished during the period of anarchy that immediately followed the downfall of the VIth Dynasty, and that the statues of the gods were broken and destroyed, and the stones of the sanctuaries used for building purposes. Amenemhat I (XIIth Dynasty) built a large and magnificent temple at Heliopolis, and his son Usertsen (Sen-Usrit) I set up two large **granite obelisks** in front of it. The later kings of the dynasty added to its old endowments, but it lost its wealth and importance during the period of anarchy that followed the rule of the kings of the XIIth Dynasty. The Hyksos kings did nothing for the priesthood of Rā, and it is not until about 1200 B.C. that we hear again of the temple, no doubt an entirely new one, of Heliopolis. Before the end of the VIIIth century B.C. the temple was in a flourishing condition, and the priesthood had regained much of their former power, for **Piānkhi,** , the Nubian conqueror of Egypt, visited it, and opened the sealed shrine and looked upon the figure of Rā within and his two sacred boats. When the Ptolemies made Alexandria the capital of Egypt, the priests of Heliopolis removed themselves thither and left their temple to fall into the hands of caretakers and others. The building remained in a more or less complete state for a couple of centuries, but little by little the walls were broken down and the stones carried off, and only the large statues and the two obelisks remained standing.

The existence of the obelisks set up by Usertsen was well known both to pagan and Christian writers. Silvestre de Sacy called attention to a passage in S. Ephrem's Commentary (IVth century A.D.) on the xxxiiird Chapter of Isaiah, in which the learned Father says: "This House of the Sun is the town in Egypt called Heliopolis, where the cult of devils and the worship of idols flourished. In this place there are two great columns which excite admiration. Each of these is 60 cubits high and stands on a pedestal 10 cubits high. The cap which rests on the top of each of these columns is of white copper, and its weight is 1,000 pounds or even more. On these columns are depicted figures of the men and animals which were worshipped by the idolaters of old time, and they also bear on them inscriptions in the priestly character containing the mysteries of paganism." Ibn Khurdâdhbah (IXth century A.D.) calls the copper caps "collars," and he and other Muslim writers describe the green marks made on one of the obelisks by the drippings of rain-water from the copper. Makrîzî says that the copper of the cap was like gold, and that there was engraved upon it the figure of a man seated on a throne facing the rising sun (de Sacy, *Relation*, page 227, note 2). Yâḳût (early XIIIth century A.D.) says that the obelisks are very high, and that from a distance they look like palm trees without tops; he goes on to say that the people call them the "MASÂLLA FIR'ÛN," *i.e.* "**Pharaoh's Packing Needles,**" As he uses the plural of *misallah* both obelisks must have been standing in his day. Yâḳût quotes Hasan ibn Ibrâhîm the Egyptian, who says that the obelisks were 50 cubits high, and describes their copper caps (Yâḳût, ed. Wüstenfeld, vol. iii, page 762).

According to 'Abd al-Latîf, an Arab physician who visited Egypt in the fourth quarter of the XIIth century, the two Pharaoh's Needles stood each on a base 10 cubits (*i.e.* about 15 feet) square, and of nearly the same height. On each base rose a square column, of pyramidal form, about 100 cubits (150 feet) high; at the base the diameter of each column was 5 cubits

($7\frac{1}{2}$ feet), and each ended in a point. The top of each was covered with a kind of copper cap, in the shape of a funnel, and hid the upper end of the column to a depth of 3 cubits (4 feet, 6 inches). Owing to the rains and the passage of time the copper had become oxidized, and the rains dropping from it had stained the shaft green. The whole surface of the obelisk was covered with inscriptions in the priestly character. 'Abd al-Latîf, who wrote in 598 A.H. (*i.e.* A.D. 1201), says that he saw one of these obelisks lying on the ground broken into two pieces, but he does not tell us when that obelisk fell. Muhammad ibn Ibrâhîm Jazîrî says that it fell on the 4th day of Ramadhân in the year 656 A.H. (*i.e.* A.D. 1258), and 200 quintals of copper were taken from it (*i.e.* from the base), and that the copper cap was worth 10,000 dînârs (about £5,000 !). But there is a mistake here, for when 'Abd al-Latîf was in Egypt about A.D. 1190 the obelisk had already fallen. Silvestre de Sacy thought that for 656 A.H. we should read 556 A.H., *i.e.* A.D. 1160, and he was probably right. Why the obelisk fell is unknown, but Lenormant says, without stating his authority, that it was wilfully thrown down by the Egyptians, who believed that treasure was hidden beneath it. Round about the obelisk 'Abd al-Latîf saw an innumerable number of small obelisks which were about one-third or one-half as high as the large obelisk, but very few of them were monolithic. For the Arabic text and a Latin translation *see* White, *Abdollatiphi Historiae Aegypti Compendium*, Oxford, 1800, and for a French rendering *see* S. de Sacy, *Relation de l'Égypte,* Paris, 1810.

The obelisk of Usertsen (Sen-Usrit) I, which is standing, and was one of a pair which stood one on each side of the first gateway of the House of the Sun at Anu, or On, may be now described. The obelisk is a monolith of red granite and is about 66 feet high. The pedestal, which is said to be made of sandstone, and a large portion of the lower part of the obelisk, are buried in mud, and the exact height of the monolith cannot therefore be given. There is a single line of hieroglyphic text down each side, and all four inscriptions read the same. The pointed top, or pyramidion, was originally covered with a casing of fine polished copper, the glint of which must have been seen from a very considerable distance. The inscriptions contain the names and titles of Usertsen I, who made, *i.e.* dedicated, the obelisk, on the first day of a solemn festival called Set. The origin of this festival is unknown, but it was certainly celebrated in very early times. The word Set means a "tail," and it has been thought that the festival was first celebrated in connection with the assumption of a lion's tail by the king as a part of his ceremonial dress. At first the festival was celebrated in the king's 30th year, but later the intervals between the Set festivals in a king's reign were shorter. It is wrong to call the festival a "jubilee," for the jubilee was celebrated every 50th year.

The inscription reads :—

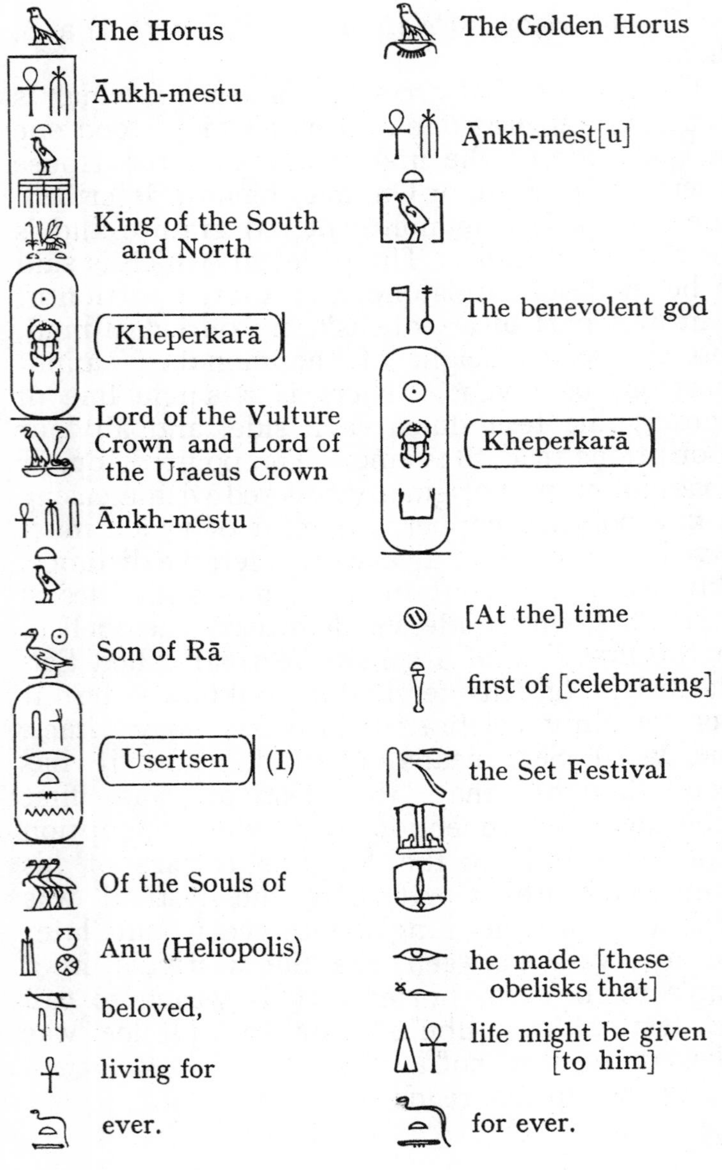
The Horus
Ānkh-mestu
King of the South and North
Kheperkarā
Lord of the Vulture Crown and Lord of the Uraeus Crown
Ānkh-mestu
Son of Rā
Usertsen (I)
Of the Souls of
Anu (Heliopolis)
beloved,
living for
ever.
The Golden Horus
Ānkh-mest[u]
The benevolent god
Kheperkarā
[At the] time
first of [celebrating]
the Set Festival
he made [these obelisks that]
life might be given [to him]
for ever.

II

THE OBELISK OF USERTSEN I AT ABGIG (BEGIG)

Usertsen I, probably realizing the importance of the Fayyûm for the agriculture of the country, built there a temple, the site of which is marked by the modern village called Abgig or Abgîg (commonly written Begig), which lies a little to the south-west of Madînat al-Fayyûm. Of the size of this temple nothing is known, and its existence is only indicated by a huge red granite monolith, now broken into two pieces, which probably stood in front of it. When complete this monolith was about 45 feet high. It is a colossal stele rather than an obelisk, for it is nearly 7 feet wide and is about 4 feet thick; but it is usually called the "obelisk of Begig." The top of it is rounded and not pointed like that of an obelisk, and in it is a deep groove which may have formed the resting-place of a bronze cap or bar. On the front of the monolith was cut a series of ten Vignettes, in which the king was represented doing homage to the various gods and goddesses of the region; the name of the king and that of each deity was given in hieroglyphs, but these are no longer legible. These were followed by a long inscription which gave the names and titles of the king in much the same order as those given on the obelisk at Heliopolis. The latter part of the inscription no doubt stated the circumstances under which the stele was set up, and the names of the gods to whom the king wished to do honour, but this can no longer be read. The names and titles of the king are repeated on the two edges of the stele, and in these inscriptions Usertsen calls himself "beloved of Ptah" of Memphis, and "beloved of Mentu," the great War-god of Southern Anu, *i.e.* Hermonthis, the modern Armant, and Thebes. The chief god of the Fayyûm was the Crocodile-god Sebek, , and the temple before which the monolith stood was probably the chief temple of Crocodilopolis, or "Crocodile-city." In the IIIrd century B.C. Ptolemy II Philadelphus made his queen Arsinoë patron goddess of the city, which was henceforth known as Crocodilopolis-Arsinoë, or simply Arsinoë, and was regarded as one of the Nomes of Egypt. Two or three generations ago the natives of the district paid honour to the two portions of the overthrown stele as the abode of a tutelary spirit, and barren wives used to go and touch it, believing that it would enable them to bear strong and healthy children. Except for its great thickness, this monolith has much in common, especially as far as its shape is concerned, with the so-called obelisks at Axum. The text is published by Lepsius, *Denkmäler*, ii, page 112, and by Caristie in the great French work, *Description de l'Égypte*, tom. iv, plate 71; for a description of it *see* tom. iv, pages 517–526 of the French text.

III

THE OBELISK OF THOTHMES I, KING OF EGYPT ABOUT 1546 B.C., AT KARNAK

Thothmes I, the son of Amenhetep I by his Queen Senseneb, , began to reign about 1546 B.C., and reigned about 30 years. On the day of his coronation, *i.e.* the 21st day of the 3rd month of the season Pert, he sent the copy of a decree to the Egyptian viceroy of Nubia, who dwelt at Elephantine, announcing his coronation and giving a list of the titles that he had adopted. Soon after he ascended the throne he made a raid into Nubia; the general of his army was Aāhmes, the son of Abana, a warrior who had fought against the Hyksos. The king was present at one engagement, and speared the leader of the enemy, and sailed down-stream with the dead body tied to the bows of his boat. The authority of Egypt in Nubia at that time seems to have been effective so far as the Island of Tombos, near the head of the Third Cataract. Thothmes next devoted himself to consolidating the power of Egypt in Syria, and his victorious troops conquered the Shasu, , a confederation of nomad tribes, and took possession of the country of Naharina, . He set up a stele at a place called Ni, , near the Euphrates, to mark the limit of his kingdom in the north, and this stele was standing in the reign of his grandson, Thothmes III. His raids in Nubia and in Syria brought him in much wealth, and a large portion of it he spent in building and repairing the temples of the great gods of Thebes and Abydos, *i.e.* Amen-Rā and Osiris.

In an inscription found at Abydos he boasts that he has made Egypt the first country in the world, and that his kingdom includes all the countries that the sun encircles. The work that he did in connection with the temple of Amen-Rā at Thebes was important. He built a court round the temple, with a colonnade of statues of Osiris, and a pylon, and made another doorway, with a copper door on which was a figure of the "Image of the god" inlaid in gold. Before the pylon he set up a series of flagstaffs, the tops of which were covered with shining, refined copper. He had two obelisks quarried at Aswân, and built a lighter nearly 200 feet long and 60 feet wide on which to transport them to Thebes, and they were set up under the direction of the official Anni in front of another pylon; the two pylons which Thothmes built were united by a colonnade. His "two great obelisks" were both standing when Richard Pococke (1704–1765) visited Thebes in 1738, but one fell subsequently and broke in pieces. Thothmes I was the first king who set up obelisks in Thebes, and in view of the later religious history of the XVIIIth Dynasty his action seems to show that he was favourably disposed to the doctrines of the priesthood of Heliopolis, and that he wished to link the cult of Rā with that of the Theban god

Amen. As Usertsen I had set up a pair of obelisks before the house of Rā at Heliopolis, so Thothmes I set up a pair before a pylon of the temple of Amen.

The obelisk that is still standing is about 90 feet high, and is in a good state of preservation. (*See* **Plate X.**) A single column of inscription originally occupied the middle of each of the four faces, and from these texts we learn that Thothmes I dedicated "two great obelisks," , to his father Amen-Rā. On the pieces of the fallen obelisk the cartouches of Thothmes III are found, and because of this some have argued that this obelisk was made by Thothmes III and not by Thothmes I, but the inscription of the latter on the standing obelisk speaks distinctly of two obelisks, and the official Anni states in his biography that he superintended the erection of two obelisks. It is probable that Thothmes I died before his inscriptions were cut on the second obelisk and that it was usurped by Thothmes III. On each side of the central columns of inscriptions on the standing obelisk are columns of hieroglyphs that were cut upon it under the XXth Dynasty; these contain the high-sounding titles of Rameses IV and Rameses VI, and their prenomens and nomens. The sides of the pyramidion of the standing obelisk are uninscribed, but it may have been furnished originally with an inscribed copper cap, like the obelisks of Usertsen I at Heliopolis. The hieroglyphic text of the obelisk of Thothmes I and translation are as follows :—

THE OBELISK OF THOTHMES I AT KARNAK

Front. Back. Right. Left.

TRANSLATION OF THE OBELISK OF THOTHMES I

FRONT.—Horus, Mighty Bull, beloved of Maāt; King of the South and the North, Ākheperkarā, emanation of Amen. He made [them, *i.e.* the obelisks] as his monument to his father, Amen-Rā, Governor of the Two Lands (*i.e.* Egypt). He set up to him two great obelisks at the two-fold doorway of the house of the god (*i.e.* temple). The pyramidion caps were made of *tchām* metal . . . .

BACK.—Horus, Mighty Bull, beloved of Maāt; King of the South and the North, lord of the vulture crown and the serpent crown, diademed with the serpent crown, great of valour, Ākheperkarā, chosen of Rā; the Horus of gold, well-doing in years, making hearts to live; son of Rā, of his body, Thothmes, diademed with beauties. He made [them] as his monument to his father Amen, Lord of the Thrones of the Two Lands (*i.e.* Egypt), President of the Apts (*i.e.* Karnak), endowed with life like Rā for ever.

RIGHT.—Horus, Mighty Bull of Rā; lord of the vulture crown and the serpent crown, conqueror of all lands; the Horus of gold, smiter of the Nine Bows; King of the South and the North, Lord of the Two Lands Ākheper-karā-merenrā. Marked out for him the lord of the gods the Set festival on the Ashet tree[1]; the son of Rā, Thothmes diademed like Rā, beloved of Amen-Rā Ka-mut-f, endowed with life for ever.

LEFT.—Horus, beloved of Rā, crowned with the White Crown; lord of the vulture crown and the serpent crown, the adorer of Temu, diademed with crowns; King of the South and the North, Lord of the Two Lands, Ākheperkarā, made of Rā; the Horus of gold, great of strength, mighty of valour, flourishing for years in the Great House of Maāt; son of Rā, Thothmes diademed like Rā, divine Governor of Anu (On), beloved of Amen-Rā, lord of the thrones of the Two Lands, endowed with life like Rā for ever.

The inscription which **Rameses IV** added to the obelisk of Thothmes I gives two of his Horus names, *i.e.* Ka-nekht-Rā-en-Kamt, , "Mighty Bull, the Sun-god of Egypt," and Ka-nekht-pehti-ma-Amen, , "Mighty Bull, strong one like Amen," and several other names of his which are well known. The king says that he has risen to open the eyes of mankind,

[1] The prototype of the lote tree of the Muslims, on each leaf of which the name of a living being was written; when a leaf fell the man whose name was written on it died. The meaning here is that the lord of the gods decreed in writing on the leaves of the Ashet-tree the Set festivals which the king should celebrate.

, and that he has made the "Temple of Amen to be like the horizon of heaven," , and he claims to have fettered the Nine Peoples of Nubia, . The inscriptions of **Rameses VI** give the king's Horus names, among them being Ka-nekht-ur-bait, , "Mighty Bull, great one of wonders." He calls himself the "Protector of Egypt," , and the "bread of Egypt," , and he "has perfected designs in the Apts and exalted Thebes like heaven," . Many parts of the inscriptions of Rameses IV and Rameses VI are obliterated.

When Thothmes I ascended the throne one of his first acts was to send out a document announcing his accession and setting forth his official titles as the successor of Horus, the chosen one of the goddesses Nekhebit and Uatchit, etc. In the first year of his reign he made a great raid into Nubia, and returned to Thebes in triumph. In the second year of his reign his troops marched as far to the south as Karmah, and he set up a memorial stele on the Island of Tombos to record his victories over the Nubians. Having made a third expedition into Nubia, he directed his attention to Rethennu, [hieroglyphs], or Northern Syria. He conquered the Shasu, [hieroglyphs], or nomad Semites of Western Asia, and made the kings of Naharina acknowledge his overlordship and pay him tribute; and he returned to Egypt with great spoil. He built a pylon at Karnak, and his architect Anni set up before it two great granite obelisks, which, as Wiedemann has noted, were both standing when Richard Pococke (1704–1765) visited Egypt (*see* his *Description of the East*, vol. i, page 95, London, 1743–1745). One of these was usurped by Thothmes III, and the other by Rameses IV and Rameses VI. The text has been published by Champollion, *Monuments*, tom. iv, plates 312, 313; Lepsius, *Denkmäler*, iii, page 6, and Sethe, *Urkunden*, Bd. i.

THE REIGN OF HATSHEPSUT. ABOUT 1500 B.C.

Hatshepsut was probably associated with her father, Thothmes I, in the rule of the kingdom during the last few years of his life, and her power became greatly increased when she married her brother, Thothmes II, either before or immediately after her father's death. Her husband died after a short, ineffective reign, and as her nephew, who later was known as Thothmes III, was then a child, she undertook to administer the kingdom. Like many Oriental women who have become queens, she had a talent for administration, and the training and experience that she had gained during her father's reign stood her in good stead when she took the reins of government into her own hands. She had the faculty of selecting wise and capable officials, whom she appears to have trusted absolutely. The expedition to Punt which she organized, and the great temple at Dêr al-Baharî, built by her architect, show that she possessed large ideas and great imagination. Her reign was a period of peace for Egypt. She was no warrior and she had no military instincts, and of this deficiency the tributaries of Egypt took full advantage. She knew the bold and warlike disposition of her nephew, and, probably with set purpose, left to him the work of recalling Egypt's tributaries in Nubia and Palestine and Syria to a right sense of their duty and obligations.

Her expedition to Punt, , in the south-east of the Sûdân, brought back an immense amount of African products, incense (*ānti*,), ebony, ivory, gold in rings, gold in dust, skins of beasts, *ānti* trees, stibium for eye-paint, boomerangs, precious woods and stones, baboons, leopards, cheetahs, monkeys, etc. The character of the expedition was purely commercial, and it was probably a great success.

In bas-reliefs she appears in the form of a man and wears male attire; only as a goddess does she take the form of a woman. When seated in a shrine she wears the headdress of a god, and a beard is attached to her chin, and masculine attributes are assigned to her. In the inscriptions masculine pronouns and verbal forms are used in speaking of her.

The funerary temple which she had built for herself and her father at Dêr al-Baharî was a very beautiful and remarkable edifice. The temple had a girdle wall, and was approached through an avenue of sphinxes. It was entered through a pylon, before which stood two obelisks. An inclined pathway led to the Eastern Terrace, the wall of which was ornamented with bas-reliefs, which were protected by a roof supported by a double row of pillars. From the platform another inclined plane or stairway led to the Western Terrace, with its portico and rows of pillars. At each end of the portico is a rock-cut shrine, the northern one being decorated with religious scenes, and the southern one with scenes describing the expedition to Punt. The total length of the whole building was about 800 feet. Hatshepsut also built a small temple at Karnak; and between the two pylons which her father, Thothmes I, had built, she set up two magnificent granite obelisks. She set up a second pair in another part of the temple of Amen, but where exactly is not known.

One of the pair erected by her in the hall built by Thothmes I is still standing (*see* **Plate X**), but the other has fallen and the upper part of it lies near its fellow. This obelisk is at once the most striking of all the known Egyptian obelisks and the highest of those still remaining on Egyptian soil. Though its proportions are fine, one of its faces is slightly convex. The inscriptions are cut with accuracy

PLATE X.

A B

The obelisks of Thothmes I (**A**) and Queen Hatshepsut (**B**) still standing at Karnak.

PLATE XI.

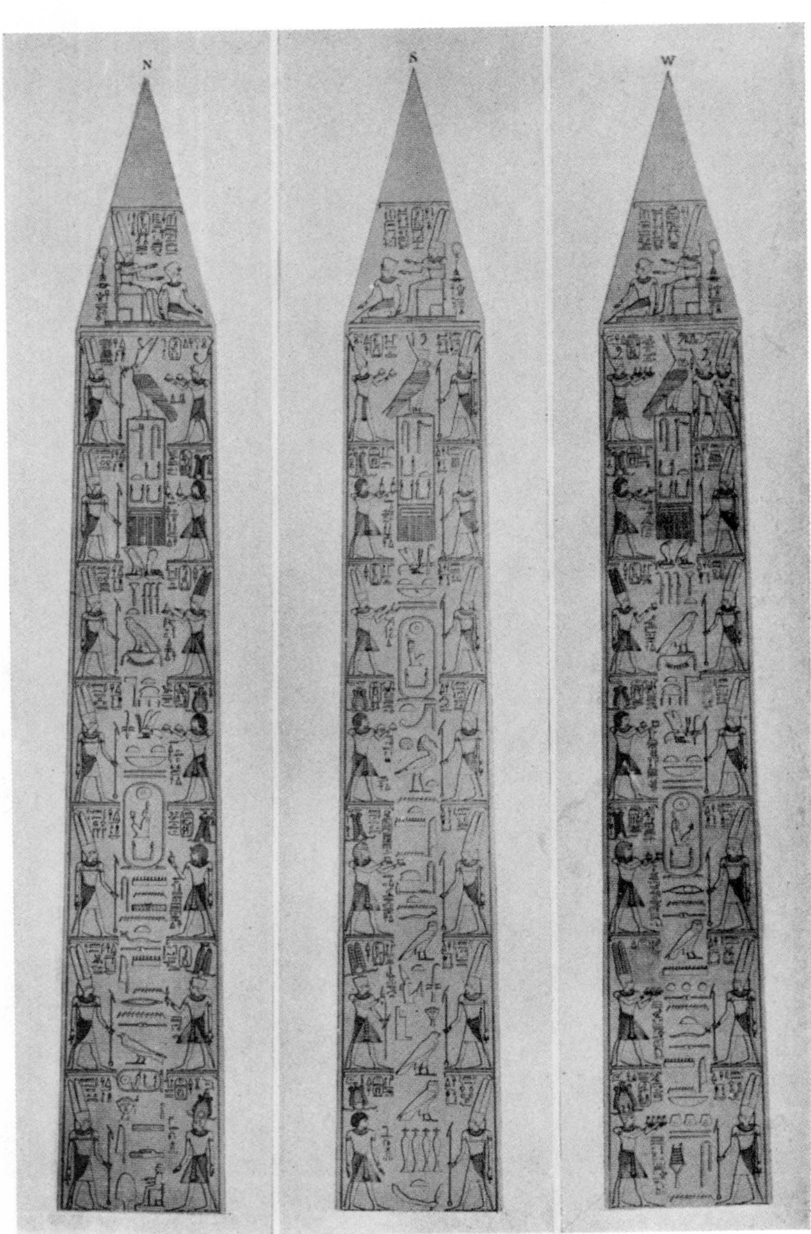

Three sides of the Obelisk of Queen Hatshepsut at Karnak showing the central lines of inscription and the Vignettes by the sides of them.

and delicacy, and the polish and finish of the monolith are worthy of admiration. The obelisk is a little more than 97 feet in height, and its diameter at the base is 8½ feet. The sides of the pyramidion are unusually long, and are sculptured with Vignettes representing the Queen, dressed in royal male attire, kneeling before Amen, whose hand is laid upon her (*see* **Plate XI**). The pyramidion was covered with a cap made of shining, refined copper, the glint of which in the sunlight could be seen from a great distance. On each face is a column of beautifully cut hieroglyphs, and on each side of the upper half of it are eight Vignettes; in those on the right are figures of Amen-Rā and in those on the left figures of the Queen, her father, and her nephew, Thothmes III, making offerings to the god. These are well illustrated by the outline drawings made from Erbkam's copies published by Lepsius in his *Denkmäler* given on pages 106–9. Amen's figures and name were obliterated by the fanatical Amenhetep IV, but were restored by Seti I. In the inscription on the base (l. 24) the Queen says that the work of quarrying the obelisks was begun [by Senmut] on the first day of the second month of the season Pert in the 15th year of her reign, and was finished on the last day of the fourth month of the season Shemut, *i.e.* in seven months, [hieroglyphs] IIII III, in the 16th year of her reign. If the statement is literally true it was a marvellously rapid piece of work, but it seems incredible. The text on the obelisk of Hatshepsut now standing reads :—

IV

THE OBELISK OF HATSHEPSUT

FRONT (West side). BACK (East side).

TRANSLATION OF THE INSCRIPTIONS ON THE SHAFT OF THE OBELISK OF HATSHEPSUT NOW STANDING

FRONT (WEST SIDE).—The Horus, Usritkau, Lord of the Vulture and Serpent Crowns (*i.e.* chosen by the goddesses Nekhebit and Uatchit), Flourishing in years, The Horus of gold, Divine one of crowns, King of the South and the North, Lord of the Two Lands, Maāt-ka-Rā. She made [them] as her monument for her father Amen, Lord of Thebes, setting up for him two great obelisks before the august pylon [called] " Amen, mighty one of terror." It is worked (*i.e.* covered over) with a very great quantity of shining, refined copper, which lights up Egypt like Athen (*i.e.* the solar Disk). Never was the like made since the world began. May it make for him, the son of Rā, Hatshepsut, the counterpart of Amen, the giving of life, like Rā, for ever.

BACK (EAST SIDE).—Usritkau, King of the South and of the North, Maāt-ka-Rā, beloved of Amen-Rā. Her Majesty made the name of her father to be established in this monument perpetually, praise being made of the King of the South and the North, Ākheperkarā (Thothmes I) by the majesty of this god. When Her Majesty set up [these] two great obelisks on the first celebration of the festival, the Lord of the Gods said: " Thy father, the King of the South and the North, Ākheperkarā, ordered the setting up of obelisks; Thy Majesty must repeat [these] monuments (*i.e.* make other obelisks) to make thee to live for ever."

RIGHT (South side).

LEFT (North side).

RIGHT (SOUTH SIDE).—Usritkau, King of the South and of the North, Maāt-ka-Rā, glorious emanation of Amen, who hath been made to rise as King of the South upon the throne of Horus, [and] as President of the holiness (?) of the Great House, the nursling of the Great Company of the Gods, Lady of all that Athen (*i.e.* the solar Disk) encircleth, whom they have joined to life, serenity, and joy of heart at the head of living beings, the son of Rā, the counterpart of Amen, Hatshepsut the beloved one of Amen-Rā, the king of the gods, unto whom life hath been given like Rā for ever

LEFT (NORTH SIDE).—Usritkau, chosen one of the goddesses Nekhebit and Uatchit, Flourishing in years, The Horus of gold, Divine one of crowns, King of the South and the North, Lord of the Two Lands, Maāt-ka-Rā. Her father, Amen, hath stablished her great name, Maāt-ka-Rā, on the holy Ashet tree. The records of her are for hundreds of thousands of years, being united to life, stability and serenity. The son of Rā, the counterpart of Amen, Hatshepsut, beloved of Amen-Rā, the king of the gods . . . this beautiful [and enduring] monument . . . which she made (*i.e.* dedicated) to him on the first day of the Set Festival, she doing this that life might be given to her for ever.[1]

[1] A scale model of this obelisk, made by the late Mr. J. Bonomi, is exhibited in the British Museum (5th Eg. Room, No. 55198) ; it is 5 feet 1½ inches in height.

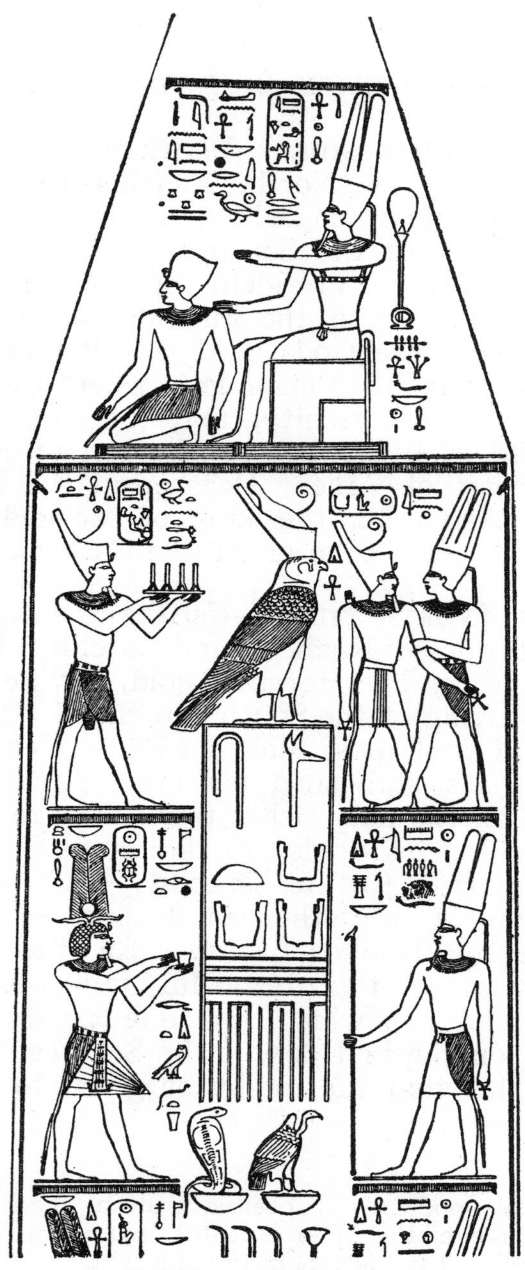

THE OBELISK OF HATSHEPSUT.

Pyramidion: Amen-Rā laying his hands on the shoulders of the Queen to infuse in her the fluid of life.

Vignettes: The Queen offering linen vestments to Amen-Rā, and being embraced by the god. Her nephew Thothmes III offering *metchet* to Amen-Rā.

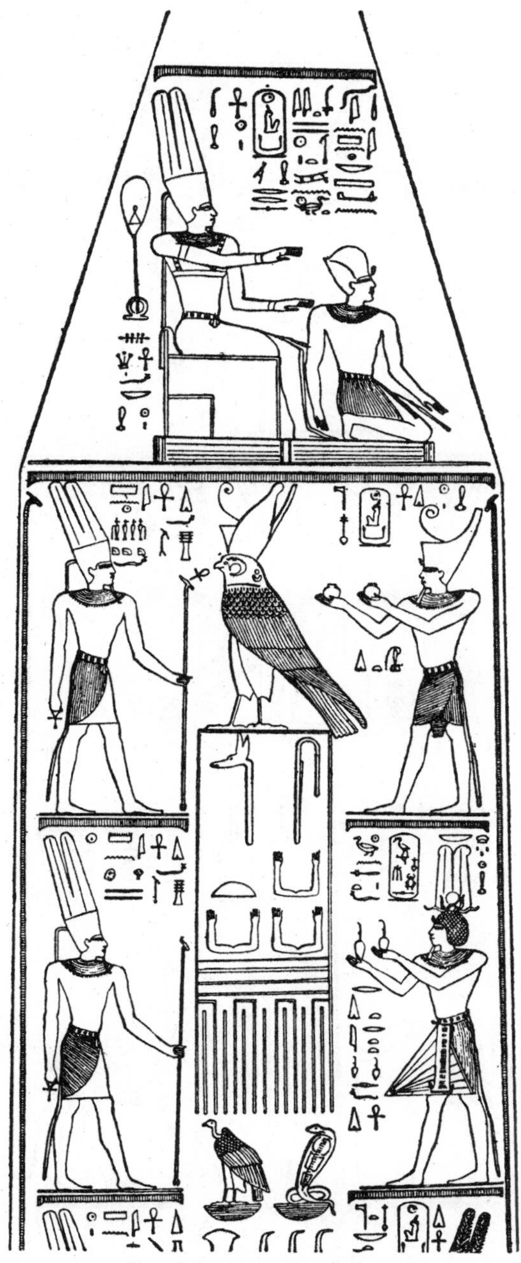

THE OBELISK OF HATSHEPSUT.

Pyramidion: Amen-Rā laying his hands on the shoulders of the Queen to infuse in her the fluid of life.

Vignettes The Queen and her father Thothmes I making offerings of wine and *metchet* to Amen-Rā.

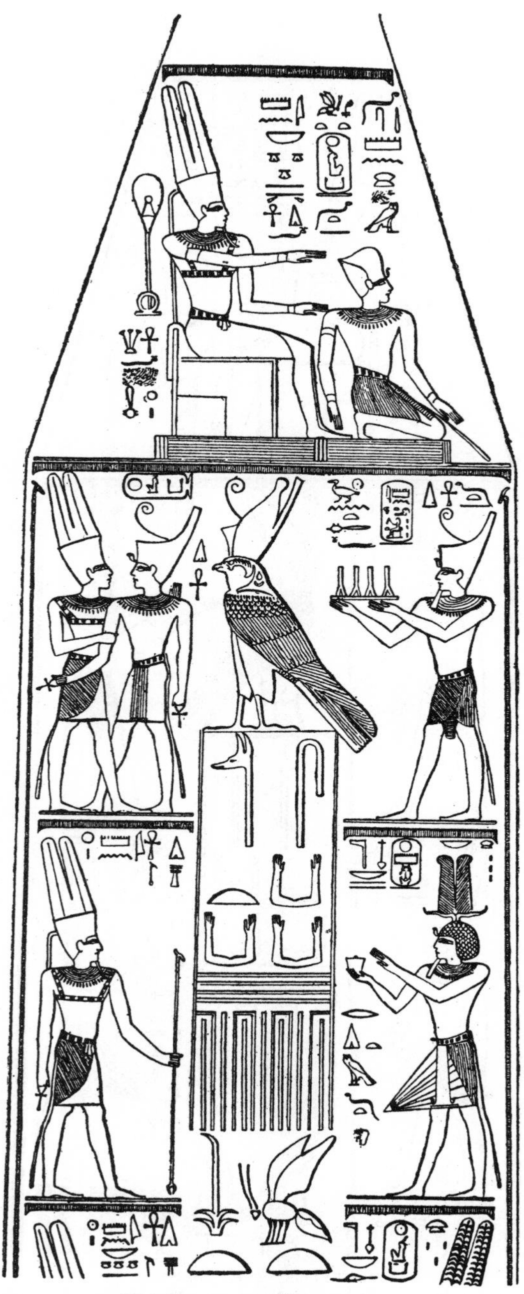

THE OBELISK OF HATSHEPSUT.

Pyramidion: Amen-Rā laying his hands on the shoulders of the Queen to infuse in her the fluid of life.

Vignettes: The Queen offering linen vestments to Amen-Rā, and being embraced by the god. Her nephew Thothmes III offering ***metchet*** to the god.

THE OBELISK OF HATSHEPSUT.

Pyramidion: Amen-Rā laying his hands on the shoulders of the Queen to infuse in her the fluid of life.

Vignettes: The Queen and her nephew Thothmes III offering wine and milk to Amen-Rā.

On the sides of the base of the obelisk is cut a long inscription in 32 lines, in which the Queen sets forth her titles and explains her reasons for making and dedicating the obelisks, and gives the history of their erection, and makes an address to her subjects, both the living and the unborn. The Queen, like the great kings her predecessors, adopted a fourfold name, but to her name as the daughter of Rā, Hatshepsut, *i.e.* "Sovereign chieftainess of the august or holy ones," she added the title "Khnemit of Amen," *i.e.* "counterpart of Amen." In other words, she asserted that she was begotten of the god Amen, and that the substance of her body was identical in every respect with that of the god. The self-created god Ari-su, , created her, and in her soul and body she possessed the attributes of all the other great gods. She believed that she was the God of All in the form of a woman, and in obeying the behests of Amen she was not only worshipping him, but adoring herself as his counterpart. In the making of her obelisks she poured out gold like grain, and even so feared that her offerings to her father were too small. The interest and importance of the inscription are very great, and it is given with a translation in the following pages :—

INSCRIPTION ON THE BASE OF THE OBELISK OF HATSHEPSUT

Hieroglyphic Text

SOUTH SIDE.—1.

2.

TRANSLATION OF THE INSCRIPTION ON THE BASE OF THE OBELISK OF HATSHEPSUT

SOUTH SIDE.—**1.** The living Horus [name] USERITKAU (Mighty of doubles). Nebti [name] UATCHIT RENPUT (Flourishing of years). Golden Horus [name] NETERIT KHĀU. Nesu-bat [name] MAĀT-KA-RĀ (Truth is the Ka of Rā). Daughter of Rā [name] HATSHEPSUT-KHNEMIT AMEN (Foremost of the holy ones, the counterpart of Amen), living for ever and ever, Daughter of Amen-Rā, darling of his heart, **2.** one and only, existing through him, glorious essence of Nebertcher (*i.e.* Lord of the Universe), her beauty was created by the Spirits of Anu (*i.e.* Rā, Shu and Tefnut), the Conquerors of the Two Lands (*i.e.* Egypt), like Ari-su (*i.e.* He who was self-made), [whom] he created to wear his crowns.

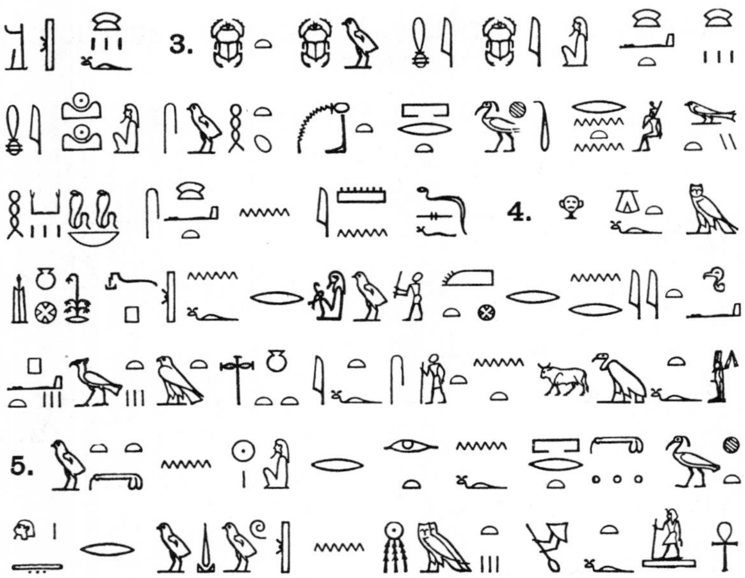

3. creatress of [many] forms like Khepera, diademed with diadems like the God of the Two Horizons (*i.e.* Her-Aakhuti), the holy egg, the glorious offspring, the suckling of the two goddesses of great magical powers, the one raised up by Amen himself **4.** upon his throne in Southern Anu (*i.e.* Hermonthis, or Armant), the one chosen by him to shepherd Egypt, to hold in check the Pāt and the Rekhit (two classes of the Egyptian people), the Horus woman who avengeth her father, the eldest daughter of Kamutef (*i.e.* the self-begotten and self-produced god), **5.** the woman begotten by Rā to make for him a glorious posterity upon earth to protect the Henmemit (a class of people ?),

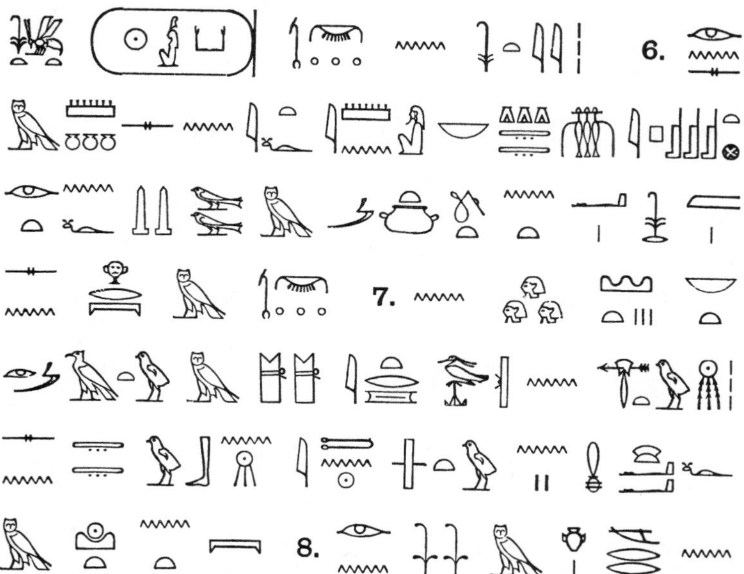

his living image, King of the South and the North, Maāt-Ka-Rā, the woman who is the *tchām* (*i.e.* either refined shining copper or "white" gold) of kings. **6.** She made [them] as her monument to her father, Amen, Lord of the Thrones of the Two Lands (*i.e.* Thebes), President of the Apts (*i.e.* Karnak). She made for him two great obelisks of the lasting (or solid) granite of the region of the South (*i.e.* the granite quarries at Aswân). The upper part[s] of [them] are of *tchām* **7.** of the best of all the mountains, and they can be seen [from afar both upstream and downstream ?]. The Two Lands (Egypt) are bathed in light when Athen (*i.e.* the solar Disk) rolleth up between them as he riseth up on the horizon of heaven. **8.** I have done this because of [my]

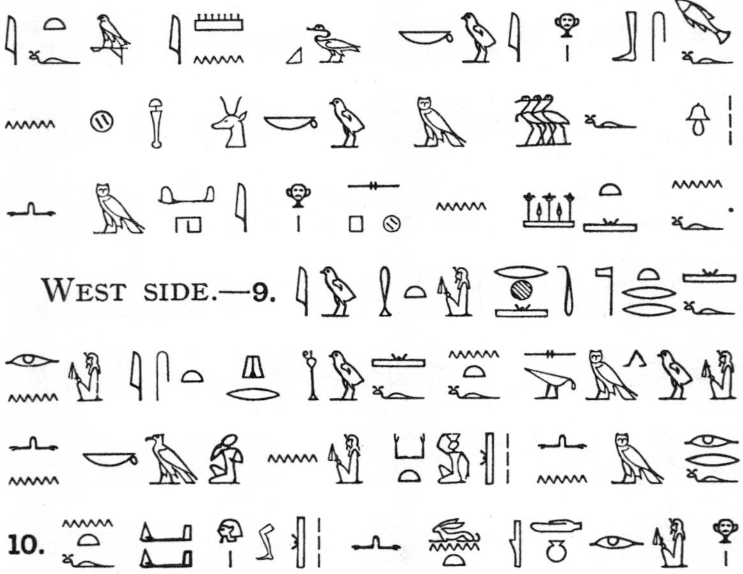

loving heart for Father Amen. I went in at his advance on the first day [of the festival ?]. I acquired knowledge from his skilled spirits. I hesitated not on any occasion when he commanded.

WEST SIDE.—**9.** My Majesty understandeth his divine power, and behold I worked under his direction ; he was my leader. I was unable to think out a plan for work without his prompting ; **10.** he was the giver of the instructions (*i.e.* specifications). I was unable to sleep because of his temple.[1] I never turned aside from any

[1] Compare, " I will not give sleep to mine eyes, *or* slumber to mine eyelids, until I find out a place for the Lord, an habitation for the mighty *God* of Jacob."—Ps. cxxxii, 4, 5.

order which he gave. My heart was like Sia (*i.e.* the god of knowledge, or wisdom personified) in respect of my father [Amen]. I entered into **11.** the plans of his heart (or mind), in no way did I neglect (*i.e.* set behind me) the city of Nebertcher (*i.e.* the Lord of the Universe), but set it before my face. I know that the Apts (*i.e.* Karnak) are the Horizon (*i.e.* the abode of the gods) upon the earth, **12.** the holy stepped building[1] of the first day (*i.e.* primeval time), the Eye of Nebertcher, the seat of his heart, the

[1] This *qai*, [hieroglyphs], is probably the equivalent of the Sumerian and Babylonian *zikkurat*, on the top of which stood the shrine containing the figure of the god.

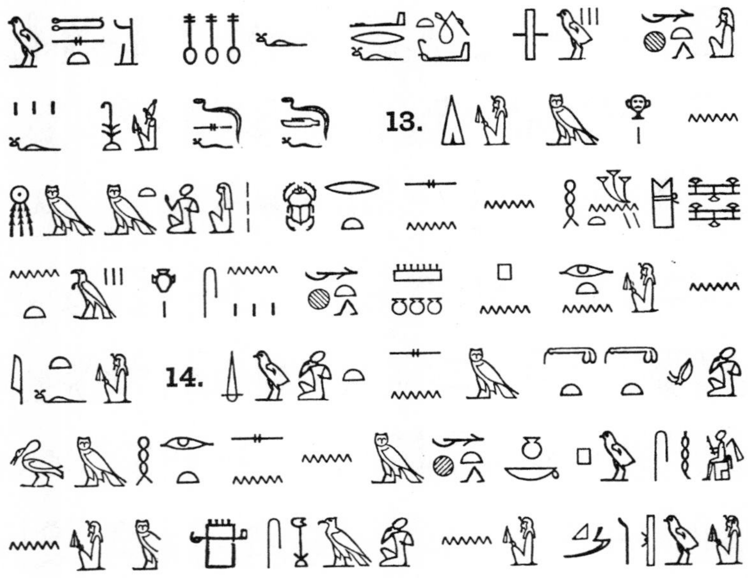

support of his beauties, the bond of those who follow him.

The king (*i.e.* the queen herself) saith: **13.** I have set [these obelisks] before the *henmemet* (*i.e.* people) who shall come into being two *hen* periods (*i.e.* 120 years) hence, whose minds shall enquire about this monument which I have made for my father, **14.** who shall speak with awe-struck (?) voices and shall seek to gaze into what is to come later. I took my seat in the Great House (*i.e.* palace), I remembered him that created me.

15. My heart urged me to make for him two obelisks with *tchām* coverings, the pyramidions (*i.e.* pointed tops) of which should pierce the sky in the august colonnade between **16.** the two great pylons [in the temple of Amen] of the KING, the mighty Bull, the King of the South and the North, Ā-Kheper-ka-Rā, the Horus, whose voice [speaks] truth. Behold, my heart (or mind) took possession (or overcame) me, leading me to utter words.

O ye men of understanding.

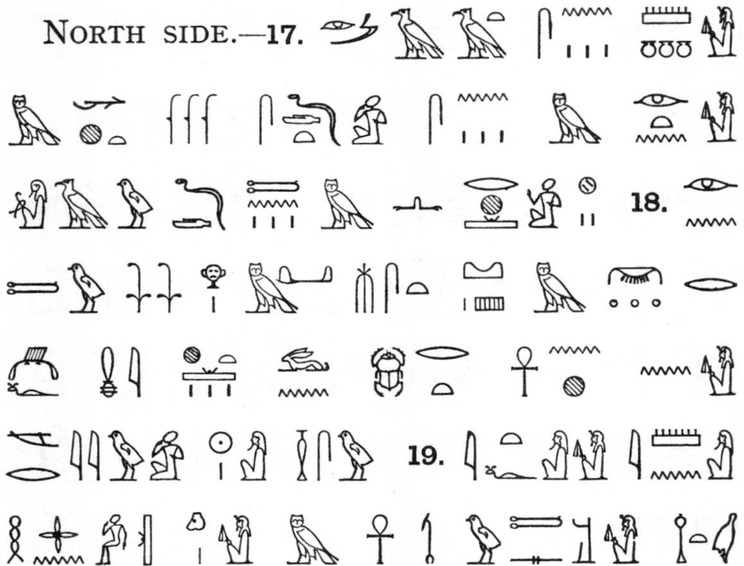

NORTH SIDE.—**17.** who shall look upon my monument after years (*i.e.* in future days), who shall discuss together what I have done, take good heed that ye say not "I know not, I know not **18.** [why] these were made, and [why] a mountain was made throughout in gold, as if it (*i.e.* gold) was one of the commonest things that exist"(?). I swear that as Rā loveth me, and as my **19.** Father Amen hath shown me favour, and as the child of my nostrils (*i.e.* breath) is with life and serenity; and as I bear the White Crown, and am crowned with the Red Crown,

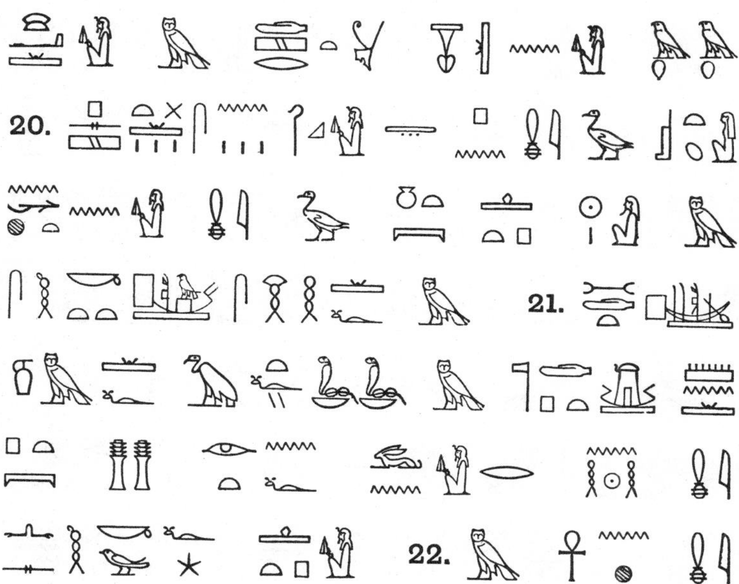

and have joined together [in amity] for the Two Hawk-gods **20**. their divisions of the world[1] (or Egypt), and have governed this land like the son of Isis (*i.e.* Horus), and am mighty like the son of Nut (*i.e.* Osiris, son of Geb and Nut); and as Rā setteth in the Sektet Boat in the evening and appeareth joyfully in the **21**. Ātet Boat in the morning, and joineth his two mothers (Isis and Nephthys ?) in the Boat of the god [Rā]; and as heaven is stablished firmly, and as what he (*i.e.* Rā) hath made is stable (or immovable), I shall have my being for ever and ever like an An-sek-f star (*i.e.* one of the circumpolar stars that never set), I shall sink to rest **22**. in [the

[1] Set was god of Lower Egypt and Horus of Upper Egypt.

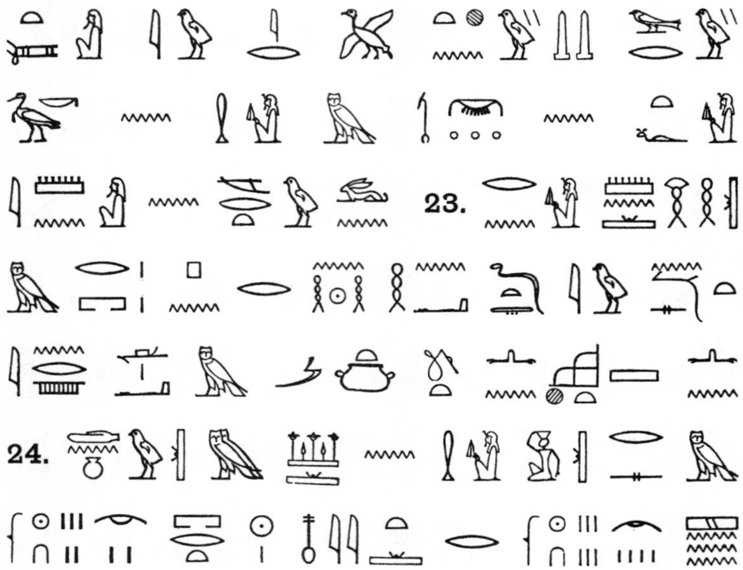

land of] life like Atem (*i.e.* the setting sun), so these two great obelisks (which my Majesty hath worked with *tchām* for my father Amen, in order that **23**. my name may abide and flourish shall stand in this temple for ever and for ever. Each obelisk is made from a single block (*i.e.* is a monolith) of granite in the quarry, without cleavage, without **24**. division. My Majesty demanded work thereon from the first day of the second month of the season Pert of the 15th year [of my reign], until the last day of the fourth month of the season Shemut, of the 16th

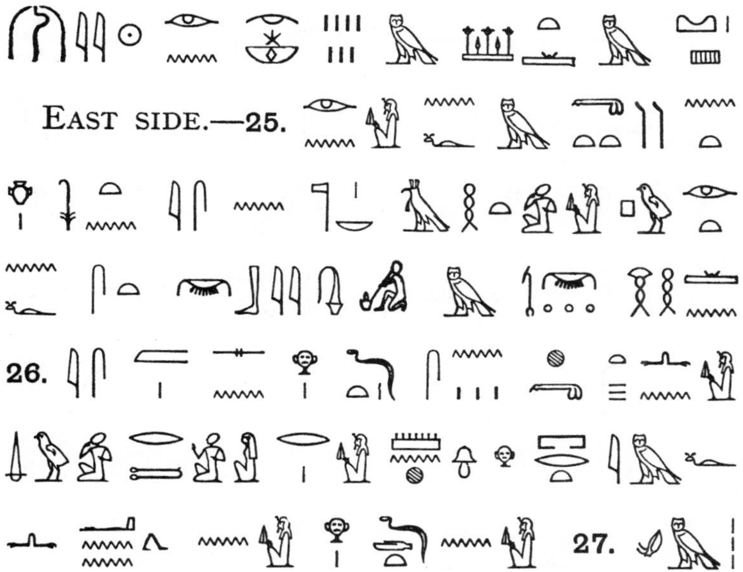

year [of my reign], making seven months since [my] demand in the mountain (*i.e.* quarry) **25**.

East side.—I made [them] for him in rectitude of heart, for [he is] thinking of every God. I longed to make them for him, plated (?) with *tchām* metal; **26**. lo! I laid their part (or, half) upon their bodies.[1] I kept in mind [what] the people would say—that my mouth was true because of what came forth from it, for I never went back on anything that I had once said. **27**. Now hearken ye to me. I gave to

[1] A difficult line to understand, but the meaning seems to be that the Queen says that she set up the upper or lighter halves upon the heavier halves, *i.e.* that she placed the obelisks in their upright positions.

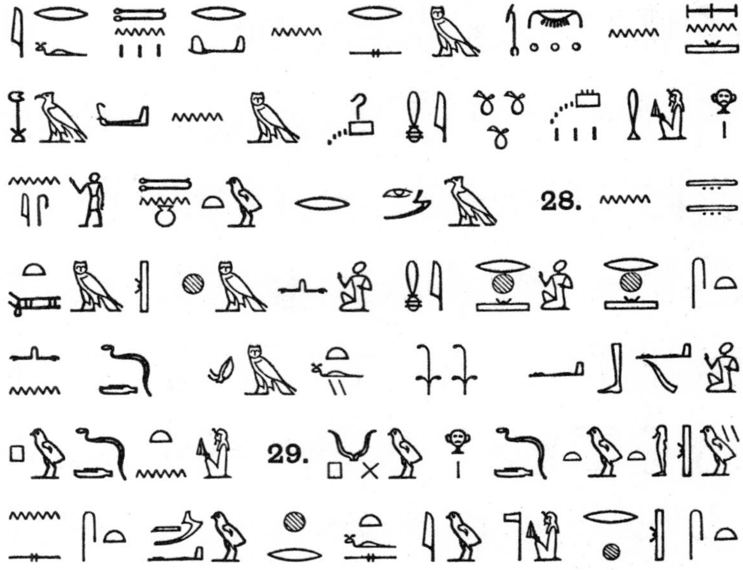

them (*i.e.* the obelisks) the best refined *tchām*, which I measured by the *heket* (bushel ?) as if it had been ordinary grain in sacks. My Majesty allotted to them a larger quantity of *tchām* than had ever been seen **28.** by the whole of the Two Lands (*i.e.* Egypt). This the fool as well as the wise man knoweth well. Let not the man who shall hear these things say that what I have said is false, but rather let him say, "It is even as she hath [said] it (or, it is exactly so)—true before her father." The God knew it [was] in me, and Amen, Lord of the thrones of

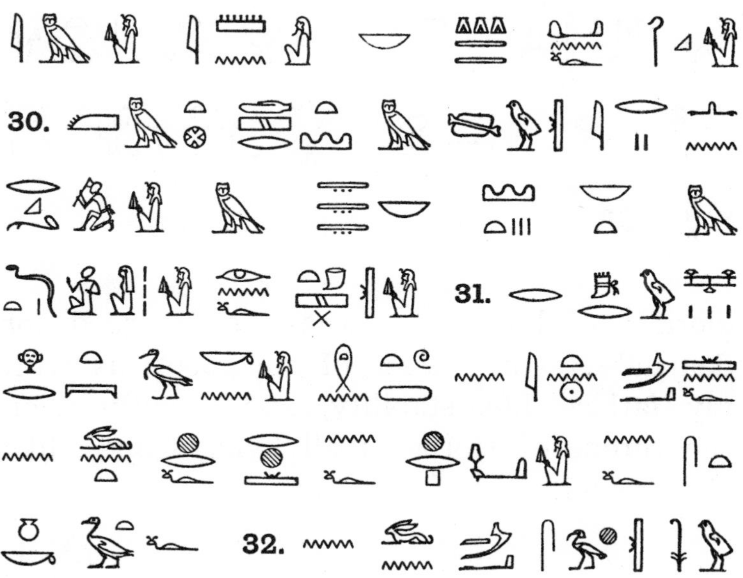

the Two Lands (Egypt), caused me to be Governor **30.** of Kamt (*i.e.* the Black Land, or Egypt proper) and Teshert (*i.e.* the Red Land or deserts on each side of the Nile) as a reward for it. None rebelleth against me in all the lands (*i.e.* the world), the dwellers in the mountains and deserts are my subjects. He hath fixed the boundary of my kingdom **31.** as far as the limits of the sky, the circuit of Aten (*i.e.* the Sun) serveth me, he hath bestowed it upon me, living through him, I present it to him. I am his daughter **32.** in very truth, the

glorifier of him. . . . what he arranged (or demanded), the vessel of my body is with my father, life, stability, and serenity upon the throne of Horus of all living beings, like Rā for ever.

THE REIGN OF THOTHMES III, 1500–1447 B.C.

The parentage of Thothmes III, the greatest of the kings of the XVIIIth Dynasty, and probably the greatest of all the kings of Egypt, has been the subject of animated discussion for many years past, and even now Egyptologists are not agreed about the matter. There is no doubt that he was associated with the great Queen Hatshepsut in the rule of the kingdom, but what was his relationship to her? Some say that he was her half-brother, arguing that Hatshepsut was the daughter of Thothmes I by his sister-wife Aāhmes, the daughter of Amenhetep I and Queen Aāhhetep, and that Thothmes III was the son of Thothmes I by another wife called Aset. But Thothmes I had yet another wife, Mutnefert, and she bore him a son who was also called Thothmes, therefore Thothmes I had two sons of that name. Other authorities say that the Thothmes who is known in history as Thothmes III was not the son of Thothmes I but of Thothmes II by his wife Aset.

According to views that have been recently promulgated, fierce quarrels broke out on the death of Thothmes I, and his daughter Hatshepsut claimed the throne and her half-brother, or half-brothers, did likewise. Hatshepsut married her half-brother, the Thothmes who became Thothmes III, before the death of Thothmes I, and reigned jointly for a time. Before Thothmes I died his son Thothmes, who is known as Thothmes II, made good his claim to the throne, and he and his half-brother, the husband of Hatshepsut, reigned jointly, their half-sister having no share in the government. When Thothmes I died, Thothmes, the son of Mutnefert, ascended the throne and reigned alone as Thothmes II; and when he died Thothmes, the son of Aset, and his sister-wife Hatshepsut, reigned jointly for several years. But Hatshepsut was the predominant partner in the government of the country, and it was not until her death that Thothmes III became King of Egypt *de facto*.

This theory is ingenious but not convincing, and, with the exception of the mutilations of Queen Hatshepsut's name which are brought forward as evidence, finds no support in the Egyptian texts and inscriptions. From time immemorial quarrels have broken out in Oriental Courts on the death of the king or ruler, by whatever title he was called, and among his children by different wives there have always been many claimants to his throne and power. It is quite possible that each of the sons of Thothmes I and their half-sister claimed the throne of their father and quarrelled bitterly over their real or fancied claims, but the present writer submits that there is no evidence of this in the inscriptions at Dêr al-Baharî, or elsewhere. The whole question of the relationship to each other of Thothmes I, II and III has been fully discussed by Maspero in the *Proceedings of the Society of Biblical Archaeology*, vol. xiv, pages 170 ff., and by Naville in *Deir el-Bahari*, London, 1894, page 13. Each has shown that we must hold Thothmes III to be the son of Thothmes II and not of Thothmes I. This is proved by a statement in the inscription of the scribe Anen, found in his tomb at Thebes. He says: "When the king of the South and the North, Ā-kheper-en-Rā (Thothmes II) reigned over Kamt (*i.e.* the Black Land), and ruled Teshert (the Red Land), and made himself master of the Two Lands (*i.e.* all Egypt) in triumph, I was filling the heart of the king in every place of his, and what he did for me was more than that which the kings before him had done, and I attained to the dignity of his most trusted friends, and I was among the favourites of His Majesty every day. Then when he went forth to heaven [and] he was united

to the gods his son stood in his place as king

of the Two Lands, he ruled on the throne of him

that begot him. His sister, the divine wife Hatshepsut,

carried out the administration of the country,

the Two Lands were according to her plans, served

her Egypt submissively. (See *Recueil de Travaux*, tom. xii, page 106; as to the words "his sister," *see* Maspero's explanation in the *Proceedings of the Society of Biblical Archaeology*, vol. xiv, page 177.)

When Hatshepsut died the tributaries of Egypt in Western Asia and in Nubia refused to acknowledge Thothmes III as their overlord and declined to pay tribute to him. The pacific rule of Hatshepsut had accustomed them to regard Egypt without fear, and the new king was obliged to undertake a series of military expeditions into Syria and Nubia on a large scale. It may be said at once that his arms were victorious everywhere, and his conquests may be briefly described. He marched from Thal in the Eastern Delta to Gâza and Ihem, where he learned that the Syrians, the Shasu, *i.e.* the nomad tribes of the deserts, and the peoples of the country of Naharina, and the Qetshu, had made a league together, and that they had assembled their armies and horses and chariots at Megiddo. Thothmes set out and, marching quickly, engaged the enemy outside the city of Megiddo. Having vanquished them he besieged the city itself and captured it, and carried off an immense amount of spoil, but very few of the enemy were slain, and the principal ringleaders escaped. During the course of the 31 years of his independent reign he made seventeen expeditions, or rather military raids, into Western Asia and Nubia, and made himself master of Palestine, Syria, Phoenicia, Assyria, Mitani, and the kings of the Babylonians, Hittites and Cyprians and others sent tribute to him. From each of his raids he brought back to Egypt immense quantities of spoil of all kinds, and Egypt became the richest country in the world. His scribes kept a diary of each expedition, in which were duly chronicled the exploits of the king and his personal bravery, and a list of the tribute obtained from each king and country. A full account of everything connected with these matters was written upon a roll of leather, which was laid up in the great temple of Amen at Thebes.

During the last ten years of his reign the tribute that he had laid upon the peoples of Western Asia and the Nubians of the Nile Valley so far south as Napata was probably collected by his governors and officers. An important share of all the spoil brought to Egypt by him was given to the temple of Amen, and the priesthood of this god became the richest in Egypt. Amen, from being merely the god of Thebes, became king of the world and king of the gods. He possessed towns in Palestine and Syria, and a very large number of slaves, male and female, and the commands of his high priest were obeyed unhesitatingly throughout the land. These gifts, which Thothmes poured into the coffers of the god, were the foundation of the wealth of Amen that provoked the jealousy of Amenhetep IV.

Thothmes was not only a great soldier but a great builder, as the famous Hall of Columns at Karnak testifies. He set up a single obelisk and two pairs of obelisks at Karnak, and two obelisks at Heliopolis, but no obelisk of his remains now at either place. Before we pass on to describe these obelisks it will be well to set before the reader a translation of the summary of the conquests of Thothmes III, which was drawn up by the priests of Amen, and cut upon a huge black granite stele (*see* **Plate XII**) that stood in the great temple of Amen-Rā in the Northern Apt (*i.e.* Karnak). The composition is rhythmical in character, and it is probable that it was chanted by the priests on the days of great festivals. In the two scenes sculptured on the upper part of the stele Thothmes is represented in the act of offering two vessels of wine, , and two vessels of burning incense, , to the god. In the text[1] Amen-Rā, Lord of the thrones of the Two Lands, says :—

THE CONQUESTS OF THOTHMES III SUMMARIZED BY AMEN-RĀ

TRANSLATION OF THE SPEECH OF AMEN-RĀ

Come to me,
Rejoice at the sight of my beneficence,
My son, my avenger, Men-kheperrā, the ever-living.
I rise in the sky for thy pleasure (or, for love of thee).
My heart dilateth with joy at thy beautiful comings to my temple.

[1] First published by Mariette, *Karnak*, plate xi ; more correctly by Sethe, *Urkunden*, ii, pages 611 ff.

Black granite stele inscribed with a text purporting to be a speech made by Amen-Rā, " King of the Gods," to Thothmes III, in which the god enumerates the conquests which he has enabled the king to make.

The Obelisk of Thothmes III in the Piazza of St. John Lateran, Rome.

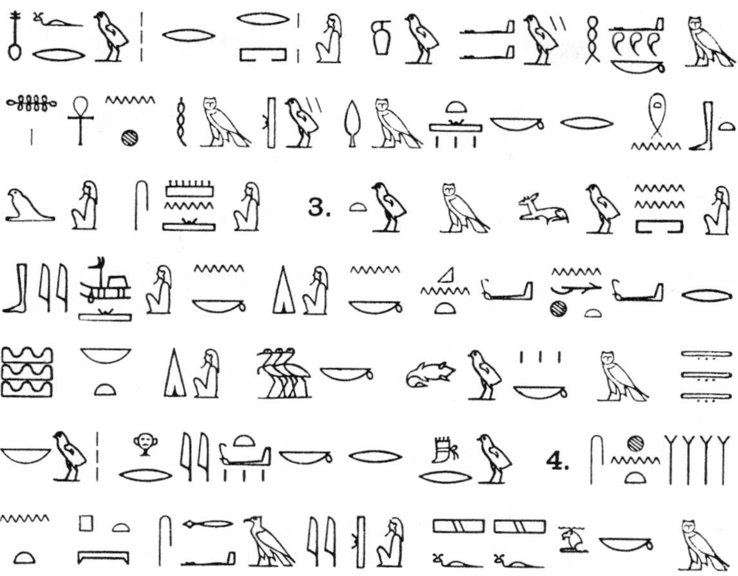

My two hands kneaded together thy body with the fluid of life.

Doubly sweet are thy benefactions to my body.

I have stablished thee in my shrine.

I have made thee to be a thing to marvel at.

I gave thee might and victory over all deserts and hills.

I have placed thy souls [and] the fear of thee in all countries.

The terror of thee reacheth to the boundary of the four pillars of the sky.

I have magnified thy boldness in the bodies of every one.

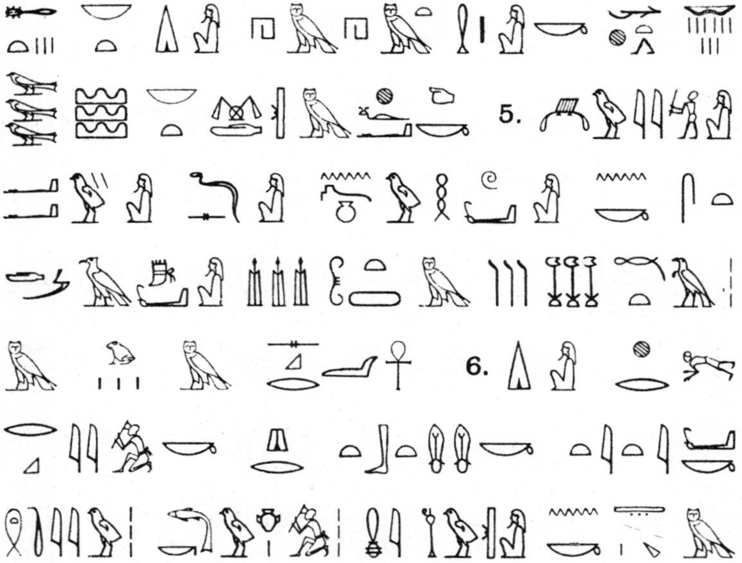

I have made thy Majesty's roar to penetrate among the Nine Peoples of Nubia ;
the chiefs of every foreign land, all of them, are in thy grasp.
I myself stretched out my two hands and bound them in fetters for thee.
I captured the Antiu of Sti (*i.e.* Nubia) by tens of thousands of thousands, and of the northern peoples I made prisoners hundreds of thousands.
I made those who rebelled against thee to hurl themselves down under thy sandals.
Thou hast crushed the seditious ones and the evil-minded folk, inasmuch as I decreed for thee the earth in its length and breadth.

The dwellers in the West [and] the dwellers in the East are beneath thy inspection.

Thou hast trampled upon every foreign land, thy heart is blithe.

There is none that dareth approach Thy Majesty, for it is I who am thy guide ; it is thou that goest forth [to attack] them.

Thou didst traverse the waters of the Great Circle (*i.e.* the Euphrates) and the country of Nehren with victory and power, for so did I decree for thee.

They heard thy roarings, they withdrew into their caves, I blocked their nostrils against the breath of life.

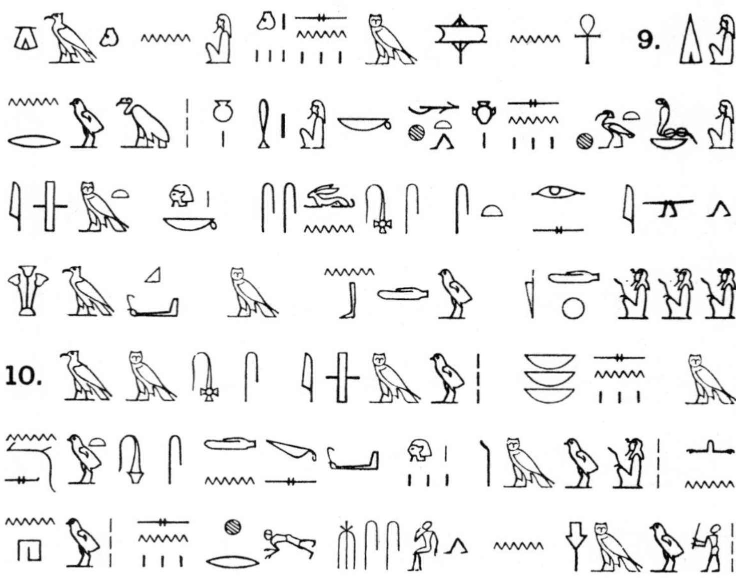

I have made the conquests of Thy Majesty to penetrate their minds.

The serpent Aakhut that is on thy head burned them up.

It maketh to come as captives grasped by the hair the Qetu peoples.

It consumeth with its flame those who dwell in their swamps.

It cutteth off the heads of the Āmu (*i.e.* the nomads of the deserts) ; none of them remaineth, the sons of their (?) mighty ones fall headlong.

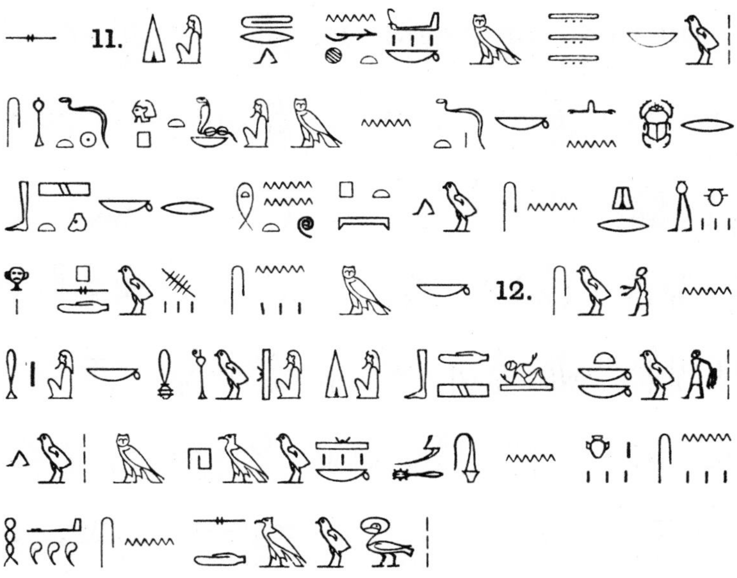

I have made thy exploits to travel round all countries, my serpent-crown illumineth thy body.

There existeth none who is disaffected in respect of thee throughout the whole circle of heaven.

They (*i.e.* the people) come bearing their offerings upon their backs, and they bow to the ground before Thy Majesty at my decree.

I have reduced to impotence the miserable folk who came to invade thy country, their hearts were scorched with fire and their members were all a-tremble.

THE SONG OF AMEN.—**13.**

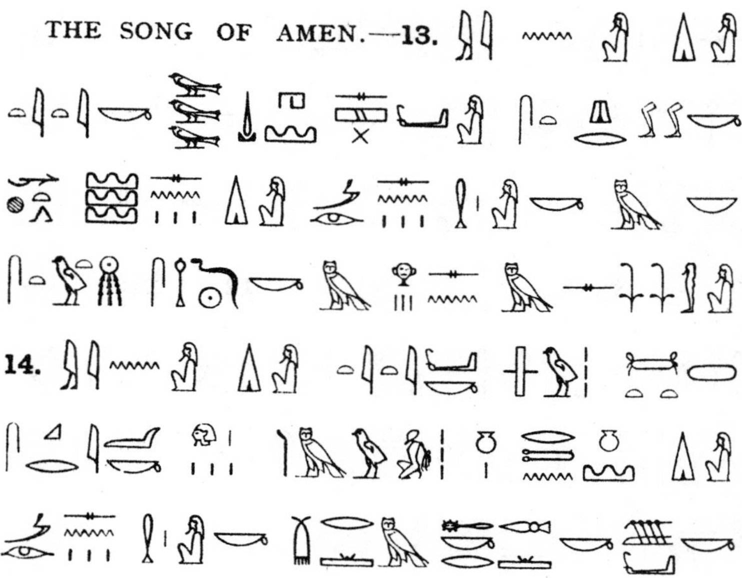

I came. I made thee to trample upon the chiefs of Tchah (Phoenicia).

I cast them down under thy feet throughout their deserts.

I made them to behold Thy Majesty as the Lord of brilliance (or light), thou didst light up their faces like an image of myself.

I came. I made thee to trample upon the dwellers in Satt (Asia), thou hast taken captive the chiefs of the Āmu (nomads) of Rethnu.

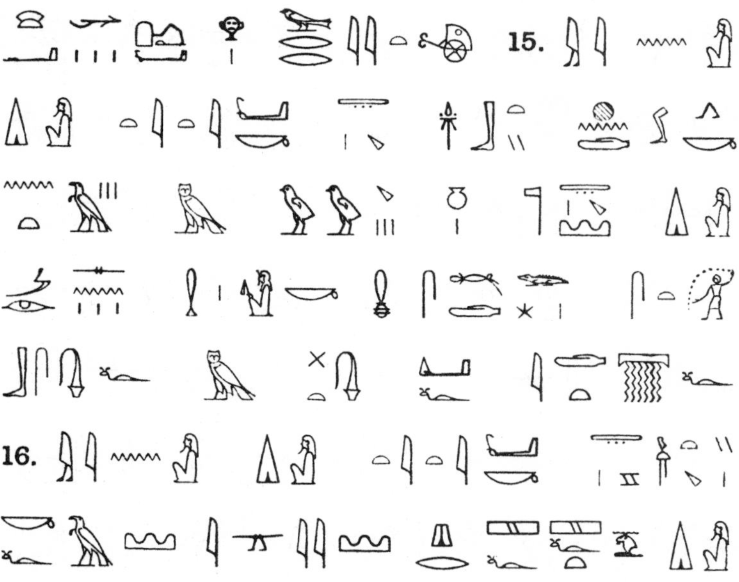

I have made them to see Thy Majesty equipped with thy gleaming arms, when thou didst take the weapons of war on the chariot.

I came. I made thee to trample under foot the Land of the East, thou hast set thy foot upon those who are in the regions of Ta-Neter (*i.e.* the Land of the God, or Southern Arabia).

I have made them to see Thy Majesty like the Seshet Star, which coruscateth in its flame of fire, and emitteth its dew (*sic*).

I came. I made thee to trample upon the Land of the West, Kefti (Phoenicia) and Asi (Cyprus) are down under thy onset.

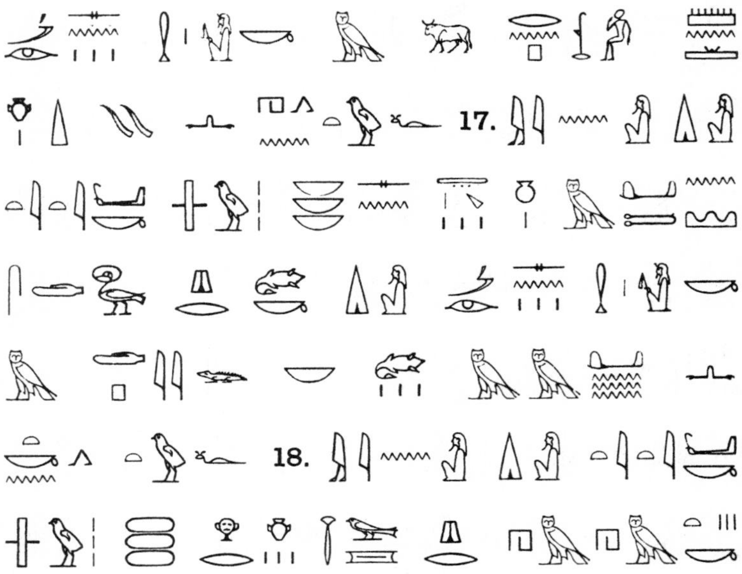

I have made them to see Thy Majesty as a young bull, determined, with horns ready [to fight], that cannot be turned back.

I came. I made thee to trample upon those who dwell in their marshes; the lands of Methen (Mitani) quake through fear of thee.

I have made them to see Thy Majesty as a *Tepi* crocodile, the terrible lord of the stream, whom none dareth go near.

I came. I made thee to trample upon those who dwell in the Islands in the Great Green [Sea] through thy bellowings.

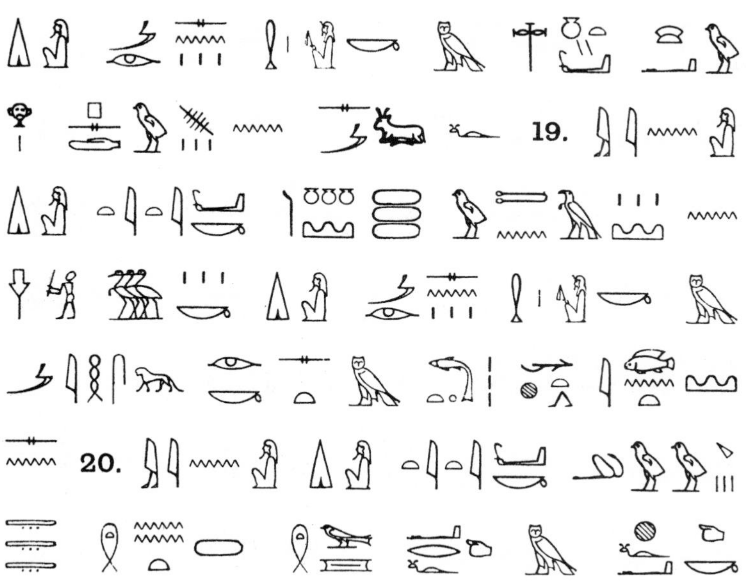

I have made them to see Thy Majesty as the striker (or slaughterer) who mounteth upon the back of the beast he hath slain.

I came. I made thee to trample upon the Tehenu (Libyans), the Islands Uthentiu (Oases ?) are [at the mercy of] the strength of thy Souls.

I have made them to see Thy Majesty as a lion fierce of eye ; thou turnest them into dead bodies throughout their deserts.

I came. I made thee to trample upon the ends of the world, the Circle of the Great Circle (*i.e.* the World-Ocean) is grasped in thy fist.

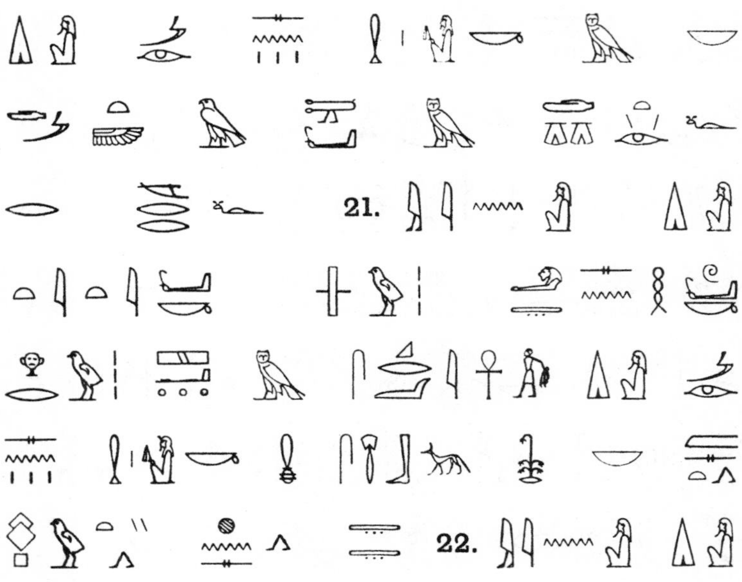

I have made them to see Thy Majesty as a hawk, the lord of the wing, who pounceth upon whatsoever he seeth at his good pleasure.

I came. I made thee to trample upon those who dwell in the foremost parts of th[eir] land; thou hast bound the Dwellers on the Sand (*i.e.* nomads) like prisoners captured alive.

I have made them to see Thy Majesty as a jackal of the South, swiftly running, the stealthy slinker, loping over the Two Lands.

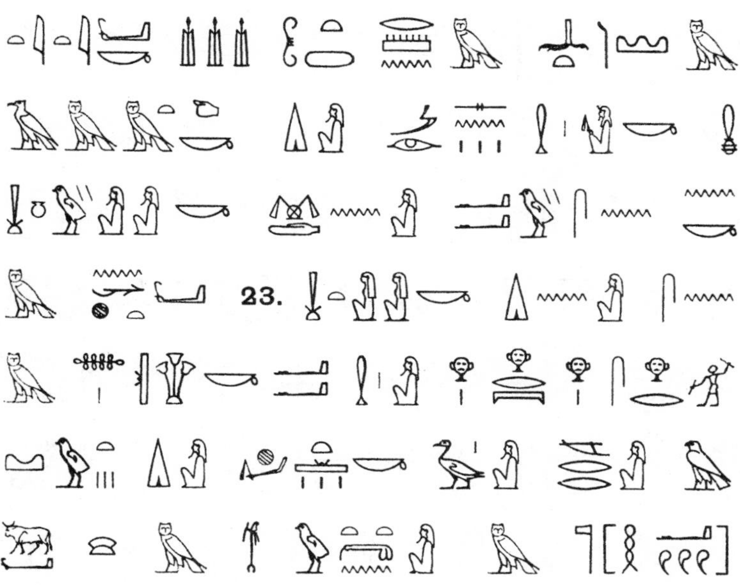

I came. I made thee to trample upon the Antiu of Sti (Nubia), as far as Shat, , they are in thy grasp.

I have made them to see Thy Majesty as the Two Divine Brethren (*i.e.* Horus and Set), I have joined together their two arms for thee in strength.

I have set thy Two Divine Sisters behind thee to protect thee, the two arms of my Majesty are on high to repel evils.

I have given thee thy splendours, my son, my beloved one, Horus, Mighty Bull, crowned in Thebes, whom I have begotten in divine flesh,

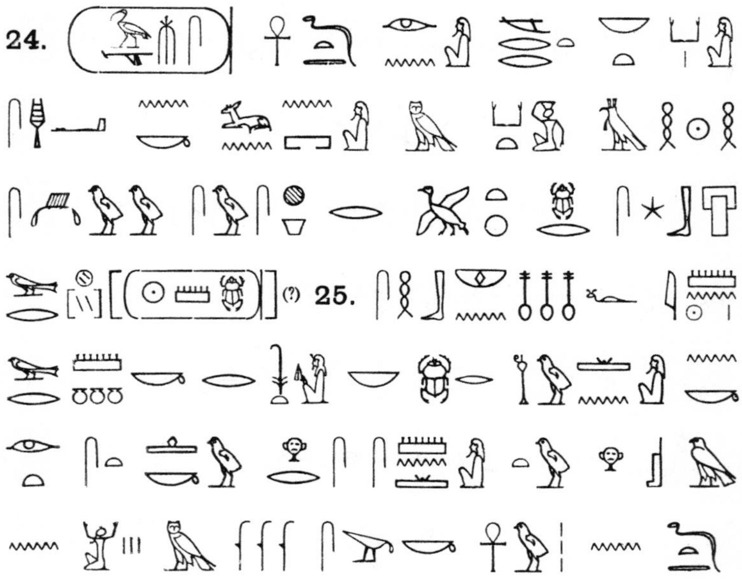

Thothmes, the ever-living, who hath done for me everything that my mind wished. Thou hast set up my sanctuary as a work of everlastingness, lengthening and broadening it more than ever before, the very Great Door, Menkheperrā, celebrating the festivals of the beauties of Amen-Rā. Thy monument is greater than that of any king who hath ever been. I commanded thee to do it. I am satisfied with it. I stablish thee on the throne of Horus of Millions of Years; thou shalt be the leader of the living for ever.

V

THE OBELISK OF THOTHMES III BEFORE ST. JOHN LATERAN

THIS obelisk, which now stands in the Piazza of St. John Lateran at Rome, was intended by Thothmes to stand in one of the courts of the temple of Amen-Rā at Karnak. It was brought from the quarries at Aswân and deposited in the temple, but the king died before it could be inscribed and set up. Thothmes III was succeeded by his son, Amenhetep II, who reigned for about 26 years, but he neither set up the uninscribed obelisk nor usurped it. His son and successor, Thothmes IV, jealous for the name and fame of his grandfather, had the obelisk inscribed with the usual dedication of Thothmes III, and then added an inscription of his own, and set up the monument in the place where he believed it was intended to go. In this inscription he tells us that it had lain untouched for 35 years. The obelisk stood in the temple of Amen until about A.D. 330, when Constantine the Great decided to remove it to the city of New Rome, which he had founded near Byzantium, and to set it up to adorn his capital. It was therefore " torn up from its place " and floated down the Nile to Memphis, and thence by canal to Alexandria. Whilst preparations were being made to take it across the Mediterranean Constantine died, and the huge block of granite, which is about 105 feet long and weighs about 460 tons, lay at Alexandria for some 25 years. In A.D. 357 Constantius, the successor of Constantine, had a lighter of immense length and beam built, and when the obelisk was slid on to it, a trireme, manned with a crew of 300 rowers, towed it to the village of Alexandria, three miles from Rome. It was then placed on a cradle laid upon rollers and drawn along and brought through the Ostian gate and the public fish-market to the Circus Maximus, where it was set up. (*See* **Plate XIII.**) Ammianus Marcellinus tells us (xvii. 4. § 15) how this was done. "Vast beams having been raised on end in a most dangerous manner, so that they looked like a grove of machines, long ropes of huge size were fastened to them, darkening the very sky with their density, as they formed a web of innumerable threads; and into them the great stone itself, covered over as it was with elements of writing, was bound, and gradually raised into the empty air, and long suspended, many thousands of men turning it round and round like a millstone, till at last it was placed in the middle of the square. And on it was placed a brazen sphere, made brighter with plates of gold, and as that was immediately afterwards struck by lightning and destroyed, a brazen figure like a torch was placed on it, also plated with gold—to look as if the torch were fully alight" (C. D. Yonge).

At some period, of which we know nothing, the obelisk either fell down or was thrown down, some think as the result of an earthquake, but others attribute it to the enemies of Rome when the city was sacked. At its fall it broke into three pieces, which were entirely forgotten until

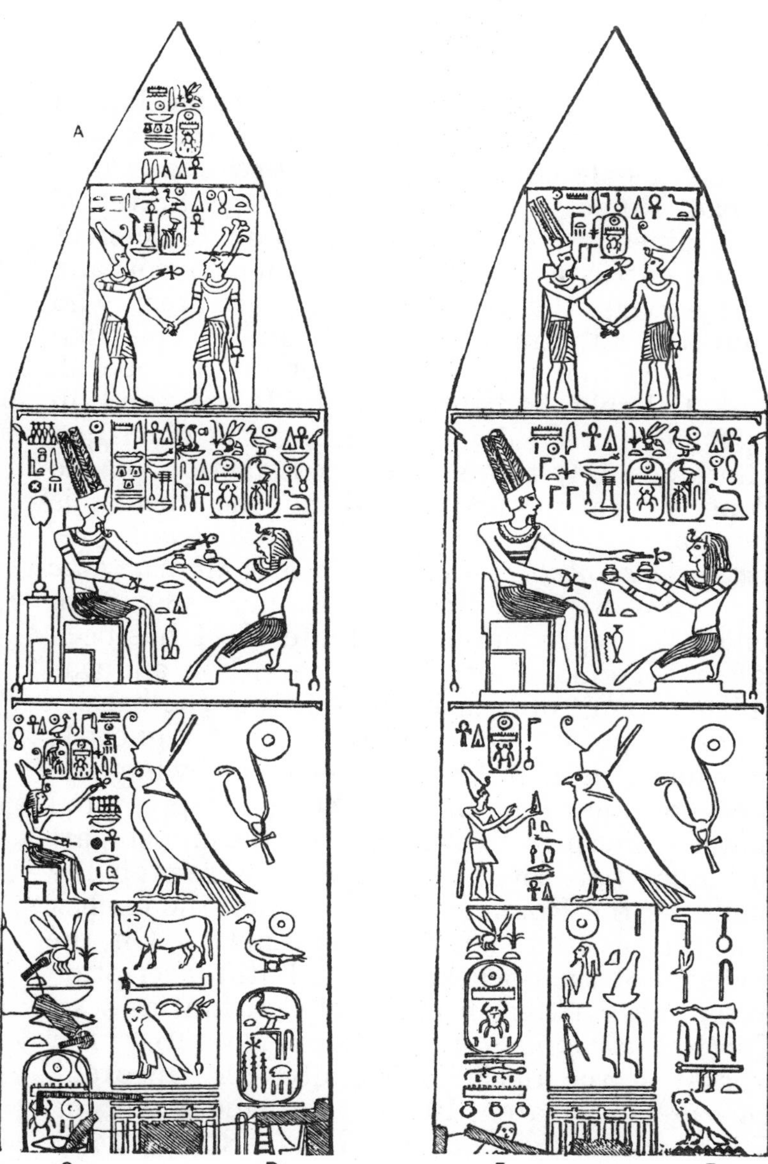

The obelisk of Thothmes III in the Piazza of St. John Lateran showing the Vignettes in which the god Amen-Rā is presenting "life" to the king and Thothmes III is making offerings to the god. At A, B, C, D, E, F, are the cartouches and inscriptions of Thothmes IV.

February 15, 1587, when they were found buried under a mass of ruins at the depth of about 24 feet, as Mercati in his work *Degli obelischi di Roma*, Rome, 1589, tells us. Pope Sixtus V determined to rejoin the pieces and to re-erect it, and entrusted the work to Domenico Fontana (1543–1607), the famous Italian architect who built the Library of the Vatican. This distinguished man had already set up the obelisk that Caligula had brought to Rome, and in 1588 he succeeded in re-erecting the obelisk of Thothmes III, to the great satisfaction of the Pope. His method of raising the obelisk is described in his work *Del modo tenuto nel trasportare l'obelisco Vaticano, e delle fabriche fatte da nostro Signore Sisto V*, Rome, 1589, from which the reproduction on Plate XIII has been taken. To make the obelisk stand Fontana was obliged to cut off nearly three feet of the base.

On the pyramidion are two series of Vignettes, in which the god Amen is seen bestowing life on Thothmes III, and the king is represented making offerings to Amen. In the upper part of the shaft are several holes, which were probably made by the Roman workmen when the obelisk was set up in the Circus Maximus. On the pedestal of the obelisk is cut a Latin inscription in 24 lines written in praise of Constantius: *see Corpus Inscriptionum Latinorum*, No. 1163. For works on the obelisk generally, *see* Ungarelli, *Interpretatio*, plate i, Rome, 1742, and Marucchi, *Gli obelischi Egiziani di Roma*, Rome, 1898. The text of the inscription of Thothmes III reads :—

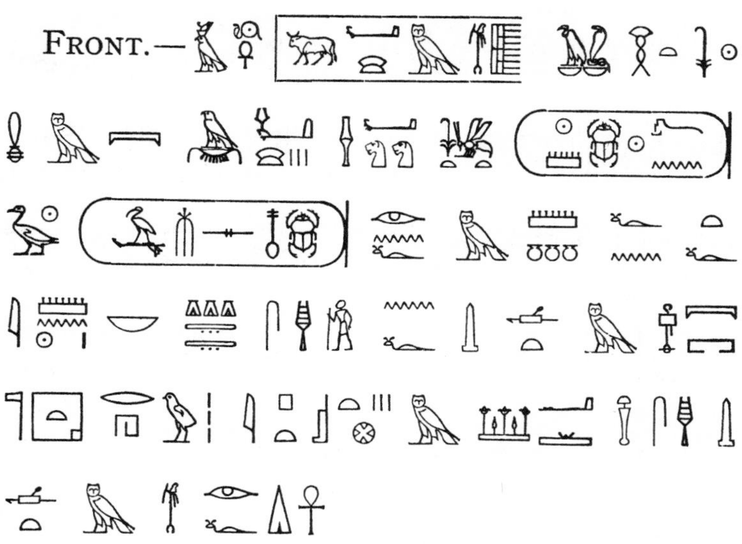

TRANSLATION OF THE OBELISK OF THOTHMES III ON THE PIAZZA OF THE LATERAN

FRONT.—Horus [name] Ka-nekht-khā-em-Uas. Nebti [name] Uaht sutenit-ma-Rā-em-pet. Golden Horus [name] Tcheser-khāu-kherp-pehti. Nesubati [name] Men-kheper-Rā-setep-en-Rā. Son of Rā [name] Tehuti-mes-nefer-kheper. He made [this obelisk] as his monument for his father Amen-Rā, lord of the thrones of the Two Lands. He set up one obelisk in the court of the temple facing the Apts (Karnak). It was the first time one[1] obelisk had been set up in Thebes. He did it that life might be given to him.

[1] They were usually erected in pairs.

RIGHT FACE.—

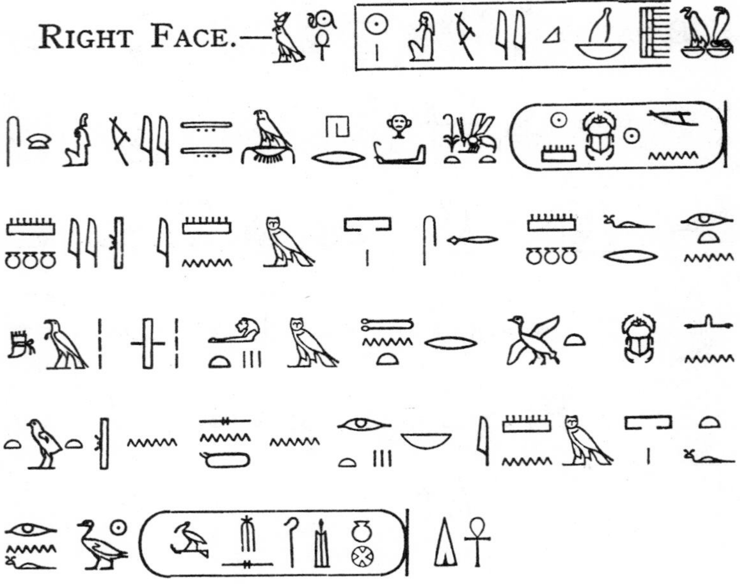

RIGHT FACE.—Horus [name] Meri - Rā - qa - hetchet. Nebti [name] Skhā - Maāt - meri - Taui. Golden Horus [name] Her-her-nekht. Nesubati [name] Men-kheper-Rā-mer-en-Rā, builder of monuments in the temple of Amen. He made his monuments greater than those made by his predecessors, larger than any that existed before, and unequalled in extent among all that had been made in the Temple of his father Amen. The son of Rā, Thothmes, governor of Anu (Heliopolis), did this that life might be given to him.

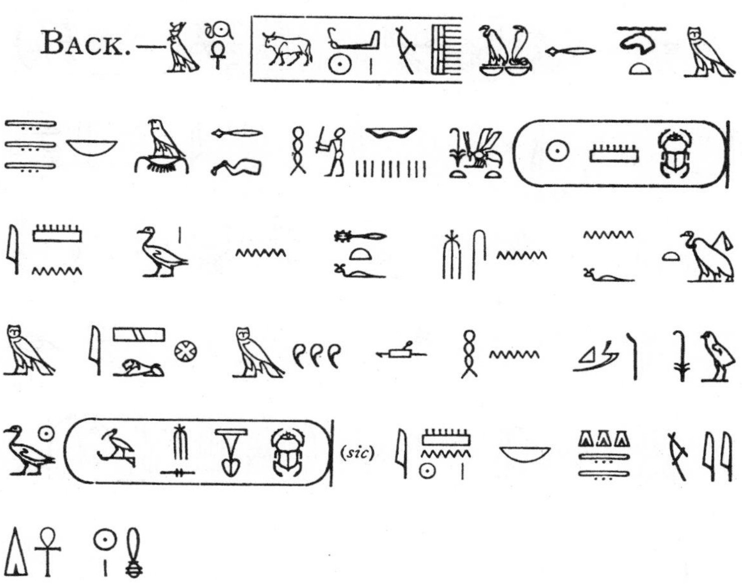

BACK.—Horus [name] Ka-nekht-meri-Rā. Nebti [name] Ā-shefit-em-taiu-nebu. Golden Horus [name] Ā-khepesh-hui-petchtiu. Nesubat [name] Men-kheper-Rā, son of Amen, of his body. The Goddess Mut in Asher brought him forth in the flesh which was one with that of him that created him. Son of Rā Thothmes nefer-kheper, beloved of Amen, lord of the thrones of the Two Lands, endowed with life like Rā.

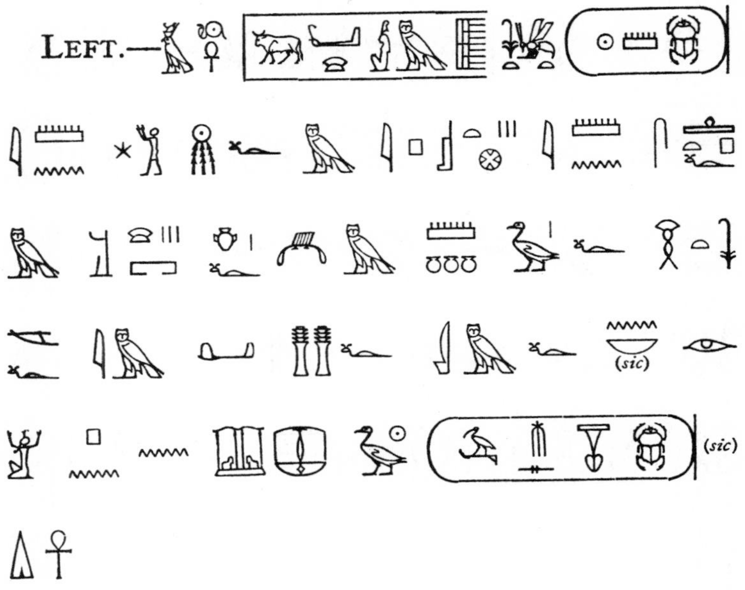

LEFT.—Horus [name] Ka-nekht-khā-em-Maāt. Nesubati [name] Men-kheper-Rā. He praiseth Amen when he riseth in the Apts. He setteth Amen to rest in the temple of Uthes-khāu, his heart rejoicing in the monuments of his son, whose sovereignty endureth, loving him there. He maketh him to be stable, that he may renew for thee the celebration of hundreds of thousands of this Set festival. Son of Rā, Thothmes, nefer-kheper, giver of (or given) life.

As already stated, Thothmes IV, the grandson of Thothmes III, found a great granite uninscribed obelisk lying near Karnak, and caused it to be inscribed in his grandfather's name, and set it up in front of the great upper gate of Karnak opposite Thebes. Some think that the obelisk was actually made for Thothmes I, who died leaving it uninscribed, and that it was annexed by Thothmes III, who either deliberately or through death left it as he had found it. The text which Thothmes IV added to it, two columns on each side, has been published by Ungarelli (*see* the plate in his *Interpretatio*, Rome, 1742) and by Marucchi (*Gli obeliscchi Egiziani*, Rome, 1898, plates i and ii), who gives a transcript of the text with an Italian translation. Copies of the text were also published by Kircher (*Oedipus* iii, page 164) and by Zoega (*De Usu et Origine Obeliscorum*, Rome, 1797). The first English translation of the text of Thothmes III was made by Birch (*Records of the Past*, iv, pages 9 ff.).

The Latin inscription on the base, which dedicates the obelisk to the Invincible Cross, reads: Sixtus V. Pont. Max. obeliscum hunc specie eximia temporum calamitate fractum Circi Max. ruinis humo limo q. alte demersum multa impensa extraxit: hunc in locum magno labore transtulit: formae. q. pristinae accurate restitutum cruci invictissimae dicavit. A.M.D.LXXXVIII. Pont. IIII. Fl. Constantinus maximus Aug. Christianae Fidei vindex et assertor obeliscum ab Aegyptio Rege impuro voto soli dedicatum sedib. avolsum suis per

Nilum transferri Alexandriam jussit ut Novam Romam ab se tunc conditam eo decoraret monumento.[1]

THE INSCRIPTION WHICH THOTHMES IV ADDED TO THE OBELISK OF HIS GRANDFATHER, THOTHMES III

NORTH SIDE. LEFT.—

TRANSLATION OF THE INSCRIPTION OF THOTHMES IV ON THE OBELISK OF THOTHMES III

NORTH SIDE. LEFT.—The King of the South and the North, the beloved of the gods. The Company of the Gods praise his beneficence. He sendeth Rā to rest in the Boat of the Evening, he praiseth Tem in the Boat of the Morning, the lord of the Two Lands, Men-kheperu-Rā, perfecter of Thebes for ever, maker of monuments in the Apts. The Company of the Gods of the House of Amen are content with what hath done the son of Tem, of his body, his heir upon his throne. Thothmes (IV) crowned with diadems, beloved of Amen-Rā.

[1] Parker, *Obelisks of Rome*, page 6.

NORTH SIDE. RIGHT.—

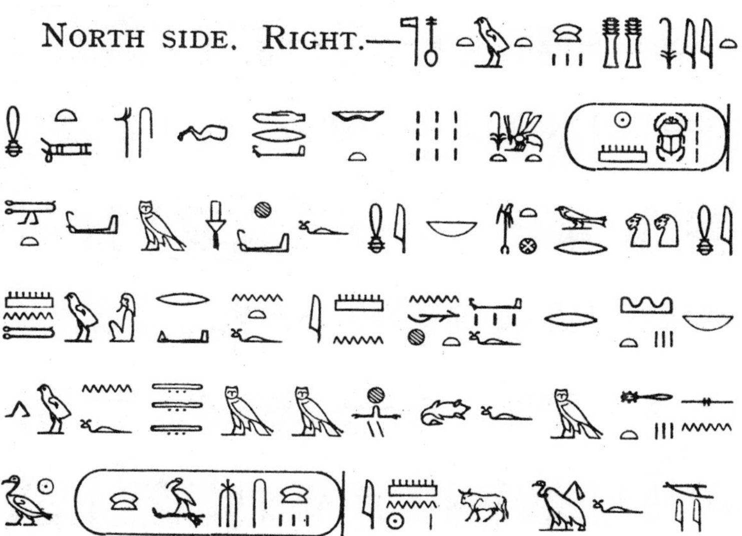

NORTH SIDE. RIGHT.—The beneficent God, the Form [with] Crowns, stablished in sovereignty like Tem, mighty one of strength, destroyer of the Nine Peoples of the Bow, King of the South and the North, Men-kheperu-Rā, victorious in his strength like the Lord of Thebes, mighty one of valour like Menthu. His Father Amen hath set his victories in all countries. Lands unknown (?) come to him with the fear of him in their bellies, son of Rā, Thothmes (IV) crowned with diadems, beloved of Amen-Rā, the Bull of his mother.

SOUTH SIDE. LEFT.—

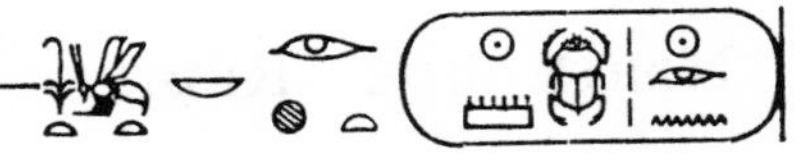

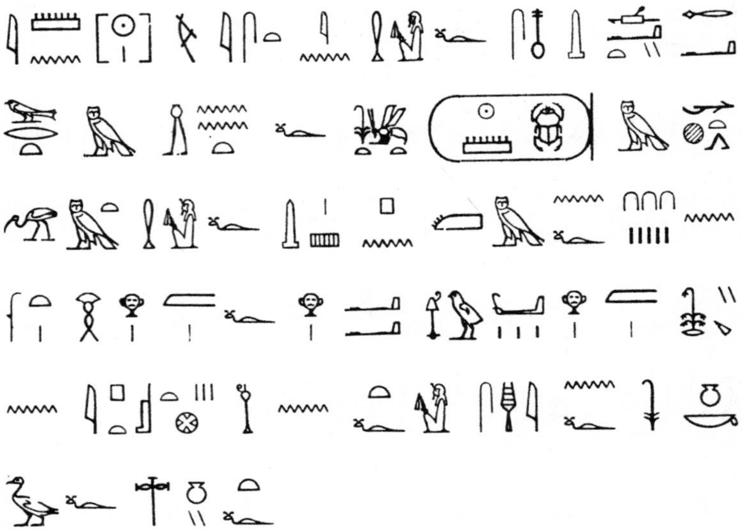

SOUTH SIDE. LEFT.—The King of the South and the North, the lord creator of things, Men-kheperu-Rā Ari-en-Rā (Thothmes IV), beloved of Amen-Rā. Behold, His Majesty decorated the one obelisk, the very great obelisk, which His Majesty Men-kheper-Rā (Thothmes III) had brought here, after his Majesty had found this obelisk, which had been lying on its side for five-and-thirty years in charge of the workmen on the south side of the Apts (Karnak), my father having commanded it to be set up to him. I am his son, the reverer of his father.

SOUTH SIDE. RIGHT.—

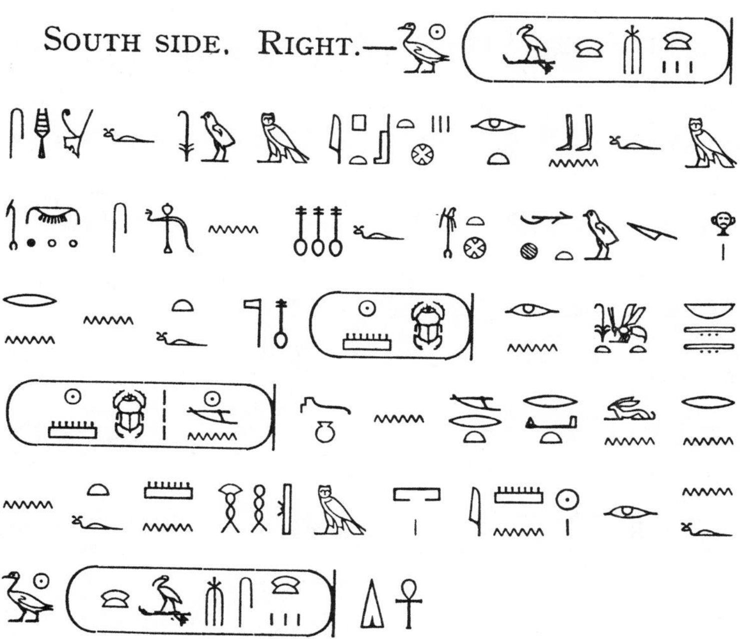

SOUTH SIDE. RIGHT.—The son of Rā, Thothmes, crowned with crowns, set it up in the Apts, and made for it a pyramidion of refined copper (or white gold), the splendours of which illumined Thebes, and inscribed it with the name of [my] father the beneficent god, Men-kheper-Rā. The King of the South and North, the lord of the Two Lands, Men-kheperu-Rā, did this in order that the name of his father might be permanent and flourish in the temple of Amen-Rā. The son of Rā, Thothmes (IV), did this for him that life might be given to him.

EAST SIDE. LEFT.—

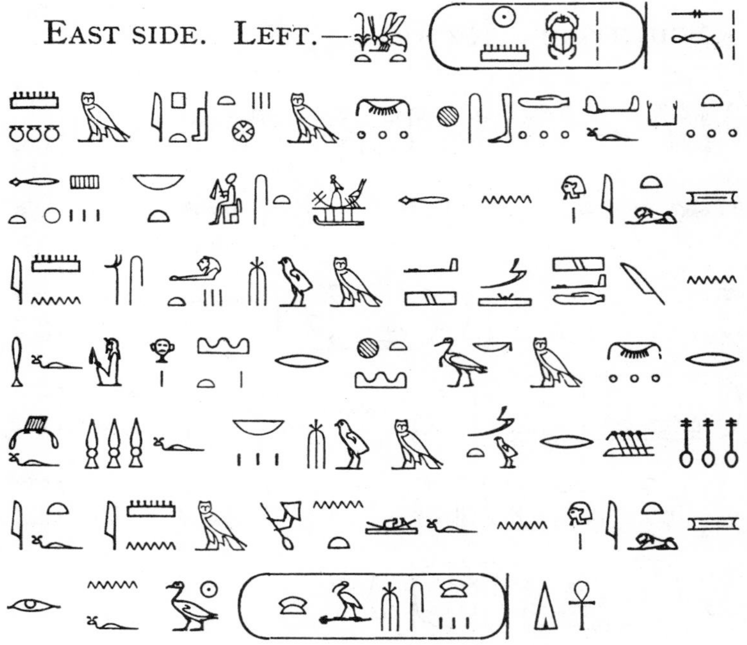

EAST SIDE. LEFT.—The King of the South and the North, Men-kheperu-Rā, who filleth the Apts with monuments in gold, lapis-lazuli, turquoise, and semi-precious stones of all kinds, made the great and august barge [used in the river festival] Tep-Atru, which was called User-hat-Amen. It was made of cedar-wood, which His Majesty cut down on the mountain of Kheta (?), and plated with gold from one end to the other. All the adornments thereof were made new to receive the beauties of Father Amen when he sailed at the festival of Tep-Atru. The son of Rā, Thothmes (IV), made it that life might be given to him.

EAST SIDE. RIGHT.—

EAST SIDE. RIGHT.—The beneficent god, mighty one of strength, who conquereth by his might, who terrifieth the Mentiu (*i.e.* the Cattle-breeding folk), whose roarings penetrate among the Antiu of Stit (*i.e.* the people of the Eastern Desert), who was trained from his babyhood by his father Amen to reign enduringly so that the princes of all lands might bow low before the will of His Majesty, who speaketh with his mouth and worketh with his hands, at whose command everything is done, the King of the South and the North, Men-kheperu-Rā, whose name shall be established in the Apts (Karnak).

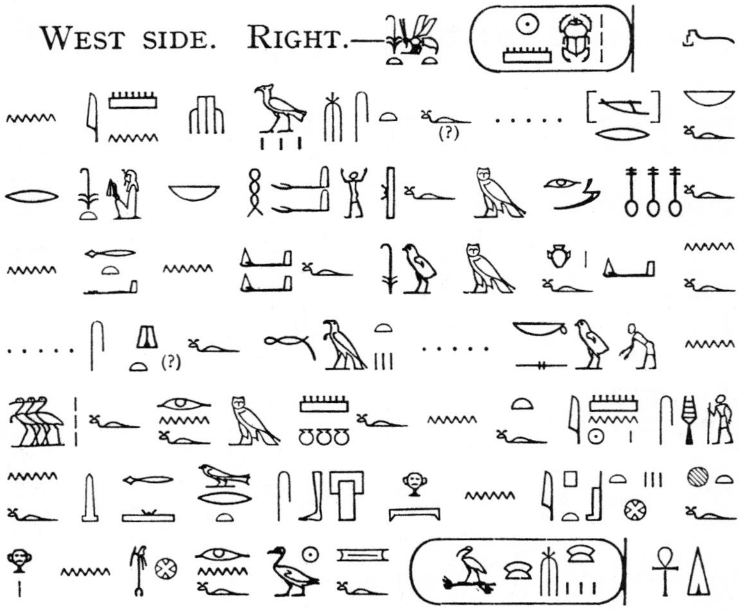

West side. Right.—King of the South and the North, Men-kheperu-Rā, chosen of Amen [to be] the President of men (?), born to him by [Mut ?], whom he loves more than any [other] king. He (*i.e.* Amen) rejoiceth at the sight of his beautiful actions, by reason of the greatness of the affection for him which he has in his heart. He hath set the Northern peoples under his rule, they bow low before his Will. He hath made it (*i.e.* the obelisk) as his monument to his father Amen-Rā. He hath set up [this] great and mighty obelisk at the upper gate of the Apts (Karnak), opposite Thebes, so that the son of Rā, his beloved Thothmes (IV), diademed with diadems, might have life given to him.

WEST SIDE. LEFT.—

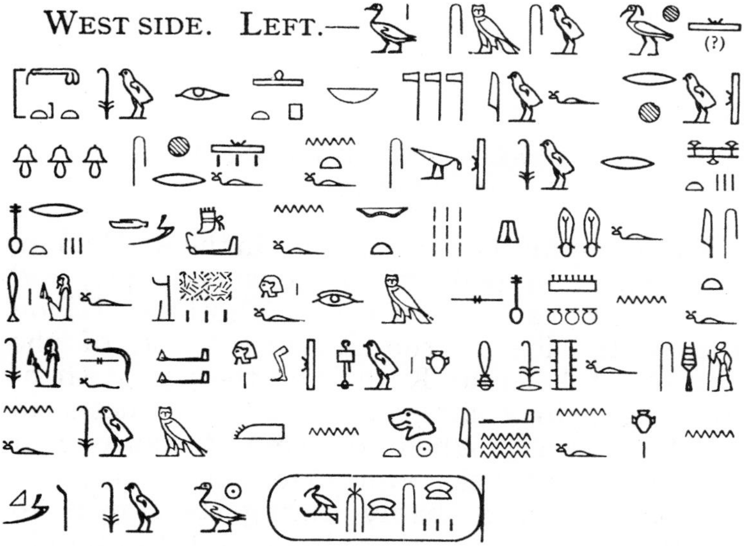

WEST SIDE. LEFT.—[Men-kheperu-Rā], the eldest son, who glorifieth him that begot him, who maketh to be satisfied the Lord of the gods, [because] he knoweth the perfections of his designs. It is he who directeth him to the paths of well-doing, it is he who hath fettered for him the Nine Peoples of the Bow under his sandals. Behold, His Majesty kept watch always to beautify the monuments of his father. The king himself issued the instructions, for he possessed the heart of the craftsman like Him of the Southern Wall (*i.e.* Ptah of Memphis). He set it (*i.e.* the obelisk) up at the end of the moment (*i.e.* at the right moment ?). He refreshed the heart of him that created him, the son of Rā, Thothmes (IV), diademed with ademdis.

VI

THE OBELISK OF THOTHMES III AT CONSTANTINOPLE

This red granite obelisk stands in the At-Meidan, the ancient hippodrome of Constantinople, and seems to have been set up by Thothmes III on the south side of the Seventh Pylon of the Temple of Amen at Karnak, in the 33rd year of his reign, to commemorate his conquests in Western Asia. When complete it was one of the largest obelisks ever made in Egypt, but it was broken probably during its transit to Constantinople, or in that city, and it is now only about 50 feet high ; the lower portion, according to Zoega, once stood in the Strategium. The upper part, which is now standing, was set up by the order of the Emperor Theodosius in the second half of the IVth century A.D., and descriptions of its pedestal and adornments are given by English travellers and others who visited Constantinople in the XVIth century (*see* above, p. 40).

On each of the four faces of the pyramidion is cut a rectangular Vignette, in which the king is seen standing before Amen, and below each of these, cut on the side of the obelisk, is a rectangular Vignette, in which the king is represented making offerings to Amen. The inscriptions read : " Amen, lord of Thebes, President of the Apts (Karnak), great god, giver of life, stability and serenity." "The beneficent god, lord of Egypt, lord creator of things, King of the South and the North, Men-kheper-Rā, son of Rā, Thothmes, to whom life is given like Rā for ever." Down each side of the shaft is a column of hieroglyphs, which read :—

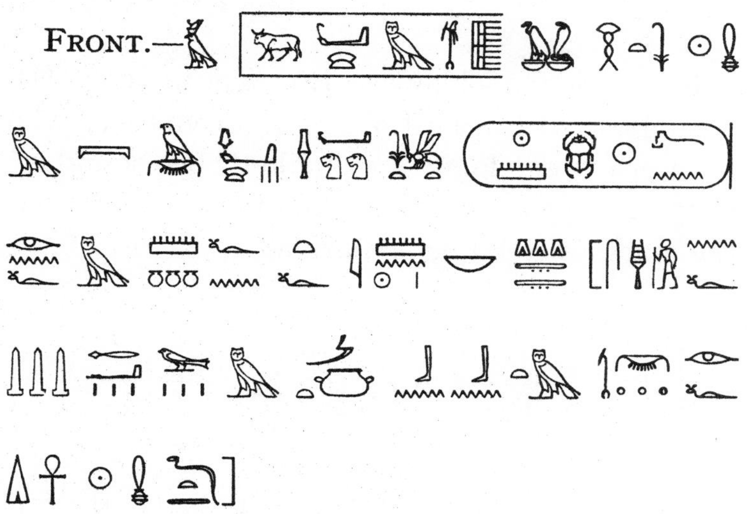

Omitting the transcriptions of the high-sounding names and titles, which have already been given, the inscriptions on the shaft of the obelisk read :—

FRONT.—He made [this obelisk] as his monument to his Father Amen-Rā, lord of the thrones of the Two Lands. [He set up for him great and mighty obelisks of granite, their pyramidions being [made] of refined copper. He did it that life might be given to him like Rā for ever.]

RIGHT.—Men - kheper - Rā (Thothmes III), emanation of Rā, lord of might (or victory), who fettereth every land, who maketh his boundary as far as Upt-ta (*i.e.* the skull of the earth) [and] the marshes as far as Naharina.

BACK.—Men-kheper-Rā Sāenrā (Thothmes III), who hath been trained, from the time when he was a babe in the arms of the Divine Mother Neith, to reign, conqueror of all lands, the master of time long-extended, lord of Set Festivals [many words illegible].

LEFT.—Men-kheper-Rā Arienrā (Thothmes III), who sailed over the Great Circle of Naharina, with valour and victory going at the head of his soldiers, and making great slaughter among the wretched people of that region.

The lower parts of all the inscriptions are wanting. Copies of the texts have been published by Lepsius, *Denkmäler*, iii, Bl. 60; Sharpe, *Egyptian Inscriptions*, ii, plate 65; and Sethe, *Urkunden*, ii.

Where this obelisk was originally set up is doubtful; Brugsch believed that it stood before the temple at Heliopolis. It is generally thought that it was taken to Alexandria by Constantine the Great (306–337), who intended to transport it to "New Rome," or Constantinople, and there to erect it, but he failed to do so. Under the influence of the Emperor Julian the Alexandrians built a special ship to carry it, and after some vicissitudes the obelisk reached

Constantinople in the reign of Theodosius. Birch thought that he set it up in the 5th quarter of the city, and that it was thrown down and broken by an earthquake; it was then removed and the upper part of it set up in its present position by Theodosius. Peter Gilles says that it was supported by four square pieces of brass, each 18 inches high. The pedestal was 12 feet square and nearly 5 feet high; built on it were two steps with a total height of 3 feet. The corners of the pedestal had been repaired with pieces of "Theban porphyry marble," each 18 inches high; but porphyry is not found at Thebes. The base on which the obelisk actually stands is nearly 8 feet high, and all its sides are sculptured with reliefs (*De Topographia Constantinopoleos*, Leyden, 1562, page 84). The bas-reliefs represent the mechanical contrivances employed in setting up the obelisk, which was done in the Praetorship of Proclus and occupied 30 or 32 days (*see* above, p. 165). These facts we learn from the two inscriptions, one in Greek and the other in Latin, which are found on one of the sides of the pedestal. They were copied by Peter Gilles and by Hobhouse (*see* his *Travels*, page 951), but are now almost illegible. The Latin text reads:—

DIFFICILIS·QVONDAM·DOMINIS·PARERE·SERENIS

IVSSVS·ET·EXTINCTIS·PALMEM·PORTARE·TYRANNIS

OMNIA·THEODOSIO·CEDVNT·SOBOLIQVE·PERENNI

TER·DENIS·SIC·VICTVS·EGO·DOMITVSQVE·DIEBVS

IVDICE·SVB·PROCLO·SVPERAS·ELATVS·AD·AVRAS

Hobhouse's rendering reads:—

"I was once unwilling to obey imperial masters,
But I was ordered to bear the palm (*i.e.* celebrate the victory) after the destruction of tyrants.
All things yield to Theodosius and his enduring offspring.
Thus I was conquered and subdued in thirty days,
And elevated towards the sky in the Praetorship of Proclus."

The Latin text says 30 days, the Greek 32, τριάκοντα δύο; see Long, *Egyptian Antiquities*, vol. i, page 332, where we have the following transcript:—

ΚΙΟΝΑ ΤΕΤΡΑΠΛΕΥΡΟΝ ΑΕΙ ΧΘΟΝΙ ΚΕΙΜΕΝΟΝ ΑΧΘΟC
ΜΟΥΝΟC ΑΝΑCΤΗCΑΙ ΘΕΥΔΟCΙΟC ΒΑCΙΛΕΥC
ΤΟΛΜΗCΑC ΠΡΟΚΛΩ ΕΠΕΚΕΚΛΕΤΟ ΚΑΙ ΤΟCΟC ΕCΤΗ
ΚΙΟΝ ΗΕΛΙΟC ΕΝ ΤΡΙΑΚΟΝΤΑ ΔΥΟ

VII, VIII

THE OBELISKS OF THOTHMES III AT HELIOPOLIS

These obelisks stood before the great pylon of the temple at Heliopolis, which was dedicated to Harakhthês, a form of the Sun-god in the morning, and to Tem, a form of the Sun-god in the evening. They were set up by Thothmes III to commemorate his celebration of the great festival of Set for the third time; the exact year of his reign in which he did this is unknown. There they stood until the reign of Augustus, who removed them to Alexandria, where they were set up before the great temple in the 18th year of Augustus Caesar's reign, *i.e.* 13–12 B.C. The architect was one Pontius, and the prefect of the day was P. Rubrius Barbarus—*Anno XVIII Caesaris Barbarus praefectus Aegypti posuit architectante Pontio* (*see* Merriam, The *Greek and Latin inscriptions on the Obelisk crab*, New York, 1883, and Dittenberger, *Orientis Graeci Inscriptiones*, Leipzig, 1895, No. 656). Both obelisks were standing when 'Abd al-Latîf visited Egypt towards the close of the XIIth century A.D., for, speaking of Alexandria, he says that he saw two obelisks in the middle of the building, which were larger than the small ones of Heliopolis (ed. de Sacy, page 181), but smaller than the two large ones. He calls them "Cleopatra's big needles." One of them fell down, probably during the earthquake which took place in 1301, when the Nile cast its boats a bowshot on the land and the walls of Alexandria were thrown down (Poole, *Middle Ages*, page 301). The obelisk lay where it fell until Mr. John Dixon removed it to London at the expense of Sir Erasmus Wilson, as has already been stated. The best copy of the text of Thothmes III is that of Sethe (*Urkunden* iv, page 590) ; of the additions by Rameses II no good copy has been published, but their non-historical character is evident from the photograph of two sides of the obelisk published by Gorringe (*op. cit.*, plate xxxvii).

The second obelisk stood on the pedestal on which the Roman engineers had placed it until it was transported in masterly fashion to New York and set up in 1880 in the Central Park by Lieut.-Commander H. H. Gorringe of the U.S. Navy (*see* **Plates XIV** and **XV**). This obelisk weighs about 220 tons, and was mounted on bronze supports, one under each angle, each bar projecting from the body of a bronze crab about 16 inches in diameter. One of these was seen in position by Mr. John Dixon, and Commander Gorringe found two, the other two having been stolen. The crab was associated with Phoebus Apollo, the Sun-god of the Greeks, who was identified with Rā, the Sun-god of the Egyptians. That the use of the crab had a religious significance which appealed to both Egyptians and Greeks seems clear. For a full account of the means used in transporting the obelisk and erecting it, and numerous plans, photographs, etc., *see* Gorringe, *Egyptian Obelisks*, London, 1885. The inscriptions of Thothmes III on both obelisks are here given.

I.—THE OBELISK ON THE THAMES EMBANKMENT

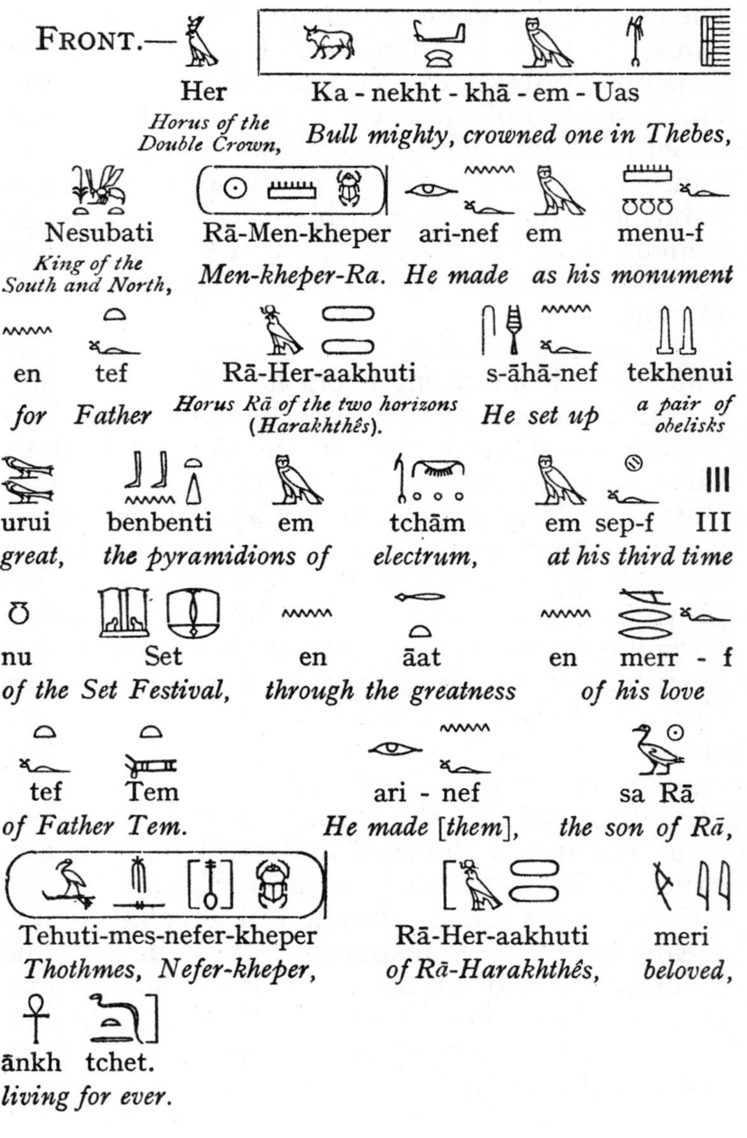

FRONT.—
Her
Horus of the Double Crown,
Ka - nekht - khā - em - Uas
Bull mighty, crowned one in Thebes,
Nesubati
King of the South and North,
Rā-Men-kheper
Men-kheper-Ra.
ari-nef
He made
em
as his
menu-f
monument
en
for
tef
Father
Rā-Her-aakhuti
Horus Rā of the two horizons (Harakhthês).
s-āhā-nef
He set up
tekhenui
a pair of obelisks
urui
great,
benbenti
the pyramidions
em
of
tchām
electrum,
em sep-f III
at his third time
nu
Set
of the Set Festival,
en
āat
through the greatness
en
merr - f
of his love
tef
Tem
of Father Tem.
ari - nef
He made [them],
sa Rā
the son of Rā,
Tehuti-mes-nefer-kheper
Thothmes, Nefer-kheper,
Rā-Her-aakhuti
of Rā-Harakhthês,
meri
beloved,
ānkh
tchet.
living for ever.

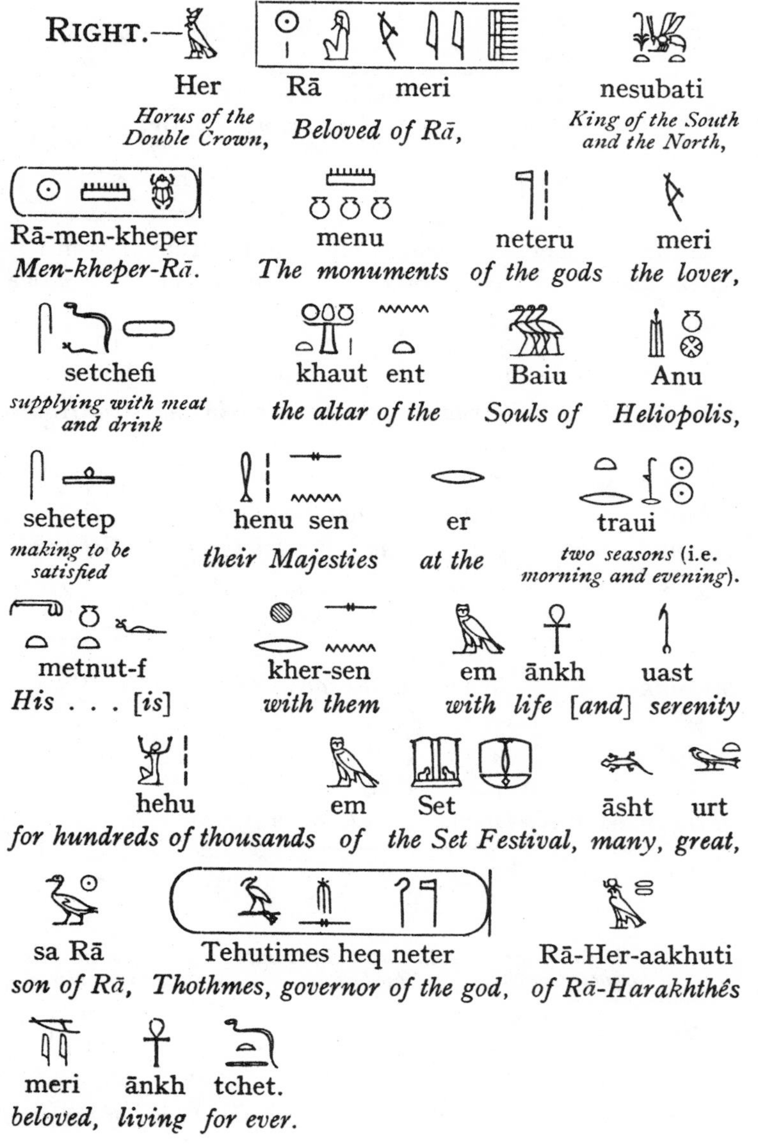
RIGHT.—
Her Rā meri nesubati
Horus of the Double Crown, Beloved of Rā, King of the South and the North,
Rā-men-kheper menu neteru meri
Men-kheper-Rā. The monuments of the gods the lover,
setchefi khaut ent Baiu Anu
supplying with meat and drink the altar of the Souls of Heliopolis,
sehetep henu sen er traui
making to be satisfied their Majesties at the two seasons (i.e. morning and evening).
metnut-f kher-sen em ānkh uast
His . . . [is] with them with life [and] serenity
hehu em Set āsht urt
for hundreds of thousands of the Set Festival, many, great,
sa Rā Tehutimes heq neter Rā-Her-aakhuti
son of Rā, Thothmes, governor of the god, of Rā-Harakhthês
meri ānkh tchet.
beloved, living for ever.

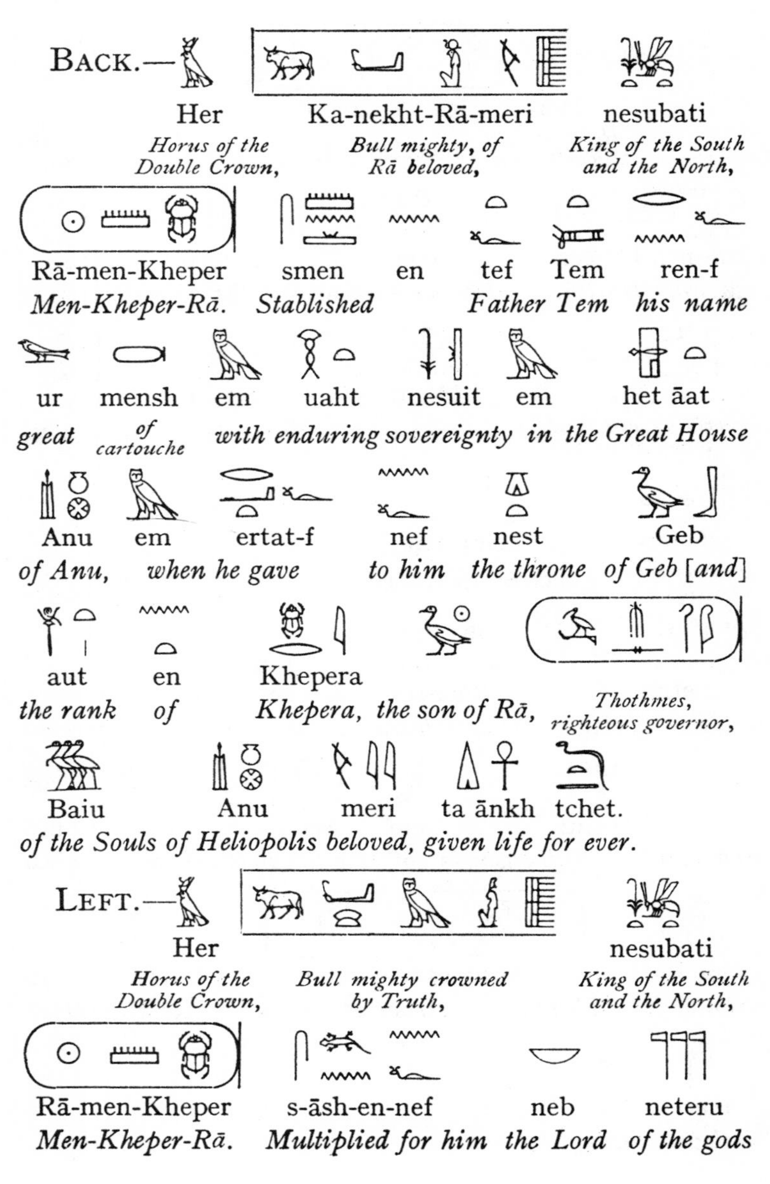

Back.—
Her
Ka-nekht-Rā-meri
nesubati
Horus of the Double Crown,
Bull mighty, of Rā beloved,
King of the South and the North,
Rā-men-Kheper
smen
en
tef
Tem
ren-f
Men-Kheper-Rā.
Stablished
Father Tem
his name
ur
mensh
em
uaht
nesuit
em
het āat
great
of cartouche
with enduring sovereignty
in the Great House
Anu
em
ertat-f
nef
nest
Geb
of Anu,
when he gave
to him
the throne
of Geb [*and*]
aut
en
Khepera
the rank
of
Khepera,
the son of Rā,
Thothmes, righteous governor,
Baiu
Anu
meri
ta ānkh
tchet.
of the Souls of Heliopolis beloved, given life for ever.
Left.—
Her
nesubati
Horus of the Double Crown,
Bull mighty crowned by Truth,
King of the South and the North,
Rā-men-Kheper
s-āsh-en-nef
neb
neteru
Men-Kheper-Rā.
Multiplied for him
the Lord
of the gods

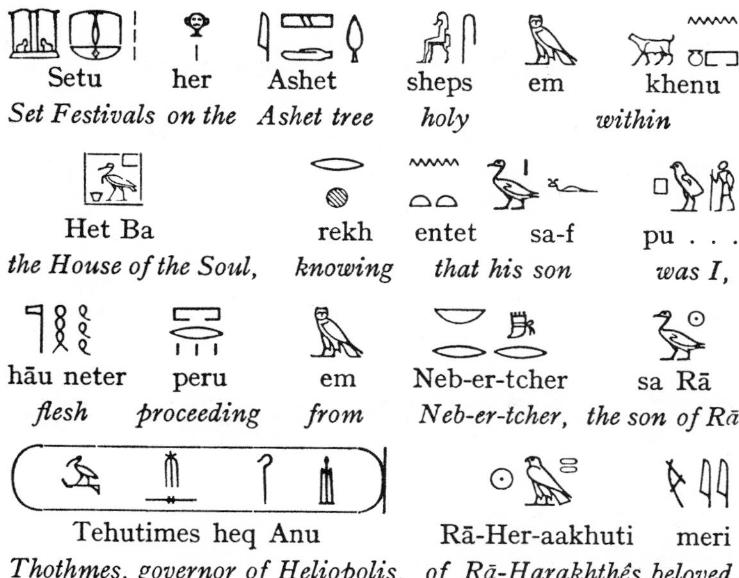

Setu her Ashet sheps em khenu
Set Festivals on the Ashet tree holy within

Het Ba rekh entet sa-f pu . . .
the House of the Soul, knowing that his son was I,

hāu neter peru em Neb-er-tcher sa Rā
flesh proceeding from Neb-er-tcher, the son of Rā

Tehutimes heq Anu Rā-Her-aakhuti meri
Thothmes, governor of Heliopolis, of Rā-Harakhthês beloved,

ānkh tchet.
living for ever.

2.—THE OBELISK IN NEW YORK

FRONT.—

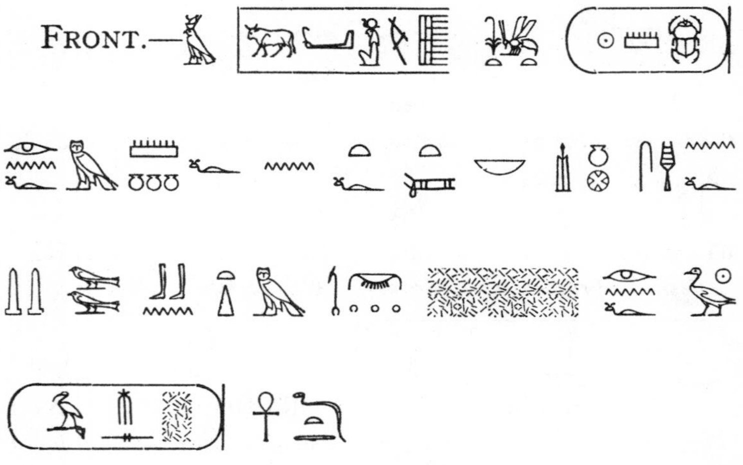

TRANSLATION

FRONT.—Horus [name]. Mighty Bull, beloved of Rā. Nesubati [name]. Men-kheper-Rā. He made [them] as his monument to Father Tem, Lord of Anu. He set up two great obelisks [with] pyramidions of electrum. The son of Rā, Thothmes, . . . the ever-living, did [this].

"Cleopatra's Needle" in the Central Park, New York.

—From Gorringe, *Egyptian Obelisks*.

The "Cleopatra's Needle" in New York being swung into position on its pedestal by Lieut.-Commander H. H. Gorringe, U.S. Navy.

Right.—Horus [name]. Mighty Bull, crowned in Thebes. Nebti [name]. Whose sovereignty flourisheth like Rā in heaven. Son of Tem, of his body. Nebt-Ant brought him forth, Thothmes. He was created by them in the Great House with the beauties of their limbs, they knowing that he would reign with a sovereignty that would flourish for ever. King of the South and North, Men-kheper-Rā, beloved of Tem the great god and the Company of his gods, to whom are given life, stability and all serenity, like Rā for ever.

BACK.—Horus [name]. Exalted one of the White Crown, beloved of Rā. Nesubati [name]. Men-kheper-Rā. Golden Horus [name]. He who reposeth on strength, smiter of the governors of the mountains and deserts remote (?) from him, according as his father Rā hath decreed for him victories over every land whatsoever, and the valour of the scimitar by the mouth (*i.e.* act) of his two arms, to increase the extent of the frontiers of Egypt. Son of Rā, Thothmes [governor of Anu], to whom everlasting life hath been given.

LEFT.—Besides the Horus and Nesubati names of the king, little else of this column remains.

On each side of the shaft of each obelisk Rameses II added two columns of hieroglyphs, one on each side of the column of hieroglyphs cut for Thothmes III. The inscriptions added by Rameses have no historical importance and contain nothing but his official names and high-sounding titles and epithets. They have been published in the *Description de l'Égypte, Antiquités*, tom. v, plates 32, 33; by Champollion, *Monuments*, tom. iv, plates 444–446; and by Burton, *Excerpta*, plates 51, 52, but these copies are very incorrect in places and useless for study. Photographs of the inscriptions on the New York obelisk have been published by Gorringe, *Egyptian Obelisks*, plate xxxi, together with a reprint of Brugsch's translation, which first appeared in the *New York Herald*, February 22, 1880. The general character and contents of the inscriptions on obelisks of Rameses II are well illustrated by the inscriptions on the Paris obelisk, of which a full translation is given later (*see* pages 197 ff.).

IX

OBELISK OF THOTHMES III FORMERLY AT SION HOUSE, BRENTFORD

From the fragment of an obelisk published by Brugsch (*Thesaurus*, page 1220), we learn that Thothmes I set up two granite obelisks before the temple of Khnemu, [hieroglyphs], at Elephantine, a fact which proves that the temple of the great god of the First Cataract was an important sanctuary. According to Birch (*Egypt*, London, 1880, page 102), Thothmes III set up a small obelisk at the same place, and he says that it was at Sion House. W. R. Cooper made the same statement (*Obelisks*, London, 1877, page 59), adding that this obelisk was unpublished. In 1880 Birch published a *Catalogue of the Egyptian Collection* of the Duke of Northumberland at Alnwick Castle, but I can find no mention of any obelisk of Thothmes III in it. On the other hand, there is a long description of the red granite obelisk of Amenhetep II on page 345, and it seems probable that both Birch and Cooper confused the names of the two kings. I have often seen the obelisk of Amenhetep II at Alnwick, but cannot remember an obelisk of Thothmes III.

X

THE OBELISKS OF AMENHETEP II, KING OF EGYPT ABOUT 1448 B.C.

Amenhetep II, the son and successor of Thothmes III, made raids on a large scale in Western Asia, and conquered the people of the Lebanon and the regions on the west bank of the Euphrates. He crossed the Orontes and set up a stele at Nī, and the Mitani chiefs paid him tribute. He took to Egypt seven chiefs of Takhsi, and sailed up to Thebes with the bodies of six of them suspended head downwards from his boat. The body of the seventh was hung on the walls of Napata in Nubia to terrify the natives. He raided the Egyptian Sûdân and rebuilt the great temple of Amâdah in Lower Nubia. He set up a pair of obelisks in honour of Khnemu, the god of the First Cataract,[1] at some place unknown, but probably at Madamûd, near Thebes, and one of these is preserved in the collection at Alnwick Castle. This obelisk is about 7 feet 3 inches high and is made of red granite. It was discovered by natives among the ruins of an Egyptian temple in the Thebaïd in 1838, and was presented in that year by Muhammad 'Alî, Viceroy of Egypt, to Algernon, fourth Duke of Northumberland, then Lord

[1] Mr. Engelbach reports the finding of a small obelisk of Amenhetep II at Aswân; he says it weighs under a ton, but gives no further details (*Problem of the Obelisks*, page 79).

Prudhoe. On the broken apex is cut a Vignette in which Amenhetep II is represented making an offering to Khnemu-Rā, who is endowing him with life and every kind of well-being. A single column of hieroglyphs is cut on one face of the shaft, and begins with the Horus name of Amenhetep II, , "Horus of the two horizons (Harakhthês), Mighty Bull, great of valour," and goes on with his Nesubati name, , " King of the South and the North, Aa-kheperu-Rā" (*i.e.* "great are the forms of Rā"), and his son-of-Rā name, " Amenhetep, god, governor of Thebes," . The remainder of the column of text reads :—" He made [the obelisk] as his own monument to his Father Khnemu-Rā. He made two obelisks for the house of the altar of Rā. He made them that everlasting life might be given to him." The hieroglyphic text reads :—

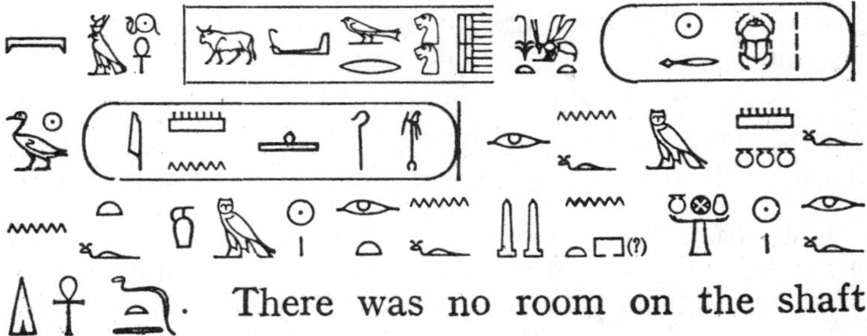

. There was no room on the shaft

to add his Nebti and golden Horus names, which were , "His power is extended, crowned in Thebes," and , "Victor, he hath gained the mastery over all lands." A full description of the monument by J. Bonomi, entitled "Description of the Alnwick Obelisk," was published in the *Transactions of the Royal Society of Literature*, Ser. II, vol. i, pages 170–175, London, 1843, and by S. Sharpe in *Egyptian Inscriptions*, Second Series, plate 69.

THE OBELISKS OF AMENHETEP III

Amenhetep III built a great temple of sandstone in the Nubian town which he calls Menenu Khā-em-Maāt , and which is known to-day by the name of Sûlb. Its ruins lie a few miles to the south of Jabal Dûsh (Dôshah) in the Third Cataract. The total length of the temple was about 520 feet. It had two pylons and two courts, the second being approached by a flight of steps, and had a colonnade which ran round all four sides, the columns being more than 6 feet in diameter. The temple was dedicated to Amen-Rā, and the king, as the son and counterpart of the god, was worshipped in it. It and the temple that he built for his wife Queen Tî at Saddênga were intended to commemorate his conquests in

Upper Nubia, now the Egyptian Sûdân. The temple was called Khā-em-Maāt, *i.e.* "rising in truth." In the great inscription which the king set up in his temple in Western Thebes he says that this temple at Sûlb was built of fine sandstone, and was decorated with gold throughout. The main door was gilded, and on each side of it stood a great obelisk. They were probably, like the walls, made of sandstone, which disintegrates early under the action of the winds, and have therefore perished. During the excavations which Mr. J. W. Crowfoot and myself made before the first pylon in 1905–6 we did not find any trace either of them or of the slabs on which they must have rested.

As long as Amenhetep III lived the cult of "Amen-Rā, king of the gods," was predominant in the region of the Third Cataract. But when his son Amenhetep IV, better known as Aakhenaten, came to the throne, he established a temple to Aten in the Sûdân, probably not far from the temple built for Tī at Saddēnga, and called it Per Gem-Aten. An inscription on a scarab from Saddēnga, and now in the British Museum (No. 51084), seems to suggest that he tried to assimilate Aten with a native Thunder-god.

XI

THE OBELISK OF SETI I IN THE PIAZZA DEL POPOLO, ROME (THE FLAMINIAN OBELISK)

This obelisk was set up by Seti I, king of Egypt about 1300 B.C., at Heliopolis ; it is about 78 feet high and weighs about 235 tons. It was transported to Rome by the Emperor Augustus, and set up about 10 B.C. by him in the Circus Maximus to commemorate his conquest of Egypt. (*See* Pliny, *Hist. Nat.* xxxvi. 9. § 14). He dedicated it to the sun, as the following inscription states :—

IMP · CAESAR · DIVI · F
AVGVSTVS
PONTIFEX MAXIMUS
IMP · $\overline{\text{XII}}$ · COS · $\overline{\text{XI}}$ · TRIB · POT · $\overline{\text{XIV}}$
AEGYPTO · IN · POTESTATEM
POPULI · ROMANI · REDACTA
SOLI · DONUM · DEDIT

At some time unknown the obelisk fell down, and it lay where it fell until the pontificate of Sixtus V, who had it dug out from the ruins under which it was buried, and instructed Domenico Fontana to set it up in the place which it now occupies. This he did in 1589. The height of the whole monument, including the pedestal and cross, is 118 feet. The obelisk was begun by Seti I and was partly inscribed during his lifetime, but he died leaving one side, the eastern, without inscription. He copied the arrangement of the text on the older obelisks, and placed one column only of hieroglyphs on each face of the shaft. Rameses II, his son and successor, completed the monument by adding two columns of hieroglyphs on each of their faces, and three on the uninscribed face, which now faces Monte Pincio. The earlier archaeologists who attempted to decipher the inscriptions on the obelisk, and to identify the king who set it up in Egypt, came to wrong conclusions as to its age and the name of its maker. They recognized that two kings were mentioned in the columns of text cut upon it, but their decipherment of their names was incorrect. Ungarelli thought that the earlier inscription was by Mer-en-Ptah and the later by Rameses III, and that the latter king was the son of the former; but the cartouches make it certain that the maker of the obelisk was Seti I, and that it was his son Rameses II who added two columns of hieroglyphs to three of the faces of the monument, and three lines to the east side. The exact year in which the obelisk was set up in Rome is not known, but it was probably some years after the conquest of Egypt by Augustus, which took place A.U.C. 731 = 23 B.C.

On three sides of the pyramidion are cut Vignettes in which Seti I, in the form of a sphinx, is offering a figure of the goddess of Truth, [hieroglyph], *Maāt*, to the Sun-god Rā; on the fourth side the king is Rameses II. The inscriptions of Seti on the three sides of the shaft read :—

NORTH SIDE.—

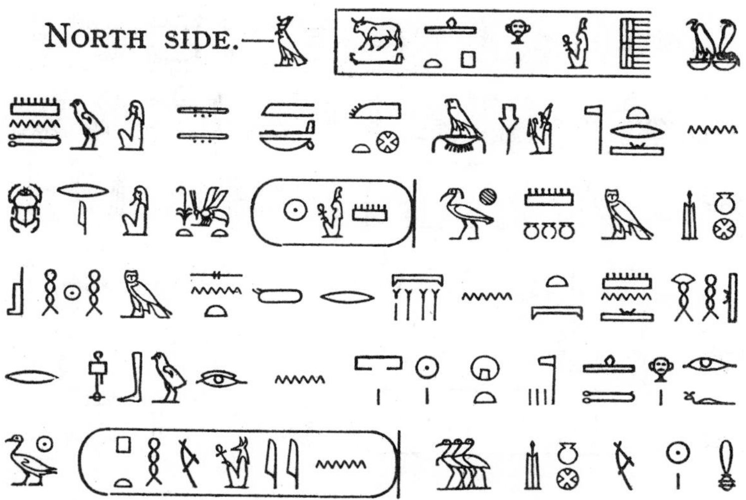

NORTH SIDE.—Horus [name] Mighty Bull, resting on Truth. Nebti [name] Menthu of the Two Lands (*i.e.* Egypt), protector of Egypt. Golden Horus [name] Chief, divine, of Khepera. Nesubati [name] Men-maāt-Rā, making splendid monuments in Anu, the everlasting seat, which is more firmly founded than the four pillars of the heavens, more stable and flourishing than the fore-court of the House of Rā. The Company of the Gods are satisfied with what hath made the son of Rā, Seti Mer-en-Ptah, , beloved of the Souls of Anu, like Rā.

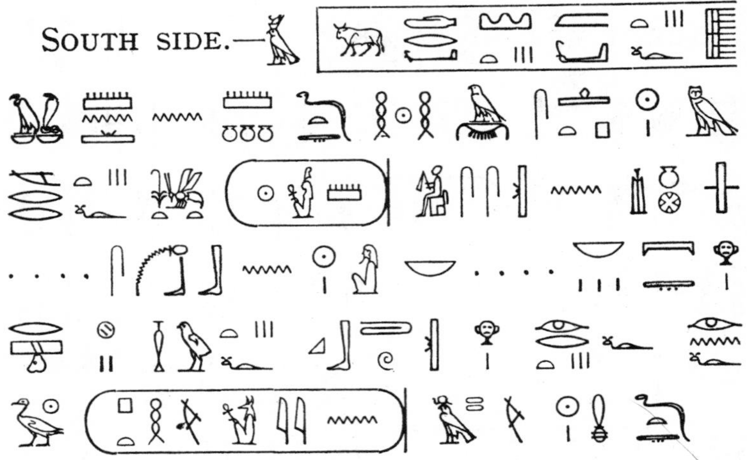

SOUTH SIDE.—Horus [name] Mighty Bull, trampler on all countries in his strength. Nebti [name] Stablisher of monuments for ever and for ever. Golden Horus [name] Satisfying Rā with his [works of] love. Nesubati [name] Men-maāt-Rā, , the august one of Anu, the dweller in . . . pourer of libations to Rā, lord of the . . . The lords of heaven and of earth rejoice and are glad in [showing] him favours, and make double what they do for him. The son of Rā, Seti Mer-en-Ptah, beloved of Her-aakhuti, worketh like Rā for ever.

On the same side is a Vignette in which Seti is seen offering two vases, , to the god. The king is described as " Horus, Mighty Bull, life of the Two Lands, lord of the Two Lands, maker of things, lord of valour, Men-maāt-Rā,

Vignettes on the pyramidion and shaft of the obelisk of Seti I, in which the king is seen offering a figure of Maāt, , and two libations, , to the god Rā Her-aakhuti, and a vase of incense, , and two vases of metchet unguent to the God Tem. Below there are six of the Horus names of the king.

son of Rā, of his body, beloved by him, lord of crowns, Seti Mer-en-Ptah, beloved of Rā the great god, lord of heaven, dweller in the Great House." And Her-aakhuti, the splendour of the Two Lands, the great god, the lord of heaven, says, "I have given to thee all lands, and all hills and deserts in peace. I unite for thee on the throne of Horus the South and the North of Egypt like Rā for ever."

WEST SIDE.—Bull of Rā, beloved of Maāt, fetterer of countries, vanquisher of the Mentiu, beloved of Rā, making great his ka, Men-maāt-Rā, who filleth Anu with obelisks, so that their rays may rise upon the House of Rā and flood it with his splendours, and that the gods may assemble in the Great House joyfully. The son of Rā, Seti Mer-en-Ptah, beloved of the Company of the Gods who dwell in the Great House did [this] that life might be given to him.

Vignettes on the pyramidion and shaft of the obelisk of Seti I, in which this king is seen offering a figure of Maāt, [hieroglyph], and two vases of metchet unguent, [hieroglyphs], to the god Rā Her-aakhuti. Below there are three of the Horus names of the king.

Vignettes added to the pyramidion and shaft of the obelisk of Seti I, by his son, Rameses II, who is seen offering a vase of unguent, and a figure of Maāt, [hieroglyph], to the god Tem, [hieroglyphs], lord of the Two Lands of Anu (Heliopolis). Below there are three of the Horus ames of Rameses II.

East side.—The Vignette on the pyramidion and the three columns of text on this side were the work of Rameses II. The central line reads:—

Mighty Bull, beloved of Maāt, User-maāt-Rā Setep-en-Rā, 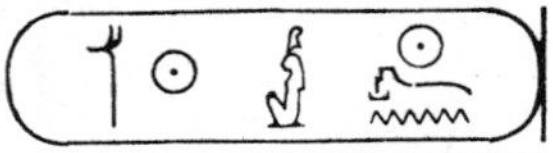 , son of Rā, Rāmessu meri-Amen, 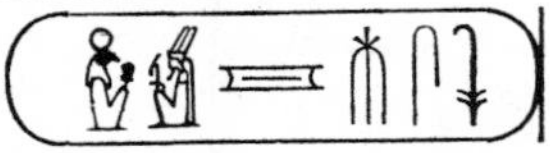 , made his monuments [as numerous] as the stars of heaven. His works join themselves to the height of heaven, Rā shineth on them and rejoiceth over them in his House of Millions of Years. His Majesty (*i.e.* Rameses II) beautified this monument of his father so that he might make his name to be stablished in the House of Rā. The son of Rā, Rāmessu meri-Amen, beloved of Tem, lord of Anu, did this so that life might be given to him for ever.

Line on left.—Horus, Mighty Bull, beloved of Maāt, strong in years, mighty one of victories, King of the South and the North, User-maāt-Rā setep-en-Rā, son of Rā, Rāmessu meri-Amen, hath made Anu splendid by his great monuments, sculpturing the gods in their forms in the Great House. To the lord of the Two Lands, User-maāt-Rā setep-en-Rā, son of Rā, Rāmessu meri-Amen, may life be given for ever.

Line on right.—Horus, Mighty Bull, beloved of Maāt, fashioner of the gods, landlord of the Two Lands, King of the South and the North, User-maāt-Rā setep-en-Rā, son of Rā, Rāmessu meri-Amen. The rays of the two horizons rejoice when they see what hath done the lord of the Two Lands, User-maāt-Rā setep-en-Rā, the son of Rā, Rāmessu-meri-Amen, to whom life hath been given like Rā.

The translation of the three lines on the east side of the obelisk will give the reader an idea of the character of the other inscriptions of Rameses II that are found upon it, and as they contain no historical information it is unnecessary to give translations of them all. The reader who wishes to study them will find transcripts of them in Marucchi, *Gli Obelischi Egiziani di Roma*, pages 51 ff. The Latin inscription of the Pope who re-erected it reads: Sixtus V. Pont. Max. | obeliscum hunc | a Caesare Aug. soli | in Circo Maximo ritu | dicatum impio | miseranda ruina | fractum obrutumq. | ervi transferri | formae suae reddi | cruciq. invictiss. | dedicari jussit | An. M.D.LXXXIX. Pont. IIII. | ante sacram | illius aedem | augustior | laetiorq. surgo. | cuius ex utero | virginali | Aug. imperante | sol iustitiae exortus est. (Parker, *Obelisks*, page 7.)

This obelisk has a special interest because when it was set up by Augustus in the Circus Maximus an Egyptian priest, of whom nothing is known except his name Hermapion, produced a translation in Greek of the hieroglyphic inscriptions upon it. This has been preserved by Ammianus Marcellinus (xvii. 4. §§ 18 ff.), and the following rendering will give an idea of the contents of some of the lines of the Greek translation :—South side, line 1: "The Sun to Ramestes the King—I have given to thee to reign with joy over the whole earth; to thee whom the Sun and Apollo love—to thee, the mighty truth-loving son of Heron—the god-born ruler of the habitable earth; whom the Sun has chosen above all men, the valiant warlike King Ramestes. Under whose power, by his valour and might, the whole world is placed. The King Ramestes, the immortal son of the Sun."

South side, line 3: "The mighty Apollo, the all-brilliant son of the Sun, whom the Sun chose above all others, and to whom the valiant Mars gave gifts. Thou whose good fortune abideth for ever. Thou whom Ammon loveth. Thou who hast filled the temple of the Phoenix with good things. Thou to whom the gods have given long life. Apollo the mighty son of Heron, Ramestes the king of the world. Who hath defended Egypt, having subdued the foreign enemy. Whom the Sun loveth. To whom the gods have given long life—the master of the world—the immortal Ramestes."

East side, line 1: "The Great God of Heliopolis, the mighty Apollo who dwelleth in Heaven, the son of Heron whom the Sun hath guided. Whom the gods have honoured. He who ruleth over all the earth: whom the Sun hath chosen before all others. The king valiant by the favour of Mars. Whom Ammon loveth, and the all-shining god who hath chosen him as a king for everlasting."

THE OBELISKS OF RAMESES II, KING OF EGYPT ABOUT 1300 B.C.

Rameses II succeeded his father Seti I (**Plate XVI**) and brought to a successful end the wars in which he had played a prominent part during the closing years of Seti's reign. The power of Egypt in Palestine had been re-established and, thanks to the raids of Seti in Syria and the great quantity of spoil that that king had taken from the Hittites and their allies, the country was prosperous and rich. Rameses raided Nubia and the country of the Libyans during the first three years of his reign ; in the fourth year he began his great attack on the Hittites and the series of inconclusive " campaigns " against them which sorely impoverished his country. The Battle of Kadesh was fought in the fifth year of his reign. He marched on Kadesh on the Orontes with a large army, and as he was nearing the city the enemy fell suddenly on two of its divisions, which were routed with considerable loss, and Rameses and his personal staff, who had outmarched the main body of the army, found themselves cut off from it and in a position of the greatest danger. But Rameses mounted his chariot and with the few troops that he had with him charged with such violence into the chariots which barred his way that he drove the enemy into the river, where many of them were drowned. He charged again and again, each time with brilliant success, and, being joined by one of his divisions, he was able to inflict such loss on the enemy that they fled to Kadesh for refuge.

The fight was continued on the following day, and the Hittites and their allies again suffered further heavy losses so that they sued for peace, and Rameses stopped the battle. He had led what was practically a forlorn hope, and it was his cool courage and personal bravery alone that saved himself and his army from destruction. There is small wonder that he was proud of the gallant feat of arms which he had performed, and that he covered the walls of all the great temples of Egypt with sculptures and texts describing the chariot charge whereat all the world wondered. But in spite of deeds of valour Kadesh remained untaken, and the Hittite power was not broken by him.

For about 15 years he raided Syria, but though he eventually made himself master of Kadesh and the Valley of the Orontes and the neighbouring countries, he failed to crush the Hittites. At length both sides were tired of fighting, and when Khattusil, king of the Hittites, offered to renew the old treaty between the Hittites and Egyptians, Rameses agreed. A copy of the new treaty was drawn up in the Egyptian and Hittite languages (the latter language being written in cuneiform), and was accepted by both kings in the 21st year of the reign of Rameses II. This treaty altered nothing, but it stopped a war which was ruining Egypt.

After this Rameses fought no more, but spent the remaining years of his long reign (about 67 years in all) in peace and comfort. He carried out building operations on a large scale. He built the rock-hewn temple of Abu

Simbel in Nubia and the temple of Hathor near it, and the little temple of Bêt al-Walî at Kalâbshah; he finished the Hall of Columns at Karnak; he built two courts and a pylon in the temple of Luxor, the Ramesseum, the town of Pithom on the old Nile–Red Sea Canal, and enlarged and beautified Tanis in the Delta, to mention only a few of his great works. He made colossal statues of himself and set up two great obelisks at Thebes and at least 14 obelisks at Tanis in the Delta. During the last forty years of his reign Egypt became exceedingly rich, commerce flourished, and the Delta became an international market, wherein men of many nationalities and tongues did their business.

The largest and finest of all the obelisks set up by Rameses II were the pair in red granite that stood, with two colossal statues of himself, in front of the pylon which he built in the temple of Amenhetep III, and are commonly known as the "Obelisks of Luxor." One was 82 feet high and weighed about 253½ tons, and the other was about 75 feet high and weighed about 222 tons. The east and west faces of both are slightly curved, a peculiarity which has induced some authorities to believe that the curvature was intended to serve some astronomical purpose; but it was probably due to some defect in "dressing" the blocks of granite after they were set up. The pyramidions are rough-hewn and plain, and were no doubt covered with metal casings. The obelisk of Rameses now standing at Luxor is the easternmost; its fellow is now in the Place de la Concorde, Paris.

Each side of each obelisk bears three columns of hieroglyphs containing the names and titles of Rameses II, and there is no reason to suppose that Rameses III added inscriptions to them. The bases of the obelisks are sculptured with figures of the dog-headed ape (*i.e.* baboon) of Thoth adoring Rā, and figures of the Nile-god Hāpi bearing his products—fruit, flowers, vegetables, fish, and feathered fowl.

It is said that after Nelson's victories the Pâshâ of Egypt offered to give to England either an obelisk of Rameses II at Luxor or the fallen obelisk of Thothmes III, commonly known as "Cleopatra's Needle," at Alexandria, but, as we have seen, the British Government accepted neither. In 1821 Muhammad 'Alî offered one of Cleopatra's Needles at Alexandria to England and the other to France, but neither Government took steps to secure an obelisk. Some years later the French Government sent out Champollion-le-Jeune to report on the Egyptian antiquities generally, and he, after examining all the obelisks in Egypt, recommended his Government to ask the Pâshâ for those of Rameses II at Luxor, as well as for the fallen obelisk at Alexandria. Thereupon Louis-Philippe instructed his Foreign Office to make application to Muhammad 'Alî for permission to remove these monuments from Luxor and Cleopatra's Needle from Alexandria, and this was granted. Meanwhile, Mr. Barker, the British Consul-General, had obtained as a gift from the Pâshâ the two Luxor obelisks, and diplomatic difficulties between the French and the English ensued. At length it was suggested that the English should have the obelisk of Thothmes I at Karnak and that the French should have the Luxor obelisks, but this suggestion had no result.

As soon as the project for bringing one of the Luxor obelisks to Paris was decided upon the Minister of Marine began to build a ship to transport it to France. This ship was called the Luxor, and was launched at Toulon on July 26, 1830, and M. Verninac de St. Maur was appointed to be her captain. She left Toulon on April 15, 1831, and arrived at Alexandria on May 3. The general control of the work of embarking the obelisk had been entrusted to the French naval constructor, M. Mimerel, but at the last moment his health failed and M. A. Le Bas took his place. The obelisk chosen for removal was the western, and its four sides faced N.W., N.E., S.E., and S.W. respectively. A number of native houses were bought and demolished in order to prepare a bed for the Luxor, which arrived on August 13. Her bow was cut off to admit the obelisk, and by December 19 the monument had been lowered from its pedestal and was safe on board. But the Luxor could not be moved until the Inundation came to float her, and it was not until August 25, 1832, that she was able to start on her way down the Nile. She reached Rosetta on October 1, and by good fortune was able to leave for Alexandria on January 1, 1833, being towed by the S.S. Sphinx. She left Alexandria on April 1 and reached Toulon, after a very stormy voyage, on May 10, 1833. She arrived at the Pont de la Concorde, Paris, in the autumn, but it was not until August, 1834, that the obelisk was drawn out of her on to dry land. After a series of delays and accidents of every kind the obelisk was successfully set up on its pedestal, a mass of granite blocks weighing in all about 236 tons, on October 25, 1836, in the presence of King Louis-Philippe and about 200,000 spectators. On the sides of the pedestal, cut in outline, are representations of the apparatus used in erecting the obelisk and illustrations of the operations of lowering and embarking it. (*See* **Plate VI** and page 48.) Models of all the apparatus used were deposited in the Musée de Marine. The total cost incurred in removing the obelisk and transporting it to Paris and re-erecting it is said to have been 2,500,000 francs, or £100,000 (25 francs to the £ sterling).

The 12 columns or lines of hieroglyphs which fill the sides of the obelisk in Paris contain nothing but repetitions of the names of Rameses II, and titles in which his kinship with the great solar gods is proclaimed and his might, majesty, and power are extolled. These have been translated and discussed by various scholars, but a handy edition of the original text has not appeared, and therefore a transcript of it is given below with an English translation. Transcripts of this King's additions to the obelisks erected by his ancestors have not been given in this book because it was felt that the inscriptions on one of his own obelisks would be sufficient to illustrate their general character.

XII

THE OBELISK OF RAMESES II IN PARIS—TEXT AND TRANSLATION

NORTH FACE, CENTRE LINE.—

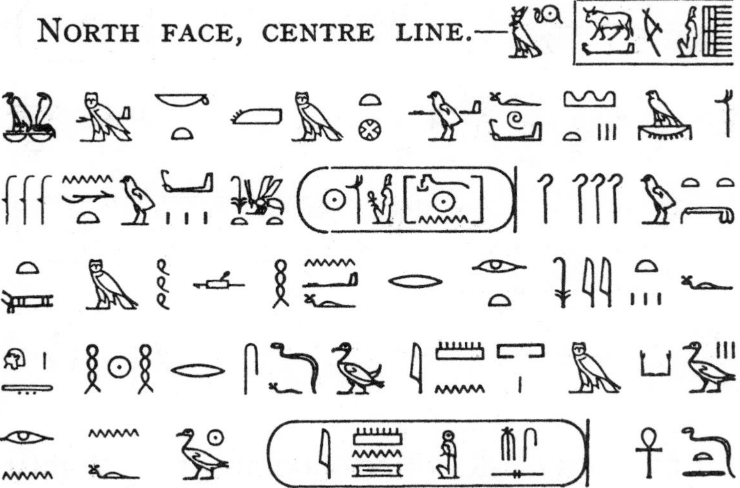

NORTH FACE, CENTRE LINE.—Rā-Her-aakhuti, the Mighty Bull, beloved of Maāt, lord of the Vulture and Uraeus Crowns, protector of Kamt (Egypt), fetterer of the countries. the Golden Horus, strong one of the years of victories, King of the South and the North, User-maāt-Rā, Governor of governors, begotten by Tem, one with him in substance, to make his sovereignty to be upon the earth for ever, provider of the House of Amen with food. The son of Rā, Rāmeses, beloved of Amen, the ever-living, made [this obelisk] for him.

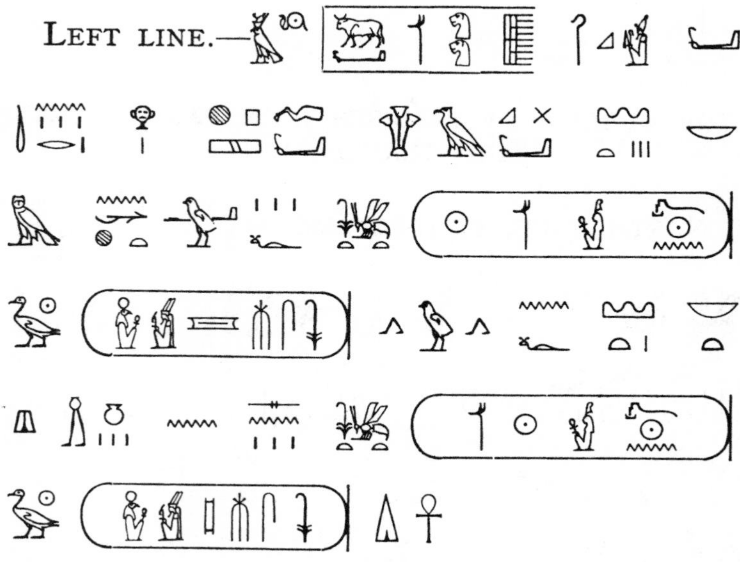

LEFT LINE.—Rā - Her - aakhuti, the Mighty Bull, mighty one of valour, Governor, mighty one of deeds with the scimitar, who hath made captive all lands by his victories, King of the South and the North, User-maāt-Rā setep-en-Rā, son of Rā, Rā-mes-su meri-Amen. Every land cometh to him bearing their offerings to the King of the South and the North, User-maāt-Rā setep-en-Rā, son of Rā, Rā-mes-su, to whom life hath been given.

RIGHT LINE.—

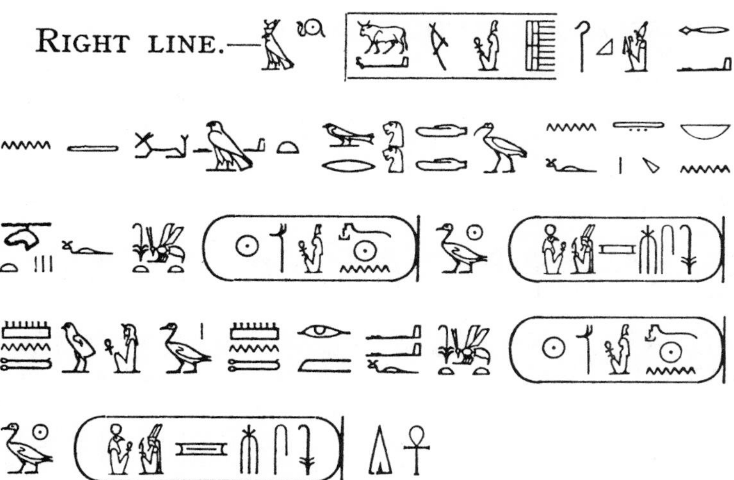

RIGHT LINE.—Rā - Her - aakhuti, the Mighty Bull, beloved of Maāt, great Governor of the domains of Horus and Set (*i.e.* Upper and Lower Egypt), mighty one of valour, before whose onslaught the whole earth trembleth, King of the South and the North, User-maāt-Rā setep-en-Rā, son of Rā, Rā-mes-su meri-Amen, the son of Menthu (the War-god of Anu Resu), whom Menthu made with his hands, King of the South and the North, User-maāt-Rā setep-en-Rā, son of Rā, Rā-mes-su, to whom life hath been given.

EAST FACE, CENTRE LINE.—

EAST FACE, CENTRE LINE.—Rā-Her-aakhuti, Mighty Bull of Rā, crusher of the Asiatics, lord of the Vulture and Uraeus Crowns, who wageth war against millions, the bold-hearted Lion, the Golden Horus, great one of victories over every land, the King of the South and the North, User-maāt-Rā, the Bull on his boundary, who maketh every land rise up and come before him by the command of his august father Amen. The son of Rā, Rā-mes-su meri-Amen, made [this obelisk] for him that he might have life for ever.

LEFT LINE.—

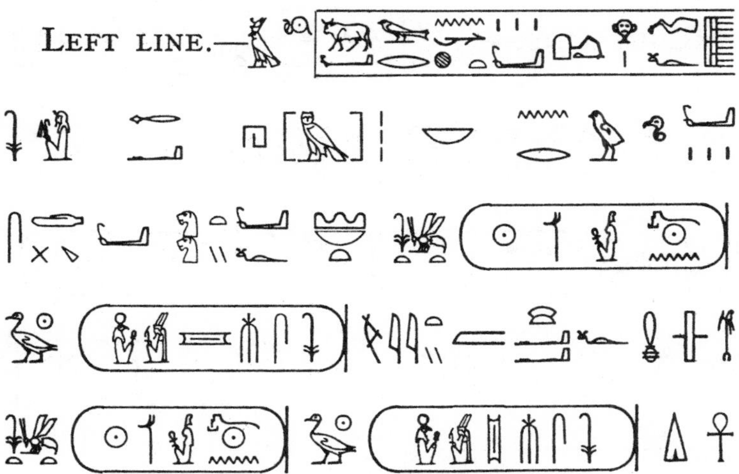

LEFT LINE.—Rā - Her - aakhuti, the Mighty Bull, great of strength, who fighteth with his hind legs, King, great one of bellowings, lord of victories, whose strength crusheth every land, King of the South and the North, User-maāt-Rā setep-en-Rā, the son of Rā, Rā-mes-su meri-Amen, who when he riseth [on his throne] is well-beloved like the dweller in Thebes (*i.e.* Amen), King of the South and the North, User-maāt-Rā setep-en-Rā, son of Rā, Rā-mes-su meri-Amen, to whom life hath been given.

RIGHT LINE.—

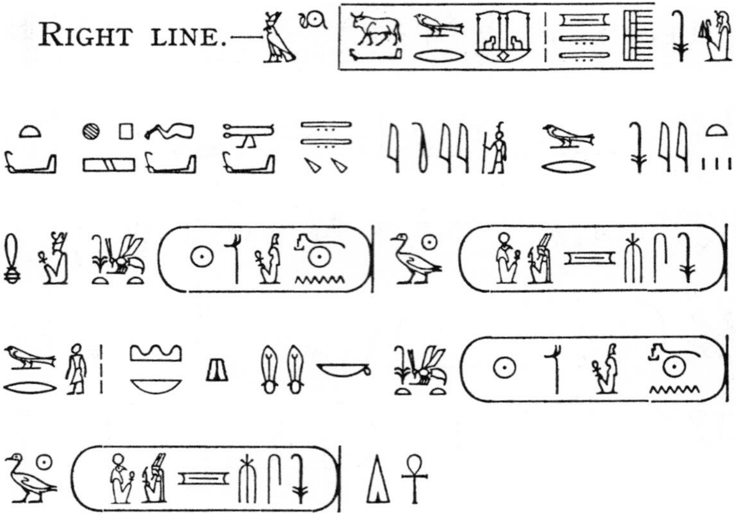

RIGHT LINE.—Rā-Her-aakhuti, Mighty Bull, great one of Set Festivals, beloved of the Two Lands, King, mighty of thigh, Conqueror of the Two Lands, Ati (Sovereign Lord), great one of sovereignty like Tem (?), King of the South and the North, User-maāt-Rā setep-en-Rā, son of Rā, Rā-mes-su meri-Amen, mighty one. The chiefs of all lands are under thy sandals, King of the South and the North, User-maāt-Rā setep-en-Rā, son of Rā, Rā-mes-su meri-Amen, to whom life hath been given.

WEST FACE, CENTRE LINE.—

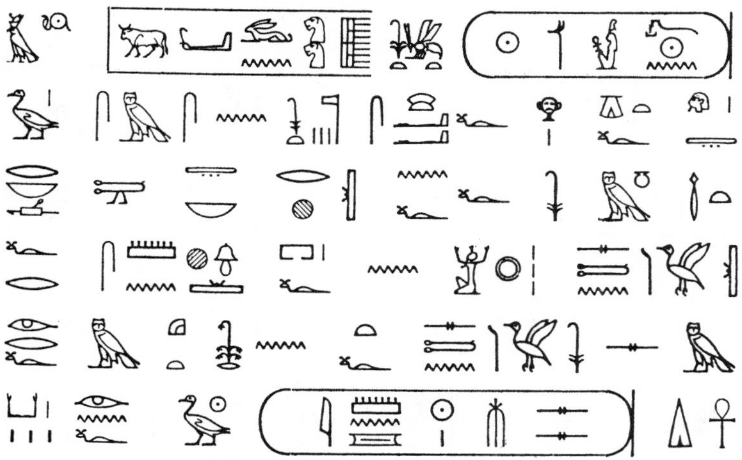

WEST FACE, CENTRE LINE.—Rā-Her-aakhuti, Mighty Bull, Being of valour, King of the South and the North, User-maāt-Rā setep-en-Rā, eldest son of the king of the gods, who hath risen upon his throne on the earth as the One Lord, conqueror of every land. He knew him . . . . . . to [establish and beautify] his House of Millions of Years. Distinguished he worked in the Southern Apt (*i.e.* the Temple of Luxor) of his father, performing distinguished works therein. This the son of Rā, Rāmeses meri-Amen, did that life might be given to him.

LEFT LINE.—

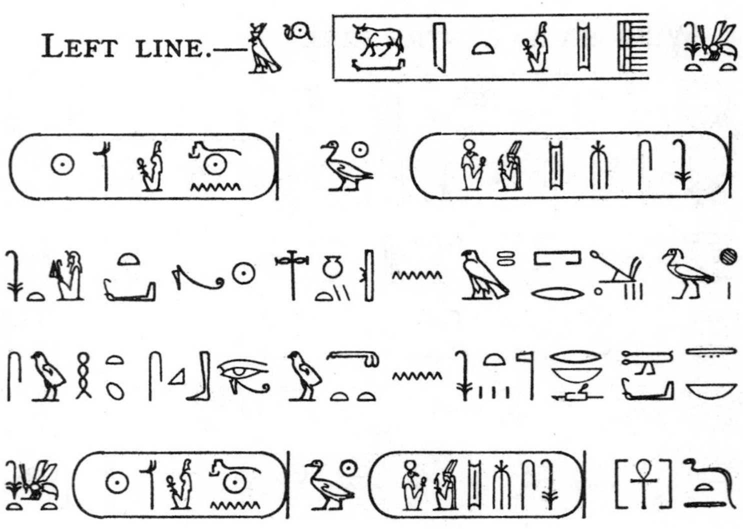

LEFT LINE.—Rā-Her-aakhuti, the Mighty Bull, beloved of Maāt, King of the South and the North, User-maāt-Rā setep-en-Rā, Son of Rā, Rā-mes-su meri-Amen. King, mighty one (?) emanation of Rā, reverer of Her-aakhuti, illustrious seed (*i.e.* offspring), the egg renewing (?) the Utchat, begotten of the King of the gods to be the One Lord, conqueror of every land, King of the South and the North, User-maāt-Rā setep-en-Rā, son of Rā, Rā-mes-su meri-Amen, the ever-living.

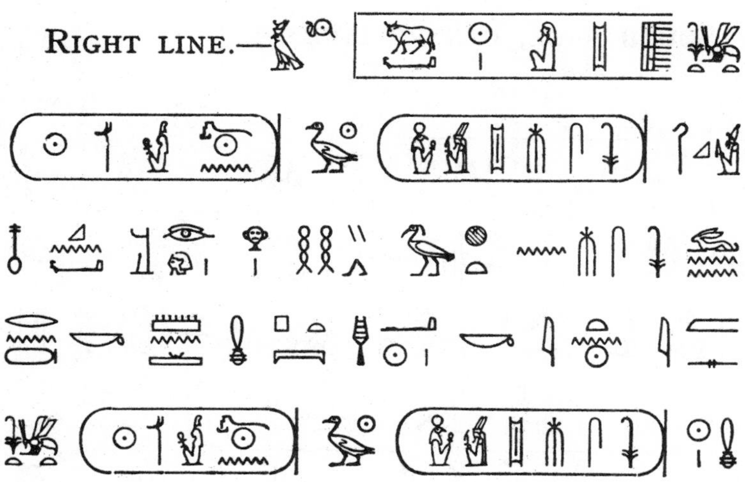

RIGHT LINE.—Rā-Her-aakhuti, Mighty Bull, beloved of Rā, King of the South and the North, User-maāt-Rā setep-en-Rā, the son of Rā, Rā-mes-su meri-Amen, the beneficent Governor, the brave [king], watching at every hour to seek after the splendour of him that begot him. Thy name is stablished as firmly as the heavens, thy period of life therein is like that of Aten (the solar disk), King of the South and the North, User-maāt-Rā setep-en-Rā, the son of Rā, Rā-mes-su meri-Amen ⌜endowed with life⌝ like Rā [for ever].

SOUTH FACE, CENTRE LINE.—

SOUTH FACE, CENTRE LINE.—Rā-Her-aakhuti, Mighty Bull, doing battle on his mighty leg[s], Lord of the Vulture and Uraeus Crowns, Rā, who casteth down him that attacketh him, bringer in (*i.e.* capturer) of the ends of the earth, the Golden Horus, whose greatness is wide-spread, valorous chief, King of the South and the North, User-maāt-Rā, the divine seed (or issue) of his father Amen, the Lord of the gods. He maketh the House of the Soul (*i.e.* a temple of Rā) to shout for joy, the Company of the Gods of the House of the Prince exult and are glad. The son of Rā, Rāmeses meri-Amen, made [it, *i.e.* this obelisk] for him that he might have life for ever.

LEFT LINE.—

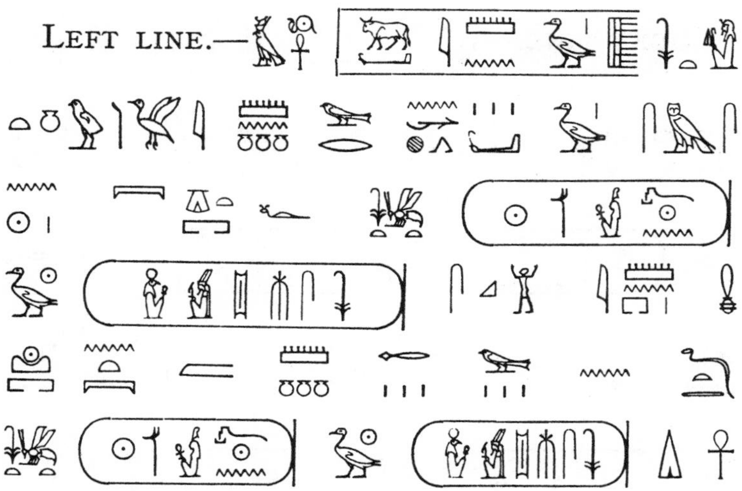

LEFT LINE.—Rā-Her-aakhuti, the Mighty Bull, the son of Amen, the king who maketh many [his] monuments, great of victories, eldest son of Rā [seated] on his throne, the King of the South and the North, User-maāt-Rā setep-en-Rā, the son of Rā, Rā-mes-su meri-Amen, who exalteth the House of Amen like the horizon of heaven with great and mighty monuments for eternity, the King of the South and the North, User-maāt-Rā setep-en-Rā, the son of Rā, Rā-mes-su meri-Amen, to whom life hath been given.

RIGHT LINE.—

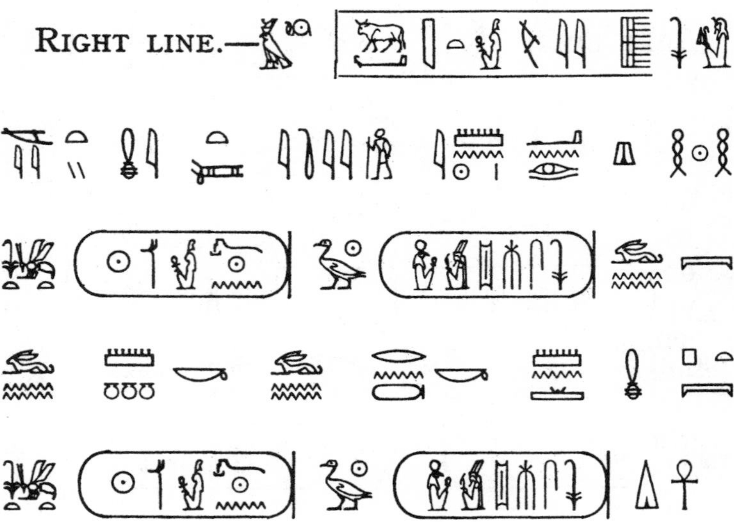

RIGHT LINE.—Rā-Her-aakhuti, Mighty Bull, beloved of Maāt, beloved one, like Tem, Prince of Amen-Rā, beautiful with eternity, King of the South and the North, User-maāt-Rā setep-en-Rā, son of Rā, Rā-mes-su meri-Amen. So long as the heavens exist, so long shall thy monuments exist; thy name shall be permanent as the heavens are permanent, King of the South and the North, User-maāt-Rā setep-en-Rā, the son of Rā, Rā-mes-su meri-Amen, to whom life hath been given.

XIII

OTHER OBELISKS OF RAMESES II, KING OF EGYPT ABOUT 1300 B.C.

I.—THE OBELISK OF THE PANTHEON

According to the Italian archaeologist Antonio Nibby (1792–1839) this obelisk is an imitation made during the period of the Roman rule over Egypt, but there is no doubt that the monument is genuine. It originally stood before one of the pylons of the House of Rā at Heliopolis. On the pyramidion are cut the prenomen and nomen of Rameses II, and on each of the faces of the shaft is one column of hieroglyphs giving the titles of this king. It is noteworthy that Rameses calls himself the "reverer of those who gave birth to him, multiplier of their days,"

It is not known when this obelisk was brought to Rome, but it and another stood before the temple of Isis and Sarapis in the Campus Martius. This temple was the centre of the cult of Egyptian gods in Rome, and was apparently a very magnificent structure. Flavius Josephus says that it was destroyed by fire about A.D. 80, but was rebuilt with great magnificence by Domitian (see *Ant. Jud.* xviii, 4). It was discovered among the ruins of this temple in 1374 during the reconstruction of the Church of St. Mary supra Minerva. In the XVIth century it stood in the piazza of St. Mahutaeus, and in 1711 it was removed by Clement XI to the place where it now stands. It is about 20 feet high.

2. THE DOGALI OBELISK

This obelisk was discovered in 1883 near the Church of St. Mary supra Minerva, and it once stood before the temple of Isis, like the obelisk of the Pantheon. It now stands before the railway station in Rome, where it was placed in memory of the 400 Italian soldiers who were cut to pieces by the Abyssinians at the Battle of Dogali, 26th January, 1887. The text and translation have been published by Schiaparelli in *Bull. Arch. Comm.*, 1883, pages 57 ff., and Marucchi, *op. cit.* pages 97 ff. The height of this obelisk is, like that of its fellow, 20 feet.

3. THE OBELISK OF THE VILLA MATTEI

This fragment was found among the ruins of the temple of Isis, and was set up by Cyriacus Matthaeius in his gardens on Monte Coelio in 1582. The inscriptions contain the titles of Rameses II, and are unimportant; they will be found in Marucchi, *op. cit.* page 101. It is said that while this obelisk was being placed upon its pedestal the architect, in his anxiety to steady the monument, incautiously placed his hand upon the pedestal at the moment when the cords were relaxed, and the monument descended upon it and crushed his fingers. As it was impossible to raise the obelisk, the architect's hand had to be cut off, leaving the bones of his fingers under it. Popular rumour says they are there to this day.

4. THE OBELISK OF THE TRINITA DEI MONTI (SALLUSTIAN OBELISK)

This obelisk is made of red granite and was quarried at Aswân; it is about 43 feet 6 inches in height and weighs about 40 tons. The pyramidion is without Vignettes. On each side of the shaft are three columns of hieroglyphs, the central lines containing the cartouches of Seti I, Men-maāt-Rā, Seti-mer-en-Ptah, and the side lines the cartouches of Rameses II, User-maāt-Rā setep-en-Rā, Rā-mes-su meri-Amen. But the style of the workmanship and the form of the hieroglyphs show conclusively that they were never cut by Egyptian workmen, and it is now generally believed by Egyptologists that the inscriptions were cut on the obelisk by Italian workmen in Rome; perhaps, as Zoega thought, in the IIIrd century A.D. There is little doubt that they were copied from the obelisk in the Piazza del Popolo. This obelisk seems to be the second which Ammianus Marcellinus refers to in his *Historia* (xvii, 4), where he says that, among the other obelisks that were brought to Rome after the reign of Augustus, one was in the

Vatican and the other in the garden of Sallust. When the Goths under Alaric sacked Rome in 410, they entered the city by the Salarian Gate and burnt the house of Sallust, and probably they threw down the obelisk, and it was damaged by its fall. It soon became buried in the ruins, and it was not seen again until the pontificate of Clement XII, who had it removed in 1733 to a place near the Scala Santa, and intended to set it up at the Lateran. In 1789 it was re-erected by the architect Antinori by the command of Pope Pius VI, who dedicated it to the Holy Trinity.

5. THE OBELISKS AT SÂN (TANIS IN THE DELTA)

In and about the temple which Rameses II built at Tanis stood a large number of red granite obelisks, some of which were erected by earlier kings, and the remains of at least fourteen have been found. Many of them were set up in pairs, which seem to have been arranged in such a way as to form an avenue; and a few of them were usurped by Rameses II, who reworked the faces and had his inscriptions cut upon them. The texts on the broken obelisks are given by Petrie in *Tanis*, Part i, London, 1885, Plates vii–xi.

6. THE OBELISK IN THE BOBOLI GARDENS, FLORENCE

This obelisk formerly stood in a temple at Heliopolis; it is about 16 feet high and weighs 4½ tons. It was removed by the Emperor

Claudius and set up by him in the Circus of Flora. In the XVIIth century it was in the grounds of the Villa Medici, Rome, but at some unknown date was transferred to the Boboli Gardens at Florence, where it is now. The cartouches of Rameses II are cut on the pyramidion, and one column of hieroglyphs occupies the centre of each face of the shaft. The text has been published by Sharpe, *Egyptian Inscriptions*, 2nd Ser., pl. 69 ; and by Bonomi in *Trans. Royal Soc. Lit.*, 2nd Ser., vol. i, page 170.

XIV

THE OBELISK OF RAMESES IV AT CAIRO

During excavations which were being made by a firm of builders in Cairo in 1887 the workmen dug out the lower portion of an inscribed sandstone obelisk, which was acquired by the Egyptian Museum the same year. The monument was cleaned, and M. Daressy copied and published the inscription upon it in *Annales du Service*, tom. iv, Cairo, 1903, page 105. There are two columns of hieroglyphs on each face of the shaft, and the cartouches

HEQ-MAĀT-RĀ SETEP-EN-AMEN, SON OF RĀ, RĀMESES MERI AMEN

show that the obelisk was erected by Rameses IV, but when and under what circumstances is not known. Rameses IV is famous chiefly on account of the interest which he took in the development of the quarries in the Wâdi Hammâmât, where he set up two stelae to record his visit to the quarries in the second year of his reign, and his despatch of a great mission thither in the third year of his reign. Acting under the direct command of his god, he went to the quarries and selected blocks of stone of Bekhen out of which to make statues of his ancestors and his gods and goddesses. A year later he sent there a great expedition under the leadership of

Rameses-nekht, high priest and clerk of the works of Amen, whose company contained 8,362 men, not counting the 900 men who died from exhaustion, heat, and fever during the progress of the work in the quarries. The arrangements made for feeding the workmen were good, for in addition to the men who came regularly with supplies of bread and meat, ten trollies, each drawn by 12 oxen, brought food and materials from Egypt. An inscription on a stele found at Abydos by Mariette, and now in Cairo, contains a very interesting prayer of the king to Rā of Heliopolis. He entreats the god to give to him, personally, health and strength and well-being; and for his country and his people he asks for great Inundations of the Nile, so that man and beast may enjoy an abundance of food and every kind of material prosperity. He claims that during the four years which he had reigned when he set up the stele he had done more for the god and his service than Rameses II had done during the whole 67 years of his reign. Therefore he asks that the god will grant him a reign of double that length, namely, 134 years. The inscriptions in the temple of Khensu at Karnak show that he did much work there.

The upper portion of the obelisk of Rameses IV found in Cairo no doubt contained his Horus names, [hieroglyphs], Ka-nekht-ānkh-em-Maāt, [hieroglyphs], Ka-nekht-Rā-en-Kamt, and [hieroglyphs], Ka-nekht-pehti-ma-Amen. The remaining portions of the columns of text, each of which begins with the king's prenomen, , read :—

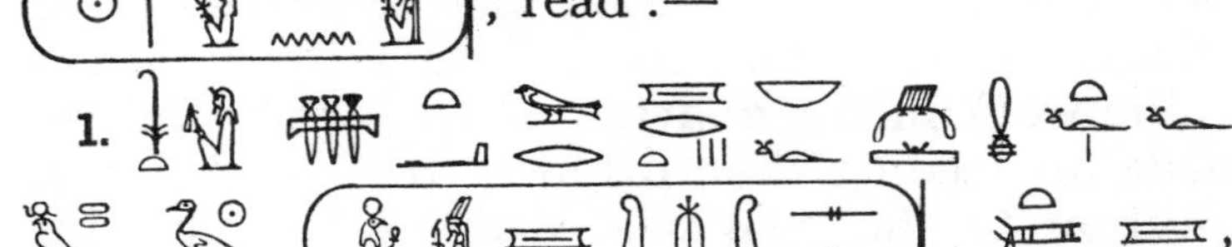

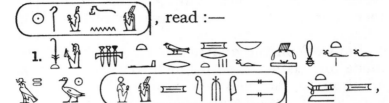

King brilliant (?), great in the love of his lord, of extended [life] like his father Rā Her-aakhuti, the son of Rā, Rameses, beloved of Amen, beloved of **Tem.**

2.

, King, perfect in ability, the prop of Maāt (*i.e.* Truth or Law), builder of the majestic temple of the Souls of Anu, the son of Rā, Rameses, beloved of Amen, beloved of **Iusās.**

3.

, King, mighty one of sovereignty like his father Rā, making the lands to live by offerings through his vigour, the son of Rā, Rameses, beloved of Amen, beloved of **Her-aakhuti.**

4. 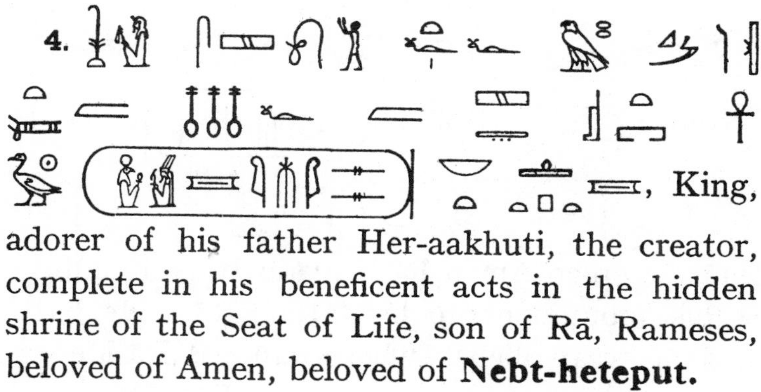, King, adorer of his father Her-aakhuti, the creator, complete in his beneficent acts in the hidden shrine of the Seat of Life, son of Rā, Rameses, beloved of Amen, beloved of **Nebt-heteput.**

5. , King, beloved one, rejoicing in Truth. His father Amen hath set him to be lord of the Nine Peoples of the Bow (Nubia), the son of Rā, Rameses, beloved of Amen, beloved of **Sepi.**

6. , King, lord of joy of heart as Governor of Kam (Egypt). His father hath dandled him. There is no limit to his love. The son of Rā, Rameses, beloved of Amen, beloved of **Isis.**

7. 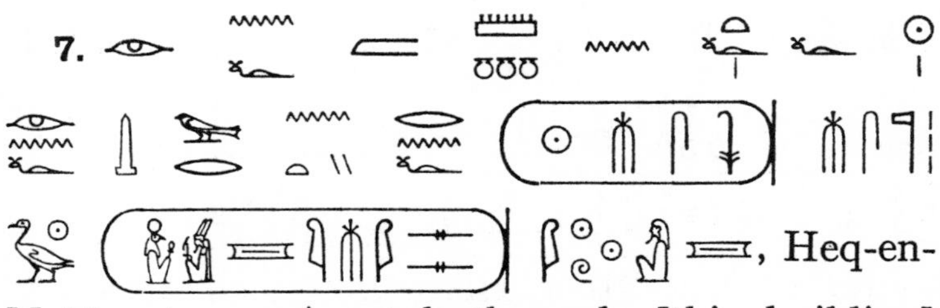, Heq-en-Maāt setep-en-Amen hath made [this building] as his monument to his father Rā. He hath made a great obelisk whose name is Rā-Messu, child of the gods, the son of Rā, Rameses, beloved of Amen, beloved of **Shu.**

8. 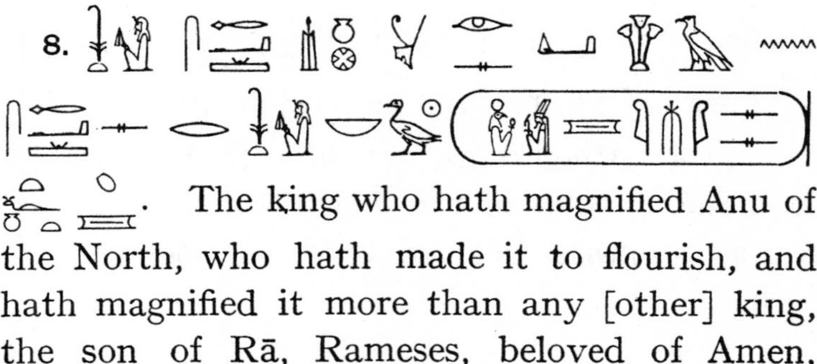. The king who hath magnified Anu of the North, who hath made it to flourish, and hath magnified it more than any [other] king, the son of Rā, Rameses, beloved of Amen, beloved of **Tefnut.**

XV

THE OBELISK OF PSAMMETICHUS II, KING OF EGYPT 593–588 B.C.

THE MONTE CITORIO OBELISK

This obelisk is about 73 feet 6 inches high and weighs about 214 tons. On the pyramidion is a relief in which the king is represented in the form of an ape making an offering to Rā-Her-aakhuti, , " the great god, lord of heaven," of whom it is said, " He gives all life and all health for ever," ; the god says to the king, " I give thee life, all serenity, all health, and all joy of heart for ever." Over the king is written, " King of the South and the North, Nefer-ab-Rā, son of Rā, Psemthek, living like Rā for ever and ever."

North side.—The inscriptions are too mutilated to be legible.

South side I.—

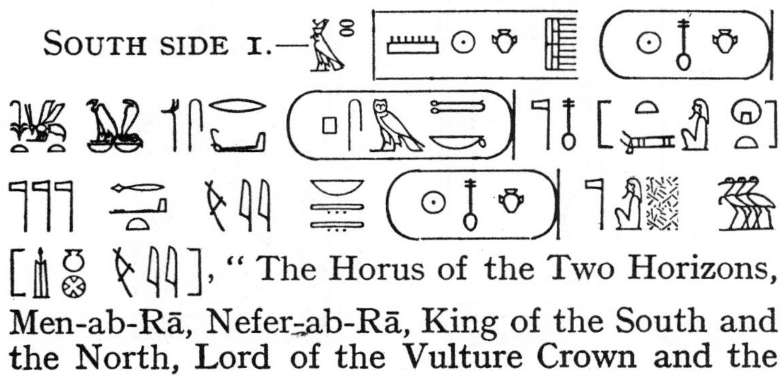

, " The Horus of the Two Horizons, Men-ab-Rā, Nefer-ab-Rā, King of the South and the North, Lord of the Vulture Crown and the

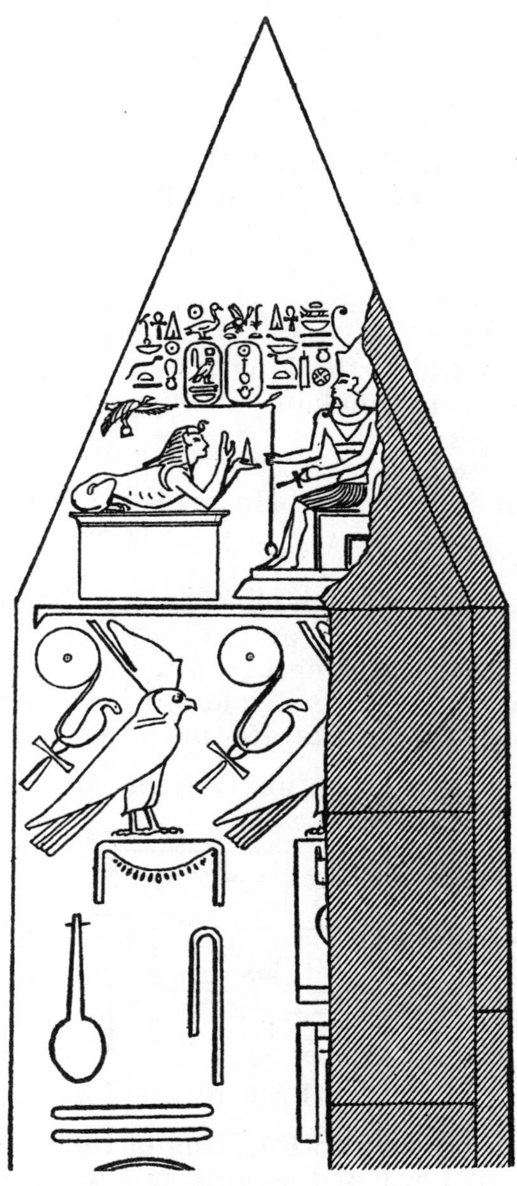

Vignette on the obelisk of Psammetichus II, in which the king, in the form of a man-headed sphinx, is offering a bread-cake, △, to Tem, "Lord of the Two Lands of Anu (Heliopolis)."

Uraeus Crown, the mighty one, Psemthek, the beneficent god, beloved of Tem and the Great Company of the gods, Lord of the Two Lands, Nefer ab-Rā, [beneficent] god, beloved of the Souls of Anu."

SOUTH SIDE 2.—

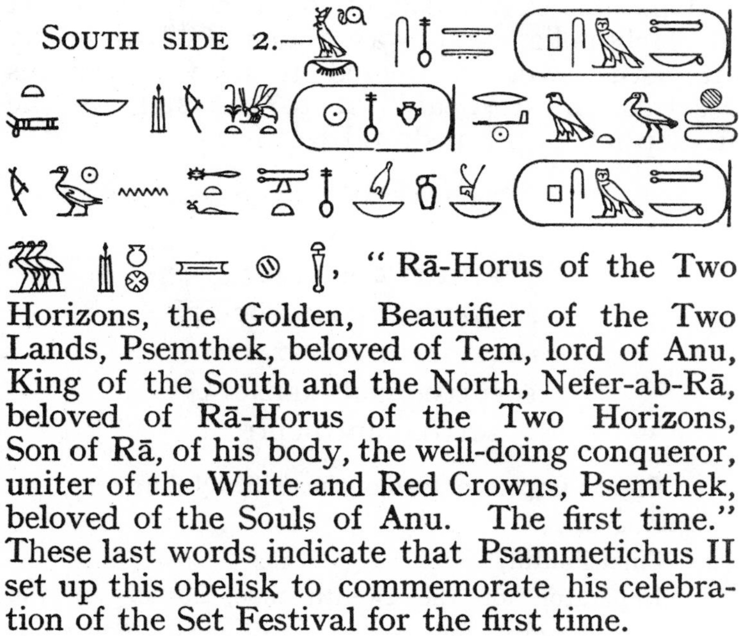

"Rā-Horus of the Two Horizons, the Golden, Beautifier of the Two Lands, Psemthek, beloved of Tem, lord of Anu, King of the South and the North, Nefer-ab-Rā, beloved of Rā-Horus of the Two Horizons, Son of Rā, of his body, the well-doing conqueror, uniter of the White and Red Crowns, Psemthek, beloved of the Souls of Anu. The first time." These last words indicate that Psammetichus II set up this obelisk to commemorate his celebration of the Set Festival for the first time.

EAST SIDE I.—This line is wanting.

EAST SIDE 2.—

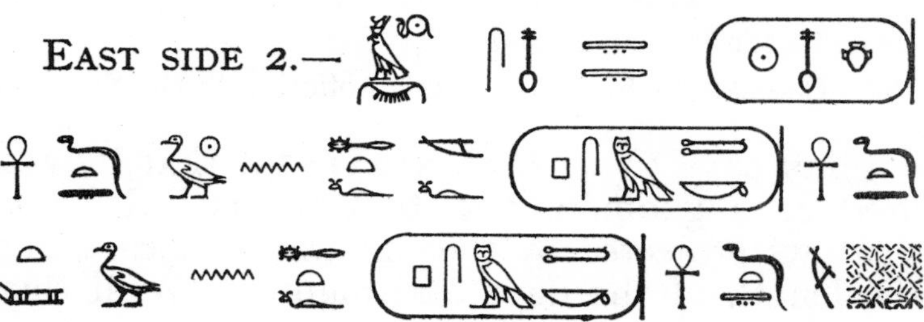

In this line the king calls himself the son of Rā-Her-aakhuti, and the son of Tem. The remaining inscriptions are repetitions of the king's names and titles which have already been given.

This obelisk was set up by Psammetichus II at Heliopolis, and was taken to Rome by Augustus, who re-erected it in the Campus Martius and dedicated it to the sun, as the inscription on its pedestal testifies—

IMP·CAESAR·DIVI·F
AVGVSTVS
PONTIFEX·MAXIMUS
IMP·$\overline{\text{XII}}$·COS·$\overline{\text{XI}}$·TRIB·POT·$\overline{\text{XIV}}$
AEGYPTO·IN·POTESTATEM
POPULI·ROMANI·REDACTA
SOLI·DONUM·DEDIT

"Caesar Imperator, son of the deified Julius,
Augustus,
Chief Pontiff,
Imperator for the twelfth time, Consul for the eleventh time, holder of tribunitian power for the fourteenth time,
Egypt having been reduced to subjection,
To the Roman People,
Dedicated [this obelisk] as an offering to the Sun."

Pliny says (*Nat. Hist.* xxxvi, 15) that it was used as a gnomon, and that it marked "the shadows projected by the sun, and so measuring the length of the days and nights. With this object, a stone monument was laid, the extreme length of which corresponded exactly with the length of the shadow thrown by the obelisk at the sixth hour [*i.e.* noon] on the day of the winter solstice. After this period, the shadow would go on, day by day, gradually decreasing, and then again would as gradually increase, correspondingly with certain lines of brass that were inserted in the stone ; a device well deserving to be known, and due to the ingenuity of Facundus Novus, the mathematician. Upon the apex of the obelisk he placed a gilded ball, in order that the shadow of the summit might be condensed and agglomerated, and so prevent the shadow of the apex itself from running to a fine point of enormous extent ; the plan being first suggested to him, it is said, by the shadow that is projected by the human head. For nearly the last 30 years, however, the observations derived from this dial have been found not to agree : whether it is that the sun itself has changed its course in consequence of some derangement of the heavenly system ; or whether that the whole earth has been in some degree displaced from its centre, a thing that, I have heard say, has been remarked in other places as well ; or whether that some earthquake, confined to this city only, has wrenched the dial from its original position ; or whether it is that in consequence of the inundation of the Tiber, the foundations of the mass have subsided, in spite of the general assertion that they are sunk as deep into the earth as the obelisk erected upon them is high."

The obelisk stood in the Campus Martius, close to the Flaminian Way and the famous monument of Augustus, at a place near the church of St. Lorenzo in Lucina. It was thrown down and suffered much damage after a fire, some think, and its pieces remained buried in ruins until 1748, when they were dug out by Benedict XIV. Finally it was repaired and re-erected in the Monte Citorio by Pius VI, in 1792, who in his inscription (given below) wrongly describes it as a monument of Sesostris.

PIVS VI. PONT. MAX.
OBELISCVM REGIS SESOSTRIDIS
A.C. CAESARE AVGVSTO HORARVM
INDICEM IN CAMPO STATVTVM
QVEM IGNIS VI ET TEMPORVM
VETVSTATE CORRVPTVM BENEDICTVS XIV
P.M. EX AGGESTA HVMO
AMOLITVM RELIQVERAT SQVALORE
DETERSO CVLTVQVE ADDITI VRBI
COELOQVE RESTITVIT
ANNO M.DCCXCII
SACRI PRINCIPATVS EIVS XVIII.

The text on the obelisk has been published by Ungarelli, *Interpretatio*, pages 125 ff. and plate 3; Zoega, *De Usu*, pages 609–644; and Marucchi, *Gli obelischi*, pages 104 ff.

XVI

THE OBELISK OF UAHABRĀ (PHARAOH HOPHRA), KING OF EGYPT ABOUT 588–566 B.C.

(OBELISK IN THE PIAZZA DELLA MINERVA)

This obelisk originally stood in a temple of Saïs, in Lower Egypt; it is about 17 feet high and weighs about 5 tons. There is a column of hieroglyphs on each side of it, and the inscriptions show that it was dedicated to the goddess Neith, , of Saïs, and to Tem of Ta-ānkh-t, . The Horus name of the king was Uah-ab-Rā, , or Suatch-taui, , his Nebti name was Neb-khepesh, , his Nesubati name was Hāā-ab-Rā, , and his son-of-Rā name was Uah-ab-Rā, whence the Hebrew Hophra and the Greek 'Απρίης. The temple of Neith was called Het-Khebit, . This obelisk was removed to Rome at some unknown period, and with another, which now stands before the Pantheon, was set up before the temple of Isis and Sarapis in the Campus Martius, near which it was found in 1665. In 1667 it was repaired and erected by Bernini, by the order of Pope Alexander VII, curiously enough on the back of a marble elephant. The text of this obelisk has been published by Ungarelli. *Interpretatio*, plate 4, pages 133 ff., and Marucchi, *Gli obelischi*, page 115 ; *see also* Kircher, *Oedipus* III, page 382, and Zoega, *De Usu*, pages 79–81.

XVII

THE OBELISKS OF NEKHT-HER-HEBIT, KING OF EGYPT ABOUT 378 B.C.

This pair of obelisks originally stood one on each side of the doorway of the chamber of a chapel dedicated to the god Thoth, the divine scribe of the gods, and the inventor of the art of writing and of mathematical and astronomical sciences. The members of Napoleon's Scientific Expedition to Egypt found the pieces of these obelisks in various parts of Cairo, where they had been seen and noted by both Pococke and Niebuhr, and they took them to Alexandria in order to send them to France. Under the Capitulations (1801), however, they passed into the hands of the British, and they, with many other objects, were sent home to King George III, who presented them to the British Museum; they now stand at the southern end of the great Egyptian Gallery (Nos. 523, 524). The pyramidion of one of them is wanting, and the other lacks both the pyramidion and the upper end of the shaft. Where they originally stood in Pharaonic times is not known, but it is probable that they were brought to Cairo from the ruined temple which Nektanebês, one of the last native kings of Egypt, built at Bahbît in honour of Horus and Osiris, about the middle of the IVth century B.C. Bahbît lies about 30 miles to the east of Tantâ, in the Delta. When complete, each obelisk was about 13 or 14 feet high and weighed about 5 tons, but the portions which now remain only measure in height 9 feet 4 inches and 8 feet 5 inches respectively. They are not made of red granite but of black basalt, a stone that was much used in late Egyptian times. Each face has a column of handsome well-cut hieroglyphs running down the centre. Each column began with the Horus, Nesubati, and son-of-Rā names of the king, which appear in these forms :—

Horus name [hieroglyphs], Mer-Taui, [hieroglyphs]

Nesubati name [hieroglyphs], Senetchem-ab-Rā setep-en-Amen, [hieroglyphs]

Son-of-Rā name, Nekht - Her - Hebit meri-Amen, [hieroglyphs]

His Nebti name was Seher - ab - neteru, [hieroglyphs], *i.e.* " satisfying the heart of the gods," and his Golden Horus name was [hieroglyphs], " stablisher of laws." After each repetition of the son-of-Rā name came the words, " living one like Rā." On No. 523 the columns read :—

Col. 1.—

Cols. 2 and 4.—

Col. 3.—[1]

TRANSLATION (523)

Col. 1.—Nekht-Her-Hebit, beloved of Thoth the Twice-great, the lord of Khemenu (*i.e.* Hermopolis), the great god, prince of Maāt (?), the holy one of all the gods.

Cols. 2 and 4.—He made [this obelisk] as his monument to his father Thoth, the lord of Khemenu. He set up in his house an obelisk of *Bekhen* stone, the pyramidion of which was of black copper, so that in return therefor he may have stability, life and serenity.

Col. 3.—Nekht-Her-Hebit, beloved of Thoth the Twice-great, the lord of Khemenu, the lord, the great god, President of the city of Hesert. President of the . . .

On No. 524 the columns read :—

[1] Inside is a sign in outline which is illegible to me.

Cols. 1 and 4.—

Col. 2.—

Col. 3.—

TRANSLATION (524)

Cols. 1 and 4.—He made [this obelisk] as his monument to his father Thoth the Twice-great, the lord of Khemenu. He set up in his house an obelisk of *Bekhen* stone, the pyramidion of which was of black copper; may they (*i.e.* the gods) give to him life and all serenity like Rā.

Col. 2.—Nekht-Her-Hebit, the beloved of Thoth the Twice-great, the lord of Khemenu, the great god, the President of beings who have knowledge, to whom all life hath been given.

Col. 3.—Nekht-Her-Hebit, the beloved of Thoth the Twice-great, the lord of Khemenu, President of the Great Company of the Gods, to whom all life hath been given.[1]

[1] Copies of the inscriptions on these obelisks and descriptions have been published in *Description de l'Égypte*, tom. v, plates 21, 22; Sharpe, *Egyptian Inscriptions*, plate 107; *Trans. R. Soc. Lit.*, IInd series ii, page 457; *Athenæum*, 1877, page 559; Long, *Egyptian Antiquities*, vol. i, page 50.

XVIII

THE PRIOLI OBELISK

G. Long (1800–79), in his work *Egyptian Antiquities*, vol. i, page 332, describes a large red granite obelisk, which he says was then in Constantinople, and adds that it was made by the order of Nectanebo[1] (Nektanebês), 378–360 B.C. This obelisk is about 35 feet high and weighs about 53 tons ; its size suggests that it was made by one of the kings of the New Kingdom, when obelisks of similar dimensions were often set up. Long further identifies this obelisk with one described by Peter Gyllius (Gilles), who says that when he first arrived in Constantinople he saw two obelisks, one being in the Circus Maximus and the other in a garden of the Palace, where it was standing upright. Later, when he saw the latter it was lying on the ground, and he was able to measure it. He says that it was 35 feet long, and that it was a monolith 6 feet square, with a compass of 24 feet. He adds that it was purchased by Antonius Priolus, who sent it to Venice, and placed it in St. Stephen's Market. See *Petri Gyllii de Topographia Constantinopoleos*, Leyden, 1562, bk. ii, chap. xi, page 84. According to Long the obelisk was never removed, and is identical with the one in red granite that still stands in the Sultân's Garden, on the most northerly eminence there. If there is an inscription upon it the date of the monument can be easily ascertained. Gorringe seems to think (*op. cit.* page 126) that it is inscribed, but that its inscriptions have never been published.

[1] Perhaps the obelisk mentioned by Pliny (*Hist. Nat.* xxxvi, 9, 14).

XIX

THE OBELISK OF PTOLEMY IX AT KINGSTON LACEY (COMMONLY KNOWN AS THE OBELISK AT PHILAE)

It seems that Nectanebus, one of the last native kings of Egypt, who reigned about the middle of the IVth century B.C., either rebuilt or founded a temple dedicated to Isis on the Island of Philae, which lies at the southern end of the First Cataract. Some of the earlier Ptolemies, *e.g.* Ptolemy II and Ptolemy III, added to this temple and had inscriptions cut on its walls, and in the second quarter of the IIIrd century B.C. Ptolemy IX built a pylon before it, and placed in front of it two figures of lions, and set up there a pair of red granite obelisks. The famous explorer Belzoni visited the Island in 1815, and found that the lions had been broken to pieces and that one of the obelisks had fallen and was in pieces. The other obelisk he succeeded in removing from the Island, and as no one in Egypt wanted it, he sold it to Mr. W. J. Bankes, of Kingston Hall, Dorset, who transported it to England and set it up in his park, at no great distance from his house, where it stands at the present day. It is 22 feet high and weighs about 6 tons. When I examined it in 1914, I found that it had suffered greatly from "weathering," and in a few years' time many portions of its inscriptions will be illegible. The pyramidion is without Vignettes, and in the centre of each face of the shaft is a column of hieroglyphs which show

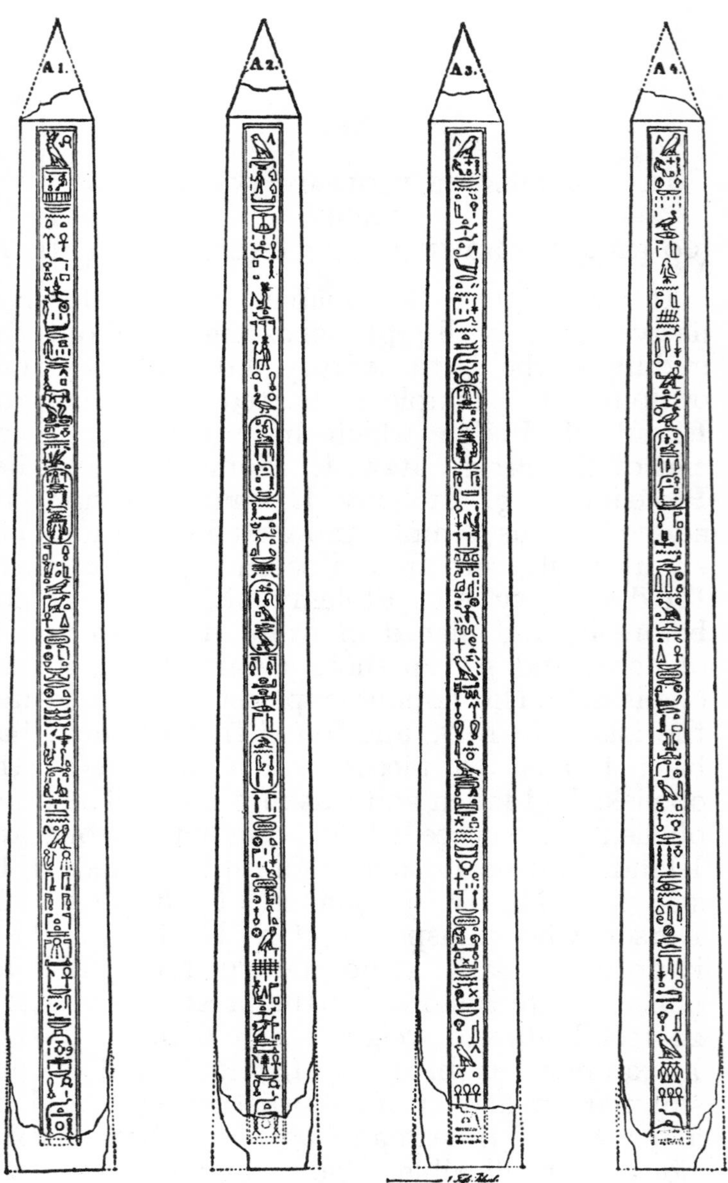

The obelisk at Kingston Lacey. It was one of a pair set up by Ptolemy IX before the great pylon of the temple of Isis at Philae.

that the obelisk was set up in honour of the goddess Isis of Philae by Ptolemy IX and his wife Cleopatra. This obelisk has a special interest in connection with Egyptian decipherment, for, with the help of the Greek inscriptions on its pedestal, Mr. W. J. Bankes was able, in 1816, to identify the cartouche that contains the name of Cleopatra. This was some years before Champollion claimed to have deciphered this queen's name. (*See* Bankes, *Essay on Dr. Young's and M. Champollion's Phonetic System*, London, 1825, pages 22, 23.) The name of Cleopatra is not found on the Rosetta Stone, as is sometimes stated. The hieroglyphic inscriptions, beyond stating the fact that Ptolemy IX dedicated the obelisk to Isis of Philae, contain no historical information. They read :—

Col. i.—

Col. i.—The Youth, rejoicing in his life, upon the throne of his father, gracious in his dispositions, august one, born to his crowns, and Apis ; the elect of the goddesses Nekhebit and Uatchit, making to be at rest the heart of the Two Lands (*i.e.* Egypt) ; the King of the South and the North, (Neterui-ubenui-auāu-en, setep-en-Ptah, ari-maāt-Amen, sekhem-ānkh-Rā),

the beneficent god (Euergetes). To Isis, the great Lady, the mother of the god, giver of life, lord of the Island of Abaton, Lord of Aleq (Philae), Lord of the countries of the South, Governor of the lands of the North, all of them [with] offerings in the step of the god Uben, the Brother gods, the Beneficent gods, the Father-loving gods, the Appearing gods, giver of life and all serenity, and all health, and all joy of heart, like Rā for ever, beloved.

Col. 2.—The Golden Horus, Chief valiant, lord of festivals, like his father Ptah Tanen, the father of the gods, Sovereign, like Rā, the Son of Rā, (Ptolemy, ever-living, beloved of Ptah), and his wife, the Governess, lady of the Two Lands (*i.e.* Egypt), Cleopatra, the Beneficent gods,

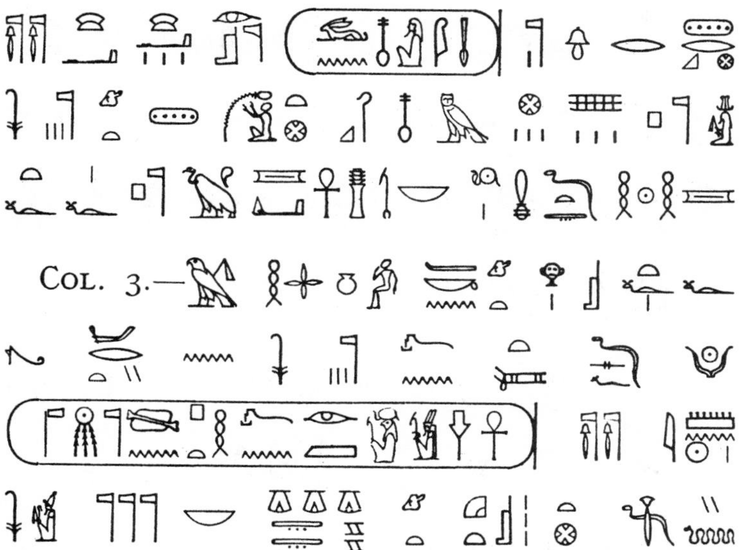

crowned with diadems, Osiris Un-Nefer, true of speech, the beneficent god, lord of Philae, King of the gods, President of the Island of Abaton, Governor beneficent in the cities and the nomes, the god Tanen was his father, the goddess was his mother beloved, giver of life, stability and all serenity, like Rā for ever and ever beloved.

COL. 3.—Horus the YOUTH, rejoicing upon the throne of his father, holy emanation of the king of the gods, chosen by Tem himself, lord of the Two Lands, (Neterui - ubenui - auāu - en, setep-en-Ptah, ari-maāt-Rā, sekhem-ānkh-Amen), the Beneficent Gods, Amen-Rā, king of the gods, lord of the thrones of the Two Lands,

President of the Apts (Karnak), making to flourish those who dwell in the domains of Horus (*i.e.* Egypt, or her temples), beautiful Image in the sanctuaries of the South and North, mighty Disk going round about the heavens and the earth, the Tuat (*i.e.* Other World), the waters, the mountains, and the dwellers in the Two Lands (?), great god, lord of the Island of Abaton, giver of all valour and of all victory [to him] that sitteth on the throne of Horus, of the President of the living ones for ever, beloved.

Col. 4.—Horus the Youth, overlord of the Nine Nations of the bow, son of Osiris, brought forth by Isis, who hath received sovereignty from his father, the son of Rā, (Ptolemy ever-living, beloved of Ptah), the Beneficent God,

hath set up two obelisks to his mother Isis, the giver of life, the Lady of Aleq (Philae), the holy shrine, President of the Island of Abaton, in this place which is beautiful through her. May her heart be pleased with what he hath done and with what shall be done by him during his great reign upon the throne of Horus, the President of the living for ever, beloved.

When the base or pedestal of the obelisk was cleared at Philae a Greek inscription on one side of it became visible, which was copied at once by Mr. Bankes; later (before the end of 1816) other copies were made by Mr. Beechy and M. Cailliaud. When the monument arrived at Kingston Hall and the pedestal was cleaned, traces of two other inscriptions in red ink were found upon it; thus the pedestal contained *three* Greek inscriptions. The longest inscription is a copy of a complaint from the priests of Philae to Ptolemy IX, and his Queen

Cleopatra, and his sister Cleopatra, a transcript of which reads :—

1. Βασιλεῖ Πτολεμαίῳ καὶ Βασιλίσσῃ Κλεοπάτρᾳ
2. τῇ ἀδελφῇ καὶ βασιλίσσῃ Κλεοπατρᾳ τῇ γυναι-
3. κί, θεοῖς Εὐεργέταις χάιρειν οἱ ἱερεῖς τῆς ἐν τῷ 'Αβά-
4. τῳ καὶ ἐν Φίλαις Ἴσιδος Θεᾶς μεγίστης ἐπεὶ οἱ παρεπι-
5. δημοῦντες εἰς τὰς Φίλας στρατηγοὶ καὶ ἐπιστάται
6. καὶ θηβάρχαι καὶ βασιλικοὶ γραμματεῖς καὶ ἐπιστάται φυ-
7. λακιτῶν καὶ οἱ ἄλλοι πρα[γ]ματικοὶ πάντες καὶ αἱ
8. ἀκολουθοῦσαι δυνάμεις καὶ ἡ λοιπὴ ὑπηρεσία ἀναγκά-
9. ζουσι ἡμᾶς παρουσίας αὐτοῖς ποιεῖσθαι οὐχ ἑκόντας

ENGLISH RENDERING

1. To King Ptolemy, and to Queen Cleopatra
2. his sister, and to Queen Cleopatra his wife,
3. the Beneficent Gods : Greeting ! We [are] the priests of Isis
4. who is worshipped in Abaton and in Philae, the great goddess. Inasmuch as
5. those travellers who visit Philae, generals, and inspectors,
6. and rulers in the Thebaïd (?), and royal officials, and scribes, and chief officers
7. of police, and all the other officers who are in the service of the Government, and the armed guards
8. who are in their following, and the rest of their servants, compel
9. us to pay the expenses of their maintenance whilst they are here,

10. *καὶ ἐκ τοῦ τοιοῦτον συμβαὶνει ἐλαττοῦσθαι τὸ ἱερὸν καὶ*
11. *κι[ν]δυνεύειν ἡμᾶς τοῦ μή ἔχειν τὰ νομιζόμενα πρὸς τὰς*
12. *γινομένας ὑπέρ τε ὑμῶν καὶ τῶν τέκνων θυσίὰς*
13. *καὶ σπονδὰς δέομεθ' ὑμῶν θεῶν μεγίστων, ἐὰν*
14. *φαίνηται, συντάξαι* Νουμηνίῳ *τῷ συγγενε[ῖ] κα[ὶ ἐπιστο]-*
15. *λογράφῳ γράψαι* Λόχῳ *τῷ συγγενεῖ καὶ στρατηγῷ τῆς*
16. Θηβαίδος *μὴ παρενοχλεῖν ἡμᾶς πρὸς ταῦτα μηδ' αλ-*
17. *λῳ μηδεν[ὶ] ἐπιτρέπειν τὸ ἀυτὸ ποιεῖν, καὶ ἡμῖν διδόναι*
18. *τοῦς καθήκοντας περὶ τοῦτων χρηματῖσμοὺς, ἐν οἷς*

10. and by reason of this [practice] the temple is becoming very poor,
11. and we are in danger of coming to possess nothing except that which will [only] suffice
12. for the cost—which is laid down by law—of the sacrifices and libations which have to be made on behalf of yourselves and your children:
13. We [therefore] beseech you, O great Gods, if it please you,
14. to give a command to Numenius, the kinsman and
15. epistolographer, to write to Lochus, the kinsman and strategos of the
16. Thebaïd, not to annoy us with these vexatious visits, and not to give
17. anyone else authority to do so: and to give us
18. a decision in writing, by a properly constituted authority, on these matters.

19. ἐπιχωρῆσαι ἡμῖν ἀναθεῖναι στήλην, ἐν ᾗ ἀναγράψομεν
20. τὴν γεγονυῖαν ἡμῖν ὑφ' ὑμῶν περὶ τούτων φιλανθρωπίαν,
21. ἵνα ἡ ὑμετέρα χάρις ἀείμνηστος ὑπάρχει παρ' αὐτῇ εἰς τὸν
22. ἅπαντα χρόνον· τούτου δὲ γενομένου ἐσόμεθα καὶ ἐν
23. τούτοις καὶ τὸ ἱερὸν τὸ τῆς Ἴσιδος εὐεργετημένοι.
24. Εὐτυχεῖτε.

19. And in this [writing] let there be included the permission to set up a stele, whereon we may inscribe
20. the gracious kindness which you will have shown us in these matters,
21. so that it (*i.e.* the stele) may preserve everlastingly the memory of the
22. act of grace which you will grant unto us. This having been done, we and
23. the temple of Isis, in this as in all other matters, shall be exceedingly grateful.
24. Fare ye well.

In answer to the petition of the priests of Isis at Philae, Ptolemy IX instructed Numenius, the epistolographer, to inform them that they might set up the stele, and with his letter he sent a copy of the letter which His Majesty ordered to be sent to Lochus. The following is a transcript of the letter of Numenius: the emendations are by Wilcken (see *Hermes*, 1887, pages 1 ff.).

1. [Βασιλεὺς Πτολεμαῖος καὶ Βασιλίσσα Κλεοπάτρα]
2. [ἡ ἀλελφὴ καὶ Βασίλισσα Κλεοπάτρα ἡ γυνὴ, θεοὶ Εὐεργέται, τοῖς ἱερεῦ]
3. [σι τῆς ἐν τῷ 'Αβάτῳ καὶ ἐν Φίλαις Ἴσιδος θεᾶς μεγίστης καὶ Θεῶν
4. ['Αδελφῶν καὶ Θε[ῶν] Εὐεργετ[ῶν καὶ Θεῶν Φιλοπατόρων]
5. [καὶ Θε]ῶν 'Επιφανῶν καὶ Θεοῦ Εὐπάτορος [καὶ Θεοῦ Φιλο]-
6. μήτορος καὶ Θεῶν Εὐεργετῶν χαίρειν· τῆ[ς γεγραμ]-
7. μένης ἐπιστολῆς πρὸς Λόχον τὸν συγγενέα καὶ
8. στρατηγὸν τὸ ἀντίγραφον ὑποτετάχαμεν. ἐπιχω-
9. ροῦμεν δὲ ὑμῖν καὶ τὴν ἀνάθεσιν, ἧς ἠξιοῦτε στήλης
10. [π]ο[ιήσ]ασθα[ι] ἔρρ[ωσθε. L . . . Πανήμ]ου β', Παχὼν κβ'.

ENGLISH RENDERING

1. King Ptolemy, and Queen Cleopatra
2. his sister, and Queen Cleopatra his wife, to the priests
3. of Isis, who is worshipped in Abaton and in Philae, and of the Brother-
4. Gods, and of the Beneficent Gods, and of the Father-loving Gods,
5. and of the Gods who appear, and of the God Eupator, and of the Mother-
6. loving Gods, and of the Beneficent Gods: Greeting.
7. Of the letter which hath been written to Lochus, the kinsman and
8. strategos, a copy we hereto affix. And we grant
9. unto you the permission, for which you have asked, to make a stele
10. and to set it up. Be of good cheer. Year . . . . Panemon 2. Pakhôn 22.

The letter of Ptolemy IX to Lochus reads :—

1. Βασιλεὺς Πτολεμαῖος καὶ Βασίλισσα Κλεο-
2. πάτρα ἡ ἀδελφὴ καὶ Βασίλισσα Κλεοπάτρα ἡ γυνὴ
3. [Λό]χῳ τῷ ἀδελφῷ χαίρειν· [τῆς δεδομένη]ς ἡ[μ]ῖν
4. [ἐντεύξε]ως παρὰ τῶν ἱ[ερέων τῆς ἐντ ῷ 'Αβάτ]ῳ καὶ [εν
5. Φίλ]αι[ς] Ἴσιδος ὑποτε[τάχαμέν σοι τὸ ἀντιγρο[φον·
6. κα]λῶς ο[ὖν] ποιήσ[ει]ς συν[τάξας, καθάπερ ἀξιοῦσι, μη-
7. δέν]α ἐνοχλεῖν αὐτοὺς, [περὶ ὧν προφέρονται παρ' ἕκαστον]·
8. ἔρρωσο.

ENGLISH RENDERING

1. King Ptolemy, and Queen Cleopatra
2. his sister, and Queen Cleopatra his wife,
3. to Lochus the brother: Greeting. Of the petition
4. which hath been presented to us by the priests of Isis [who is worshipped]
5. in Abaton and in Philae, we append hereto a copy.
6. It will be good then that thou shouldst make suitable arrangements so
7. that no one under any pretext whatsoever should cause [the priests] annoyance in respect of the matters that they have set out in detail.
8. Be of good cheer.

It was to be expected that the letter of Numenius to the priests, and the letter of Ptolemy IX to Lochus, would have been cut on the pedestal like the petition of the priests, but evidently this was not done. The probable reason why was furnished by Mr. Bankes. According to him the red colour in which he found the inscriptions to have been traced was only the foundation for the gold in which both dispatches were painted. In other words, the priests, in order to pay special honour to the royal mandate to Lochus and to the King's answer to themselves, inscribed the texts of both in gold upon the pedestal and steps of one of the two obelisks which Ptolemy IX had set up in honour of Isis of Philae. The pedestal is about 6 feet high, and on it is fixed a metal plate with an inscription stating that the obelisk was re-erected in Kingston Park by Mr. Bankes in the presence of the Duke of Wellington in 1839.

XX

THE OBELISK OF THE EMPEROR DOMITIAN

(THE PAMPHYLIAN OBELISK IN THE PIAZZA NAVONA)

This obelisk, which is about 54 feet high and weighs about 93 tons, was quarried at Syene by the order of the Emperor Domitian, and some authorities think that it was erected by him in one of the great temples of Egypt, but of this there is no evidence. It is well known, as Birch pointed out many years ago, that Domitian built a temple in honour of Sarapis and Isis in the Campus Martius, and it is very probable that he had the obelisk quarried to set up before it. The only thing about the obelisk that is certainly Egyptian is the granite of which it is composed; no Egyptian ever cut the inscriptions on it. In the Vignettes on the pyramidion Domitian is seen worshipping the gods, and like a Pharaoh of old he bears names as Rā-Her-aakhuti and the Golden Horus, and Nebti and Nesubati names. He calls Rā-Her-aakhuti his father, and says that he "set up a great obelisk to him,"

1 2

THE OBELISK OF DOMITIAN IN THE PIAZZA NAVONA.

1. The king wearing a crown with horns, disk, cobras and plumes, offering the Utchat, 𓂀, to Amen-Rā.

2. The king offering bread, wine, and incense to Thoth, Lord of Khemenu (Hermopolis). Thoth and Osiris promise to give him life, health, strength, and serenity.

The pyramidion is a modern restoration.

He gives his name and titles in cartouches thus :— [cartouche] AUTOCRATOR [cartouche] Caesar Domitianus Sebastus. A single column of poorly cut hieroglyphs occupies the centre of each face of the shaft. The titles of Domitian given in these lines are copied from those of Thothmes III, Rameses II and others ; for copies, *see* Ungarelli, *Interpretatio, Obelis.*, plate 4, and Marucchi, *Gli obelischi*, page 125. The names of Vespasian, [cartouche], and Titus, [cartouche], *Tchits p-ur, i.e.* "Titus the Great," are mentioned on the eastern face of the shaft thus :—He hath received the kingdom of his father, [hieroglyphs], Vespasian, in the place of his brother, [hieroglyphs], Titus the Great, after his soul flew up into heaven, [hieroglyphs], *tcher pai ba-f er hert.*

Where this obelisk originally stood is not known, but it is certain that in the fourth century of our Era it was removed to the

Circus of Romulus, the son of Maxentius, not far from the Appian Way and near the Mausoleum of Cecilia Metella. It was then believed to be a monument set up in honour of Romulus. At some unknown time it fell down, or was thrown down, and Poggio, the Florentine, saw it among the ruins at the beginning of the XVth century. It lay where it fell until the middle of the XVIth century, as Fulvius says, and a quarter of a century later Mercati suggested to Pope Sixtus V to re-erect it before the basilica of Saint Sebastian. Nothing was done, however, and the obelisk lay in the ruins of the Circus of Romulus until 1651, when Pope Innocent X ordered its five pieces to be dug out and taken to the Piazza Navona, where he instructed Bernini to restore it and set it up on a pedestal 40 feet high in the centre of a great fountain with four figures representing the great rivers of Europe. Popular tradition says that it now stands on the spot in the Stadium of Domitian where the Christian martyr Saint Agnes was burnt to death during the persecution of Valerian, A.D. 258. At any rate, it is a "triumphant ornament" of her church, which was built on a magnificent scale by Innocent X and stands opposite to it (Marucchi, page 131). On each side of the pedestal Innocent had a Latin inscription cut, and the general history of the re-erection of the obelisk is given in the lines on the south, east, and west sides in flowery language. The inscription on the north side which states that the obelisk was brought to Rome by

The fragments of the obelisk of Domitian at Benevento.

Caracalla, and gives the date of its re-erection, reads :—

OBELISCUM
AB·IMP·ANT·CARACALLA·ROMAM
ADVECTVM
CUM·INTER·CIRCI·CASTRENSIS
RVDERA
CONFRACTUS·DIV·IACVESSIT
INNOCENTIUS·DECIMUS·PONT.·OPT
MAX.
AD·FONTIS·FORIQ·ORNATVM
TRANSTVLIT·INSTAVRAVIT·EREXIT
ANNO·SAL·M.D.CLI·PONTIF·VII[1]

But it is doubtful if Caracalla had anything to do with this monument.

A medal was struck to celebrate the re-erection of the obelisk ; on one side was a representation of the monument with the legend "Abluto aqua virgine agonalium cruore."

THE OBELISK OF DOMITIAN AT BENEVENTO

There stands in the square of the Cathedral at Benevento in Italy a part of the shaft of a small broken red granite obelisk which is about 9 feet high and weighs about 2½ tons ; the pyramidion and part of the base are wanting. On each face of the shaft is a column of hieroglyphs containing the cartouche of Domitian. A portion of a similar obelisk is built into a wall of the bishop's palace. Birch thought that this pair of obelisks were set up before the temple of Isis in Beneventum by the Emperor Domitian ; the founder of the temple was Lucilius Lupus, whose name appears on the standing obelisk.

[1] All four texts are given in Parker, *Egyptian Obelisks*, page 8.

XXI

THE OBELISK OF THE EMPEROR HADRIAN (OBELISK OF MONTE PINCIO)

This obelisk is sometimes called the "Varianian Obelisk," because it stood at one time in the Circus Varianus, and the "Barberini Obelisk," because it was discovered in the time of Pope Urban VIII, and the "Obelisk of Passeggiata," from the name of the place where it now stands. It was quarried at Aswân (Syene) by the command of the Emperor Hadrian, and is about 30 feet high; its weight is nearly 18 tons. The style of the inscriptions and the forms of the hieroglyphs show that they were the work of the Roman Period, and the scribes who drafted the inscriptions prove by their compositions that they possessed little knowledge of the Egyptian language, and were unfamiliar with its syllabary and alphabet. Whether this obelisk was one of a pair cannot be said, but there seems to be little doubt that Hadrian set it up before the funerary temple which he built in the city of Antinoë, A.D. 131, to commemorate the suicide of his favourite Antinous, who drowned himself in the Nile to secure the happiness of his beloved Emperor.

The pyramidion is uninscribed, and there are two columns of ill-shaped and ill-cut hieroglyphs on each face of the shaft. On the north side we see the Emperor Hadrian offering a figure of the goddess Maāt, , to the god

Her-aakhuti, and he is called "lord of crowns, Hatrānes (Hadrianus) Ksr (Caesar)," . His wife Sābina, *Sābina,* is called "August one, living for ever," . The inscriptions on the south and east sides of the shaft make it clear that Hadrian ordered that Antinous was to be worshipped as an Egyptian god, and we may be sure that native Egyptian ceremonies were performed daily in the temple to secure everlasting life for the Emperor's favourite. In the Vignettes we see Antinous presenting vessels of wine and other offerings to Amen and to Thoth, who reaches out to him , the symbol of life. Antinous is called Osiris, , and he is said to "breathe the breath of life," , and his soul to be like that of Rā, . He, like Osiris, is called the "truth speaker," indicating that his soul was believed to have been weighed in the Great Scales and "found to be a speaker of the truth"; he follows Osiris wherever he goes in Ta-tcheser (the Holy Land of the dead), and the guardians of the portals of heaven throw open wide the gates for him to enter.

Time after time Antinous is identified with Osiris, the truth speaker, [hieroglyphs]. All this happened in Egypt, but both Birch (in Parker, *The Twelve Obelisks in Rome*, Oxford, 1879, pages 52–60) and Erman (*Der Obelisk des Antinous*, Berlin, 1896), have shown that there is good reason for supposing that there was a tomb, or at least a cenotaph, of Antinous in Rome. In the inscriptions on the west side of the shaft it is distinctly said that the deceased "Antinous rests in the sanctuary which is within Sekhtiqet, [hieroglyphs], of the Lady of Thebes (?), [hieroglyph], Harma," [hieroglyphs], *i.e.* Rome. The text goes on to say: "He is known as a god in all the divine shrines of Kam (*i.e.* Egypt), a temple has been built for him, and he is worshipped as a god by the priests and libationers of the South and the North. A city is named after him . . . , and the *Atmiti* soldiers of the Lords of the North (*i.e.* Greeks) come thither, camps are provided for them, and they make happy their life there. A temple of this god is there called by the name of 'Osiris Antinous'; it is built of beautiful stone and has sphinxes and many statues similar to those which the Greeks make, all the goddesses give to him the breath of life, and he breathes the air which makes him young again.” 

 (Marucchi, page 137).

Now if Antinous was worshipped as an Osiris in his temple in Egypt, we must suppose that he was mummified, as Birch suggested, otherwise all the funerary ceremonies of the Egyptians performed for him would be meaningless. But it is quite clear that there was a tomb or a cenotaph of Antinous in Rome; if a tomb, Hadrian must have had his mummy brought from Egypt. Whether there was a tomb or a cenotaph Hadrian certainly transported the obelisk at Monte Pincio from Egypt and set it up in Rome. Erman believes that the Sekhti-qet mentioned in the text was a district close to Rome, and that its situation was marked by the obelisk which was found outside the great gate of the vineyard Saccoccia ; some archaeologists, indeed, call that site the "Circus Varianus." There, according to Erman and others, the tomb of Antinous stood (Marucchi, *Gli obelischi*, page 138). Birch thought that the obelisk was removed to the Circus Varianus from some other locality, and Parker says that it was set up there by Heliogabalus about A.D. 220. It was probably thrown down and broken at the sacking of Rome by the Goths, and it remained where it fell until the time of Pope Urban VIII (1623–44), when it was found broken into three pieces near the church of St. Croce in Gerusalemme, which had been built on the site of the Circus Varianus. Pope Urban wished to set it up near the Barberini palace, but nothing was done, and it remained buried in ruins until Domina Cornelia Barberini, the last relative of Urban, gave it to Pope Clement XIV. It was then transported to the garden of the Pigna in the Vatican, where it lay until 1822 ; in that year Pius VII had it repaired and set up in "Passeggiata" of Pincio. For fuller descriptions and details, especially copies of the text on this obelisk, *see* Ungarelli, *Interpretatio*, plate iv ; Kircher, *Obeliscus Pamphilius* ; Parker, *The Twelve Obelisks*, plate iv, and Marucchi, *op. cit.* pages 134 ff.

XXII

UNINSCRIBED OBELISKS

The largest uninscribed obelisk in the world is that which stands in the Piazza of St. Peter in Rome, and is commonly known as the "Vatican Obelisk." It is second in height only to that of Queen Hatshepsut at Karnak; it is a little more than 83 feet high, and weighs about 326 tons. It is mentioned by Pliny (*Nat. Hist.* xxxvi, 11), who calls it the "third obelisk," and says that it was in the garden of one Vaticanus in the Circus of the Emperors Caius (*i.e.* Caligula, A.D. 37–41) and Nero, and that it was an imitation made by Nuncoreus, the son of Sesostris. This obelisk was certainly quarried in Egypt, but by the order of which king cannot be said, and what the original Egyptian name (of which "Nuncoreus" is a corruption) was is not known. It is generally assumed that the obelisk was intended to be set up at Heliopolis, and that Caius Caligula transported it to Rome, where he set it up in the Circus of Caligula, later known as the Circus of Nero because of the slaughter of the Christians which he had carried out there in July, 67. Caligula dedicated the monument to his predecessors Augustus and Tiberius, as the inscription on the front and back of the pedestal shows :—

DIVO CAESARI DIVI IVLII F AVGVSTO
TI CAESARI DIVI AVGVSTI F AVGVSTO
SACRVM.

To this Sixtus V added the following :—

SIXTO V. PONT. MAX. OPT. PRINC.
FELICI PERETTO DE MONTE ALTO PA.
PA. OB PVRGATAM PRAEDONIB. ITA-
LIAM RESTITVTAM INSTAVRATAMQ.
VRB. OBELISCVM CAES. E CIRCO NERON.
IN MEDIAM D. PETRI AREAM INCREDIB.
SVMPTV TRALAT. ET VERAE RELIGIONI
DEDICATVM S.P.Q.R AD REI MEMOR.
OBELISC. HVNC P.

Thanks probably to the strong solid base on which the obelisk stood, it remained upright, or nearly so, for 1500 years; when the architect Fontana examined it in 1585 he found that it was leaning toward the Basilica of St. Peter and that its pyramidion was 1 foot 5 inches from the perpendicular. The question of removing it to a more suitable site had been often discussed, but nothing was done until the Pontificate of Sixtus V, who decided to dig out the obelisks which were known to be lying among the ruins in various parts of the city, and to re-erect them to the honour of Christ and His Cross. This great work he committed to Domenico Fontana, and he instructed him to remove the obelisk of Caligula from the Circus of Nero to the Piazza of St. Peter's. He began to dig the trench for the foundation on September 25, 1585, and in April, 1586, the obelisk was successfully lowered from its pedestal and laid flat, and was re-erected on September 10 following. A bronze cross 7 feet 4 inches high was set in the pyramidion, but was removed in 1740, when a cavity was cut in it and certain relics of our Lord were placed in it. There are several short Latin inscriptions on the pedestal :—That on the north side records the dedication of the obelisk to the Invincible Cross. Sixtus V. Pont. Max. | cruci invictae | obeliscum vaticanum | ab impura superstitione | expiatum iustius | et felicius consecravit. | An. MDLXXXVI. Pont. II. That on the south side records that Sixtus V removed the obelisk, which had been dedicated to the wicked cult of heathen gods, with great toil and labour into the precincts of the Apostles. Sixtus V. Pont. Max. | obeliscum vaticanum diis gentium | impio cultu dicatum | ad apostolorum limina | operoso labore transtulit | An. MDLXXXVI. Pont. II. That on the east side calls upon those who are hostile to the Cross to flee, for the Lion of the Tribe of Judah conquers. Ecce crux Domini | fugite partes | adversae | vicit Leo | de Tribu Juda. On the west side Christ's conquest and rule are proclaimed, and He is asked to protect His people from all evil. Christus vincit | Christus regnat | Christus imperat | Christus ab omni malo | plebem suam defendat. The inscription referring to the cross which Sixtus V added to the obelisk is at the top of the face opposite St. Peter's, and reads :—Sanctissimae Cruci | Sixtus V. Pont. Max. consecravit. | E priore sede avulsum | et Caess. Augg. ac Tib | ablatum. M.D.LXXXVI. The cost of removing and re-erecting the obelisk was 20,000 scudi, or about £11,000. The total height of the monument, including the pedestal and the cross, is between 132 and 133 feet.

XXIII

THE OBELISKS OF S. MARIA MAGGIORE AND MONTE CAVALLO

Both these obelisks were quarried in Egypt, and brought to Rome probably in the reign of Domitian; each is uninscribed. The larger is about 48 feet high and weighs about 45 tons, and the smaller is 45 feet high and weighs about 43 tons. They were found among the ruins of the Mausoleum of Augustus, behind the Church of St. Rocco, in the XVIth century, and there seems to be no doubt that they are the two obelisks mentioned by Ammianus Marcellinus :—Duo in Augusti monumento erecti sunt. The one was re-erected by Domenico Fontana for Pope Sixtus V in 1587 near the great Basilica of the Esquilino. The other lay behind the Church of St. Rocco until 1786, when Pope Pius VI had it dug out from the ruins and set up in the Piazza of the Quirinale with the statues of the two Dioscuri, which had been found close by in the Bath of Constantine. Who brought them to Rome cannot be said, but they can hardly have been there in the days of Pliny, and Strabo, who describes the Mausoleum of Augustus (v. 3. § 8), does not mention them. Zoega, Nibby and Marucchi think that they were brought to Egypt by Domitian, because after the time of Nerva the Mausoleum of Augustus was no longer used as a place of sepulture. The story of the obelisk of St. Maria Maggiore is told by Sixtus V in his Latin inscription :— Sixtus V. Pont. Max. | obeliscum | Aegypto advectum | Augusto | in eius mausoleo | dicatum | eversum deinde et | in plures confractum partes | in via ad S. Rochum | iacentem | in pristinam faciem | restitutum | Salutiferae cruci | felicius | hic erigi iussit An. D. | M.D.LXXXVII. Pont. III.

On the other three sides are cut :—

1. Christus | per invictam | crucem | populo pacem | praebeat | qui | Augusti paci | in praesepe nasci | volvit |
2. Christum dominum | quem augustus | de virgine | nasciturum | vivens adoravit | seq. deinceps | dominum | dici vetvit | adoro: |
3. Christi dei | in aeternum viventis | cvnabvla | lactissime colo | qvi mortvi | sepvlchro Avgvsti | tristis serviebam |

XXIV

THE SEPULCHRAL OBELISK OF PRINCE BEB,

This obelisk is preserved in the Collection of the Duke of Northumberland at Alnwick Castle; it is made of fine limestone and is about 1 foot 8 inches high and 1 foot square. The pyramidion is without Vignette or inscription. On the upper part of one face is a figure of the deceased, seated on a chair of state and smelling a lotus flower, , which he holds in his left hand. Before him stands a figure of the "overseer of the throne, Amenemhat," , who presents to him a censer with burning incense, , in it, and raises his right hand in salutation to him. On another face is a figure of the god of virility and reproduction, Menu, , ithyphallic, wearing plumes, and holding a whip, , in his left hand, which is raised above his shoulder, . On each of the two other sides is a figure of the deceased, with his arms hanging by his sides and wearing a tunic with a projection in front and held in position by a belt. Below these Vignettes is a series of prayers cut in well-shaped hieroglyphs, presumably under the XIIth Dynasty.

Many small funerary obelisks which were made under the Old Kingdom are known, but on none of them do we find inscribed anything but the name and rank of the person commemorated by the obelisk. As the Alnwick obelisk is one of the finest of all the known funerary obelisks, and the inscriptions upon it are interesting, they are reproduced in full here, with translations. Three of the prayers begin with the words NESU TA HETEP, , which mean, "The king gives an offering." This formula is very old, and dates from the time when the king not only gave a man permission to be buried in a tomb, but contributed a gift to the funerary offerings. It was used throughout the whole period of Egyptian history, and even to this day kings and chiefs make "dashes," *i.e.* gifts for the funerary offerings of their subjects and friends when they are about to be buried.

FACE A.—

TRANSLATION

FACE A.—May Geb (the Earth-god) give the sweet breath of the north wind, and splendour, and strength, and [the verdict of] truth-speaker to the Ka (the double) of the Great Chief of the Southern Thirty, Hennu, the truth-speaker,

lord of reverent service, born of the lady of the house, Renefānkh, begotten by the Great Chief of the Southern Thirty, Babu, the truth-speaker, lord of reverent service.

Behold, it is Amenemhat, the truth-speaker, the overseer of the throne, who hath the entry into the storehouse of fruit and plants, who maketh [his] name to live (*i.e.* who has set up the obelisk to perpetuate the name of Hennu).

Face B.—Praise be given to Osiris, the great god, the lord of Abydos, and to Up-Uatu, the lord of Ta-tcheser, and Menu-Her-nekhti, and to the gods who dwell in Abydos! May they grant sepulchral meals of oxen, geese,

bread-cakes, changes of linen apparel, and things of every kind pure [and beautiful], unguents, and bitumen oil, and the breath of life, to the Ka of prince Beb—may he repeat his life! (*i.e.* live again)—born of the king's concubine Aurera the truth-speaker, the lord of reverent service! He saith :—Praise and thanksgiving be to thee, Osiris, Khenti Amenti (*i.e.* President of Amenti), and to Up-Uatu [*sic*], lord of Abydos, sovereign prince of all the gods, Governor of governors, lord of victory and power and truth-speaking, lord of that which existeth and of that which doth not exist, at whose wish Rā shineth! The

gods exult at the sight of him advancing and shedding light, and there is expanding of the heart through joy among the gods, which the Truth-speaker giveth. Thou risest up crowned, thou risest up crowned in thy beautiful progressions at thy festivals at each season of thy . . . . Thy Father Rā giveth to thee expansion of heart in them. Thou art praised by gods, and by men, and by the Pāt,[1] and by the Rekhit,[1] thou the living one who renewest thyself like Rā for ever.

[1] Orders of spiritual beings, perhaps the beatified souls of men dead.

FACE C.—

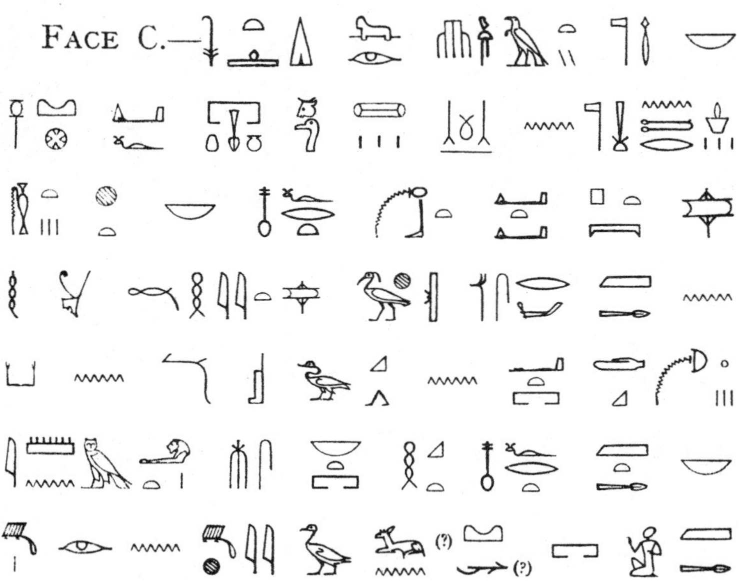

FACE C.—May Osiris, Khenti Amenti, the great god, lord of Abydos, give sepulchral meals of oxen, geese, and bread-cakes, and changes of linen apparel, incense, libations, and every kind of good and pure product that heaven giveth, and the sweet breath of the north wind, and splendour, and power, and [the verdict] of truth-speaker to the Ka of the overseer of the throne, who hath the entry to the chamber of fruit and flowers, Amenemhat, born of the lady of the house Heqit-Nefrit (*i.e.* the Pretty Frog), whose word is truth, the lady of reverent devotion, begotten by the devoted one Sa-Auntu (?), the truth-speaker.

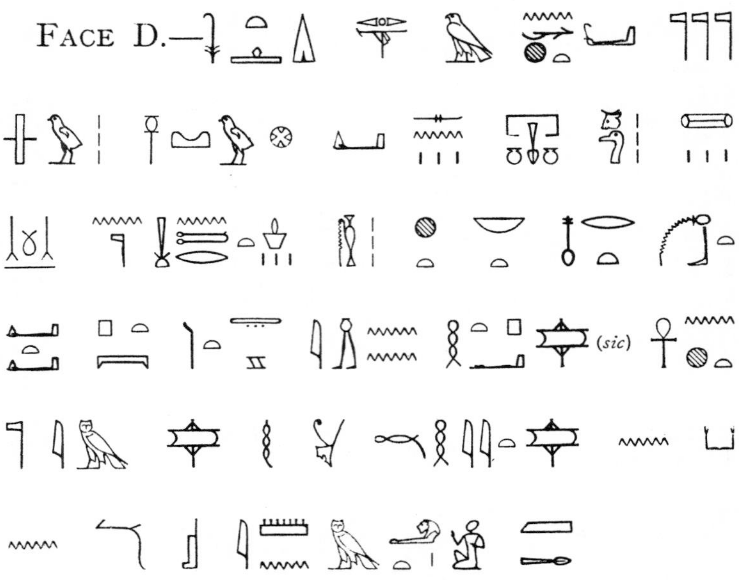

FACE D.—May Menu-Her-Nekhti, and the gods who dwell in Abydos, give sepulchral meals of oxen, geese, and cakes, and changes of linen apparel, incense, libations, and every kind of good and pure thing that the heavens give, and the earth produceth, and Hāp (the Nile) bringeth [from his caverns], whereon the god liveth, and the sweet breath of the north wind to the ka of the overseer of the throne, Amen-emhat, whose word is true.

The above inscriptions show that the obelisk was made for Prince Beb, the son of a king (name unknown) and his concubine Aurera (Face B), and that the dedicator was Amenemhat, the son of Heqit-Nefrit and Sa-Auntu, who served in his master's fruit house (Face C), and whose prayer is on Face D. On Face A he caused an inscription to be cut to commemorate one Hennu, the son of Babu by his wife Renefānkh.

XXV

THE SEPULCHRAL OBELISK OF NUBKHEPERRĀ ANTEF

Mr. Villiers Stuart, the distinguished Irish traveller who visited Egypt in the third quarter of the XIXth century, saw lying about among the ruins of the tombs of Drah Abu'l Nekkah, in Western Thebes, fragments of several inscribed obelisks belonging to the period immediately before or after the XIIth Dynasty. To some of these he called Mariette's attention, and they were dug out and several fragments were rejoined. In his *Nile Gleanings*, London, 1879, page 273, Stuart gave a drawing of two faces of one of these obelisks, and later Mariette published the text on all four faces of an obelisk of the king whose prenomen appears on the Karnak List thus:— , "Beneficent god, the lord making things, Nub-kheper-Rā" (Mariette, *Mon. Div.*, plate 50*a*). The Horus name of this king was either Nefer-kheperu or Kheper-kheperu; his Nebti name was Her-her-nest-f; his Nesubati name was Nub-kheper-Rā, and his Son-of-Rā name was

Antef. On one face of the shaft of the reconstructed obelisk we have :—

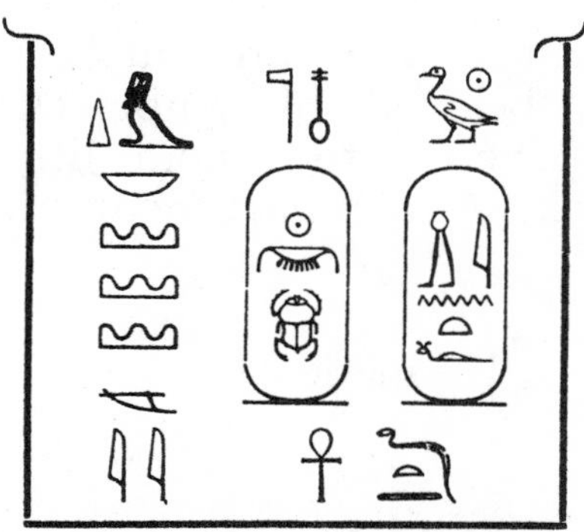

"Beneficent god, Nubkheperrā, son of Rā, Antef, beloved of Horus-Sept, lord of all foreign lands, living for ever." The inscriptions on the other three faces read :—1.

"Chosen one of the Vulture and Uraeus goddesses, resting upon his throne, son of Rā, of his body, Antef, beloved of Osiris, President of Amenti, to whom life hath been given for ever."

2. 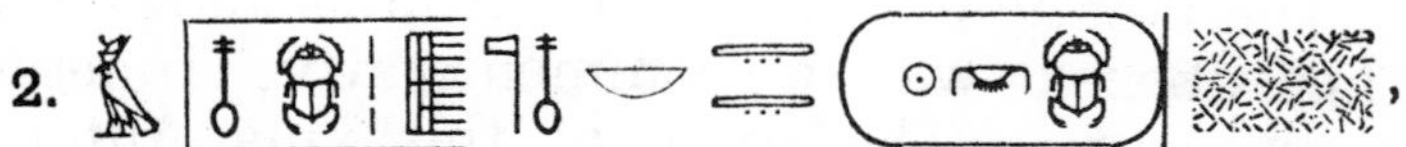

"Rā-Her-aakhuti, Nefer-kheperu, the beneficent god, lord of the Two Lands, Nubkheperrā . . . ." By the side are the signs , "restorer."

3. , "Beneficent god, lord of the Two Lands, the lord, maker of things, son of Rā, beloved of Anpu (Anubis), the lord of Ta-tcheser, to whom life hath been given for ever." In Stuart's copy we have the short line:

The mention of Osiris and Anubis shows that this obelisk was a commemorative funerary monument. The tomb of this king Antef is referred to in the Abbott Papyrus. Legrain gives , Kheper-kheperu, as a variant of his Horus name (*Annales*, iii. 14).

XXVI

THE UNDETACHED OBELISK IN A QUARRY AT ASWÂN

Every traveller who has visited the granite quarries at Aswân has been shown by his guide the upper part of an immense granite obelisk lying in a narrow trench, and marvelled how it was possible for such a mighty monolith to be got out of the quarry. Wilkinson, a great authority on Egyptian archaeology, examined it carefully, and concluded that it had been separated from the living rock, but had been abandoned by the quarrymen after they had finished it because it was "broken in the centre" (*Ancient Egyptians*, ed. Birch, vol. ii, page 307). Gorringe likewise examined the obelisk, and states in his work (*Egyptian Obelisks*, London, 1885, page 143) that it is "finished on three sides, but is still united to the quarry by its lower face." In 1922 Mr. Engelbach, of the Egyptian Service of Antiquities, cleared out the trench in which the obelisk lies, and now the entire length of it is visible. He, like Wilkinson, found that the obelisk was left there because of an unexpected fissure in the rock. He found also on examining the upper surface the outline of a smaller obelisk of about the same size as the obelisk of Thothmes III now standing in the Piazza of the Lateran in Rome. The Aswân obelisk is 137 feet long, and the smaller one, which it was proposed to cut out of it, would therefore have been about 105 feet long. Mr. Engelbach thinks that the Aswân obelisk weighs about 1,168 tons, and the Lateran obelisk 455 tons (*Problem of the Obelisks*, page 24); Gorringe says the Aswân obelisk weighs 1,540,000 lb., *i.e.* 687½ tons (*Egyptian Obelisks*, page 145).

LIST OF THE MOST IMPORTANT INSCRIBED OBELISKS NOW IN EXISTENCE

	Height (approximate)
XIth Dynasty.	
Obelisk of Nubkheperrā Antef in Cairo	8 or 9 feet
XIIth Dynasty.	
Obelisk of Usertsen I at Matarîyah (Heliopolis)	67 ,,
Obelisk of Usertsen I at Abgig ..	43 ,,
XVIIIth Dynasty.	
Obelisk of Thothmes I at Karnak	71½ ,,
Obelisk of Hatshepsut at Karnak	97½ ,,
Obelisk of Thothmes III in Constantinople	55½ ,,
Obelisk of Thothmes III in Rome	105½ ,,
Obelisk of Thothmes III in London	68½ ,,
Obelisk of Thothmes III at Karnak (fragment)	19 ,,
Obelisk of Thothmes III in New York	69½ ,,
Obelisk of Amenhetep II at Alnwick Castle	7¼ ,,
Obelisk of Amenhetep II at Aswân	(Weight unknown)

XIXth Dynasty.	Height (approximate)
Obelisk of Seti I and Rameses II in Rome	83 feet
Obelisk of Rameses II at Luxor ..	82 ,,
Obelisk of Rameses II in Paris ..	75 ,,
Three Obelisks of Rameses II in Rome	20 ,, 17½ ,, 8¼ ,,
Obelisks of Rameses II in fragments at Sân (Tanis)	—
Obelisk of Rameses II in Florence	7 ,,

XXth Dynasty.

Portion of an obelisk of Rameses IV in Cairo	(Height and weight unknown)

XXVIth Dynasty.	Height (approximate)
Obelisk of Psammetichus II in Rome	71½ feet
Obelisk of Hophra in Rome ..	18 ,,

XXXth Dynasty.

Two obelisks of Nectanebus I in London	20 ,,
Obelisk of Nectanebus I in Constantinople	35 ,,

Ptolemaïc Period.

Obelisk of Ptolemy IX at Kingston Lacey	22 ,,

Roman Period.	Height (approximate)
Obelisk of the Piazza del Popolo, Roman imitation	78½ feet
Obelisk of Domitian in the Piazza Navona, Rome	54½ ,,
Obelisk of Domitian (Borgian) in Naples	6½ ,,
Obelisk of Domitian in Benevento	9 ,,
Obelisk of Hadrian in Rome (Monte Pincio)	30 ,,
Two small obelisks in Florence ..	6 ,,
Obelisk in Sicily (Catania), Roman imitation	12¼ ,,

SEPULCHRAL OBELISKS of the IVth and XIIth Dynasties in London and Berlin.

Obelisk of Beb or Babu at Alnwick Castle.

THE MONOLITHIC MONUMENTS, COMMONLY CALLED "OBELISKS," AT AKSÛM IN ABYSSINIA

Many writers on the obelisks of Egypt have referred to the monolithic monuments at Aksûm, and nearly all of them have tried to show that the use of them was derived from Egypt, and that the meaning and symbolism of both classes of monuments were the same. But before considering the accuracy of this view it will be useful to report what travellers have written about the monoliths of Aksûm, for not having seen them I am unable to give a description of them from knowledge at first hand. One of the oldest accounts of these we owe to Father Alvarez, who lived in Abyssinia from 1520–1527; *see* his *Narrative,* edited by Lord Stanley, London, 1881, page 82. He says: Above this town there are many stones standing up, and others on the ground, very large and beautiful, and wrought with handsome designs, among which is one raised upon another, and worked like an altar stone, except that it is of very great size, and it is set in the other as if inchased. This raised stone is 64 ells in length and 6 wide; and the sides are 3 ells wide. It is very straight and well worked, made with arcades below, as far as a head (*i.e.* apex) made like a half moon; and the side which has this half moon is towards the south. There appear in it five nails, which do not show more on account of the rust; and they are like fives of dice in compass. And that it may not be said, "How could so high a stone be measured?" I have already said how it was all in arcades as far as the foot of the half moon, and these are all of one size; and we measured those we could reach to, and by those reckoned up the others, and we found 60 ells, and we gave four to the half moon, although it would be more, and so it made 64 ells. This very long stone, on its south side, and where the nails in the half moon are, at the height of a man, has the form of a portal carved in the stone itself, with a bolt and a lock, as if it were shut up. The stone on which it is set up has an ell in thickness, and is well worked; it is placed on other large stones, and surrounded by other smaller stones, and no man can tell how much of it enters the other stone, or if it reaches to the ground. There are other stones raised above the ground, and very well worked; some of them will be quite 40 ells long, and others 30. There are more than 30 of these stones, and they have no patterns on them; most of them have large inscriptions, which the country people cannot read, neither could we read them; according to their appearance, these characters must be Hebrew. There are two of these stones, very large and beautiful, with designs of large arcades, and ornaments of good size, which are lying on the ground entire, and one of them is broken into three pieces, and each of these exceeds 80 ells, and is 10 ells in width. Close to them are stones, in which these had to be, or had been let in, which were bored and very well worked.

Father Jerome Lobo calls the stones "obélisques," and says that they vary in size;

some have been overthrown by the Turks, and others are still standing upright (*Voyage Historique*, Paris, 1728, page 203). Bruce, who lived in Abyssinia from 1768 to 1773, says in his *Travels* (vol. iii, page 457): "In one square there are forty obelisks, none of which have any hieroglyphics upon them [Poncet mistook the carvings for hieroglyphs]. There is one larger than the rest still standing, but there are two larger than this still fallen. They are all of one piece of granite; and on the top of that which is standing there is a patera exceedingly well carved in the Greek taste [by patera, *i.e.* a broad flat dish or libation bowl, he means the top which Alvarez says was like a half moon]. Below, there is the door-bolt and lock, which Poncet speaks of, carved on the obelisk, as if to represent an entrance through it to some building behind. The lock and bolt are precisely the same as those used at this day in Egypt and Palestine, but were never seen, as far as I know, in Ethiopia, or at any time in use there. I apprehend this obelisk, and the two larger that are fallen, to be the work of Ptolemy Evergetes. There is a great deal of carving upon the face of the obelisk in a Gothic taste, something like metopes, triglyphs, and guttae, disposed rudely, and without order, but there are no characters or figures. The face of this pyramid (*sic*) looks due south; has been placed with great exactness and preserves its perpendicular position till this day. As this obelisk has been otherwise described as to its ornaments, I have given a geometrical elevation of it servilely copied, without shading or perspective, that all kind of readers may understand it."

We may note, in passing, that Lord Valentia was satisfied that "Bruce's pretended knowledge of drawing was not to be depended upon, the present instance affording a striking example both of his want of veracity and uncommon assurance, in giving, with a view to correct others, 'as a geometrical elevation,' so very false a sketch of this monument" (*Voyages and Travels*, vol. iii, page 94). Lord Valentia gave a better drawing of the monument on the plate facing page 87 of his work.

Henry Salt describes the "obelisk" as a "very magnificent work of art, formed of a single block of granite and measuring full 60 feet in height, . . . and as the most admirable and perfect monument of its kind. All its ornaments are very boldly relieved, which, together with the hollow space running up the centre and the patera at top, give a lightness and elegance to the whole form that is probably unrivalled . . . The order of the architecture is strictly Grecian and was, therefore, not likely to have been introduced at an earlier period [*i.e.* than the time of the Ptolemies]. The tradition of the country ascribes these monoliths to the reign of the Emperor Aeizana, about A.D. 300. There cannot exist a doubt but that they were erected by Grecian workmen from Egypt" (*Voyage*, London, 1814, page 405). Parkyns, who lived in Abyssinia for three years, says: "The principal 'obelisk' is carved on the south side, as if to represent a door, windows, cornices, etc., while under the protecting arms of the venerable tree stand five or six smaller ones, without ornament, most of which have considerably deviated from the perpendicular. Altogether they form a very interesting family party" (*Life in Abyssinia*, London, 1853, vol. i, page 208).

Mr. J. T. Bent, who travelled in Abyssinia in 1893, examined the monuments of Aksûm with great care, and came to the conclusion that they are older than the line of statues in precious metal which led up to the city. In all he thought there might be fifty. Many of the fallen ones are hidden away in gardens, built into houses, and so forth. He divided the monuments into two classes, namely "obelisks" and rough unhewn stones, like the menhirs of Brittany, "the monoliths of Zimbabwe in Mashonaland, and the Stonehenge of Wiltshire" (*Sacred City*, London, 1896, page 182). Now the "Book of Aksûm" መጽሐፈ ፡ አክሱም ፡ published by Conti Rossini (*Liber Axumae*, Paris, 1909), says that there were at Aksûm when it was written "58 monolithic stone (*sic*) stelae, some fallen and some still standing," ወሐውልት ፡ ዐብንሂ ፡ ሀሎ ፡ ይእዜ ፡ ኀበ ፡ ዘወድቀ ፡ ወኀበ ፡ ሀሎ ፡ ቀዊሞ ፡ ፶ ፡ ወ፰ ፡፡ Therefore Mr. Bent's guess was very near the truth. The exact positions of the monuments are well shown in the Stadtplan of Aksûm which Littmann has published (*Aksûm*, Bd. i, Taf. ii). They all lie in the valley to the north-east of the town in two groups. At the end of the valley nearest the town are the three largest monoliths, one standing and the other two fallen. The two largest, which are lying down, are 110 feet and 80 feet long respectively, and the one still standing is about 67 feet long; the other monoliths, all of which have fallen, vary greatly in height, say from 12 feet to 26 feet, and they are not ornamented with sculptured reliefs.

Now the rough unhewn monoliths that are seen standing about, many of them very much out of the perpendicular, may well have been set up at a comparatively early period as memorial stelae of great warriors. They cannot all have been objects of a cult, and it is possible that the flat open spaces in which they stand were cemeteries. For a time those who set them up were content to leave them undecorated, and in the form in which they have been found. Then under some impulse, of which we know nothing, the mason's chisel was set to work, and the first attempt to give the monolith a definite form is illustrated by a stele about 16 feet high, which has the corners squared, and a series of nine or ten notches cut on one side of it, and several holes. On another of about the same height the stone is divided into four sections by four bands; judging from the large monolith these sections represent the four storeys of a building. The sculptured reliefs on the large monoliths, which are carefully executed, suggest that each monolith was intended to represent a building of many storeys, and additional support is given to this view by the door, with its lock and key, or handle simply, which is sculptured below the storeys, at the lower end of the monolith. The space above the door represents an antechamber.

The large standing Monolith at Aksûm.

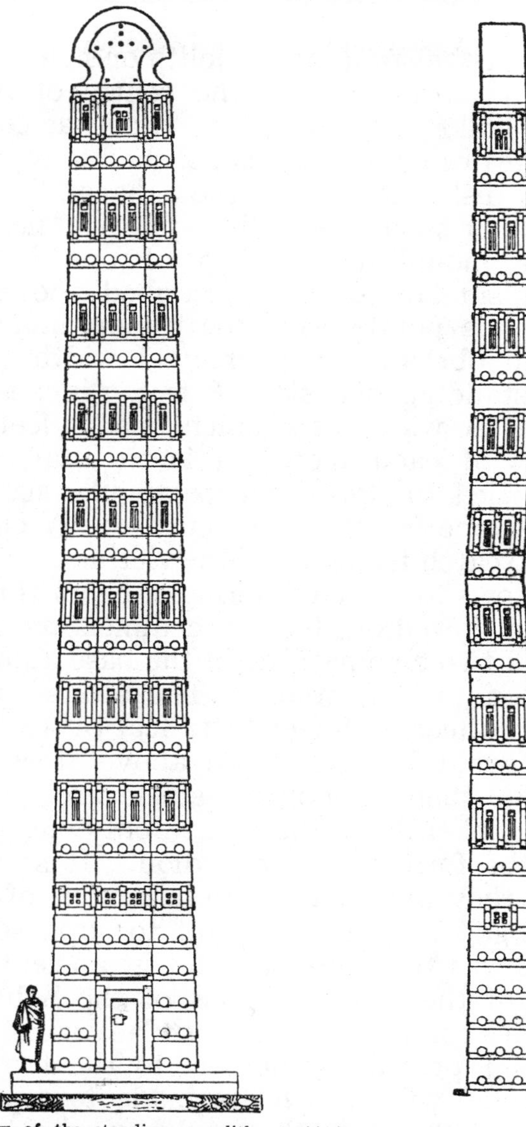

Front view of the standing monolith at Aksûm showing the sculptured door with its bolt lock, and the nine rows of sculptures representing stages, and the rounded top on which a metal disk was fixed. The monolith is oriented to the south. Drawn from Littmann and Lüpke, *Deutsche Aksûm-Expedition*, Band III, Berlin, 1913.

View of one of the sides of the standing monolith showing the sculptured bands, bosses and doors.

The top of the standing monolith or stele is semicircular in form, and in the centre of it is a circular hollow, which at one time was covered by a plate of metal, perhaps polished to represent the solar disk, a symbol of the Sabaean Sun-god. Two smaller stelae are still in position near the standing monolith; the top of one is semicircular, similar to that described above, and the other is pointed like the pyramidion of an Egyptian obelisk. The greatest width of the largest standing obelisk is 8 feet 7 inches, and the greatest width of a fallen one 13 feet. At the foot of each monolith is an altar, which usually takes the form of a rectangular slab on a base of stone in which are cut:—1. A circular hollow to catch the blood of the victim. 2. Three oval hollows to receive offerings. From this slab the blood flowed out by two channels on to the base, and two channels cut in the base allowed it to drip on to the ground. The altars vary in size from 9 feet by 8 feet to 14 feet by 12 feet.

From what has been said above it is quite clear that these monolithic stelae are not like Egyptian obelisks in shape, and only one has its top in the form of a pyramidion. It seems to me that they were not set up in honour of kings but of a god, and it is natural to suppose that that god was the Sun-god, who in ancient days was one of the principal gods of the Sabaeans. Mr. Bent compared these stelae, with their divisions representing houses, to the tombs in Cilicia and Lycia which are made to represent houses, and therefore the workmen who cut the imitation doors and windows upon them may have been, as Salt thought, European, and most probably Greek. But they have many characteristics that suggest Egyptian and perhaps Sumerian influence. It will be remembered that altars on which blood sacrifices were

FACE OF THE ALTAR OF ONE OF THE LARGE FALLEN MONOLITHS AT AKSÛM.

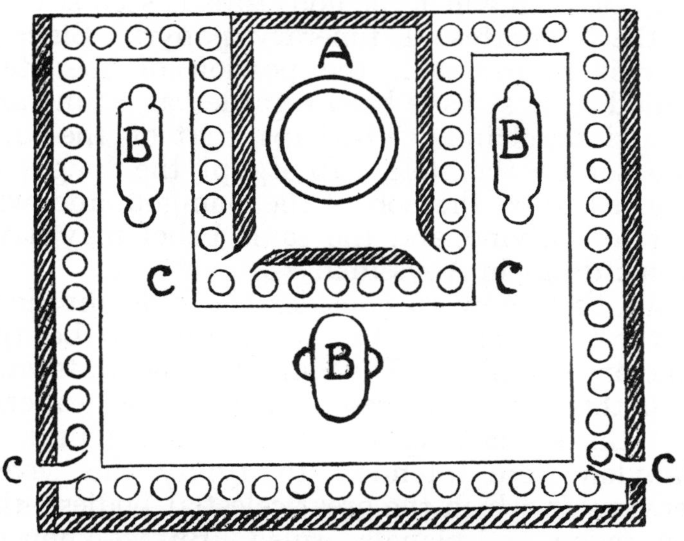

A. Raised slab with a circular hollow to receive the blood of the victims, the throats of which were cut over it.
B. Oval hollows in which offerings were made.
C. Channels along which the blood flowed on to the face of the altar and thence to the ground.

offered up stood before the Sun-stones that were worshipped in the Sun-temples under the Vth Dynasty in Egypt, and there are altars before the stelae at Aksûm. In Egypt the sacrifices were offered to the Sun-god, whose spirit was, at certain times, believed to be present in the Sun-stone. The disk, with its metal covering, which is found on the top of the stelae at Aksûm, suggests that the blood sacrifices made on the altars before them were offered up to the sun; if this be so the stele at Aksûm is the equivalent of the Sun-stone in Egypt. The door with its bolt or lock reminds us of the folding doors of the funerary coffer, with their two bolts, on which the god Osiris is seen seated, in the Vignettes of funerary papyri. Since a door is represented, the portion of the stele behind it must have been regarded as a funerary temple or chamber, perhaps that of the king who set up the stele. In Egypt the king was believed to be the son of the Sun-god, and was therefore divine, and the same belief may have been current in Abyssinia.

We have now to consider the nine divisions of the stele above what we assume to be the funerary chamber. The Sumerian ziggurats with their three stages represented the three heavens, and the seven stages of the great ziggurat at Babylon were intended to typify the seven heavens in which the great celestial bodies—the sun, moon, and planets—ruled. But we know of no ziggurat with nine stages, and in this respect the Aksûm stelae stood alone. On the top stage of the ziggurat the shrine containing a figure of the god Bêl, or Bêl Marduk, was placed, and on the Aksûm stele we have the Sun-god to whom it was dedicated, in the form of the solar disk. To sum up, the stele at Aksûm, in its most complete form, was, I believe, intended to be a representation of the heavens above the earth, and the disk on its top was the symbol of the lord of them all—

the Sun-god. The Egyptian papyri contain no information about the kingdom of Rā, the Sun-god, and whether it was divided into heavens or not cannot be said. But it is well known that the Tuat, or kingdom of Osiris, was situated in the earth, and we know that it was divided into seven sections in comparatively early times. In the Vignettes to Chap. cxlvii of the Book of the Dead pictures of the doors of the Seven Ārits, or "Halls," of the kingdom of Osiris are given, and the general shape of them is similar to that of the doors of the sections on the stele of Aksûm. It is probable that these "Halls" were believed to be situated one below the other, but it is not so stated. A papyrus in the British Museum (No. 10478, sheets 2–7) shows that the Tuat was sometimes believed to be divided into Twelve Circles, or Spheres, but how these were arranged is not known. The seven heavens of the Babylonians were believed to be situated one above the other, and the seven hells one below the other, as in the figure here given; the thick line represents the earth. The stelae at

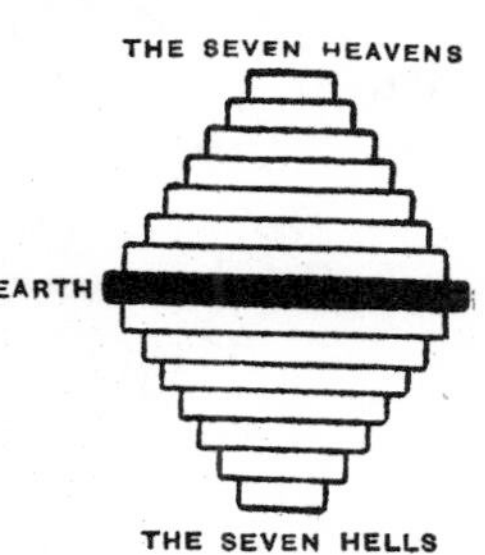

Aksûm were dedicated, I believe, to the Sun-god, like the obelisks of Egypt, but the character of the theological ideas connected with them appears to be different. Mr. Bent regarded the stelae of Aksûm as "Bethels," or "Houses of God," terminating in the firmament, in which the Sabaean Sun-god was supposed to reside, and his view is probably correct.

BIBLIOGRAPHY

'ABD AL-LATÎF. *Relation de l'Égypte*, ed. De Sacy, Paris, 1810.

AMMIANUS MARCELLINUS. *Roman History*, Bk. IV, §§ 4 ff.

ANGELIN, J. P. *Expédition du Louxor*, Paris, 1833.

ANGELLO DA BARGA, P. *P.A.B. Commentarius de obelisco*, Venetiis, 1732.

ARNAUD D'AGNEL, G. *Marseille et le second obélisque de Louqsor*, Valence, 1906.

BECK, T. *Domenico Fontana* (1543–1607) *und der Transport des Vaticanischen Obelisken*, Hannover, 1898.

BIRCH, S. *Notes upon Obelisks*, London, 1852–53.

" Obelisk of the Lateran " (*Records of the Past*, Vol. IV, pages 9 ff.).

" Observations on the obelisk of the Atmeidan at Constantinople " (*Trans. R. Soc. Lit.*, Vol. II, 1847, page 218 f.).

Translations of the Obelisks in London and New York in WEISSE, J. A. *The Obelisk and Freemasonry*, New York, 1880.

BONOMI, J. " Description of the Alnwick Obelisk " (*Trans. R. Soc. Lit.*, London, 1843, Vol. II, pages 170 ff.).

" Notes on Obelisks," *Ibid.* page 158.

BREASTED, J. H. " The Obelisks of Thothmes III " (*Aeg. Zeit.*, 1901, Bd. 39, pages 55 ff.).

Builder. " On Cleopatra's Needle," Vol. IX, pages 478 ff.

" Obelisks and their Pedestals " (*Ibid.* Vol. XXXVI, pages 55, 410).

BURTON, J. *Excerpta Hieroglyphica*, Cairo, 1825.

CHABAS, F. J. " Obelisk of Alexandria," and " Obelisk of Rameses II " (*Records of the Past*, Vol. IV, page 17; Vol. V, page 21). For the French originals, *see* Maspero, *Bibl. Égyptol.*, Tom. XI.

CHAMPOLLION, J. F. *Monuments de l'Égypte*, Tom. IV.

" De l'obélisque Égyptien de l'île de Philae " (*Revue encyclopédique*, Paris, 1822).

CHAMPOLLION-FIGEAC. Notice sur un ouvrage intitulé : *Interpretatio Obeliscorum* . . . , Paris, 1842.

COOPER, W. R. *A Short History of Egyptian Obelisks*, London, 1877.

DARESSY, G. " L'obélisque de Qaha " (*Annales du Service*, Cairo, 1920, Tom. XIX, pages 131 ff.).

On the obelisk of Rameses IV (*Annales*, Tom. IV, Cairo, 1903, page 105).

Description de l'Égypte, Paris, 1809–28, Vol. V, plates.

ENGELBACH, R. *The Aswân Obelisk*, Cairo, 1922.

The Problem of the Obelisks, London (no date).

Engineering. " The Cleopatra Needle," London, 1877–78.

ERMAN, A. " Die Obelisken der Kaiserzeit " (*Aeg. Zeit.*, 1896, Bd. 34, pages 149 ff).

FERRY, H. *L'Obélisque de Louxor*, Paris, 1868.

FONTANA, D. *Della Trasportatione dell' Obelisco Vaticano, ed delle Fabriche di Nostro Signore Papa Sisto V. Libro primo con tavole,* Roma, 1590.

GILLES, P. *De Topographia Constantinopoleos et de illius Antiquitatibus,* Libri IV, Leyden, 1562.

GORRINGE, H. H. *Egyptian Obelisks,* London, 1885.

HERMAPION. [For his Greek translation of the text of an obelisk, *see* the Roman History of Ammianus Marcellinus.]

JENNINGS, H. *The Obelisk,* London, 1877.

KING, J. *Cleopatra's Needle,* London, 1884.

LABORDE, A. L. J. *Description des Obélisques de Louqsor,* Paris, 1833.

LAUTH, F. J. " Der Obelisk in der Münchener Glyptothek " (*Aeg. Zeit.*, 1866, Bd. 4, pages 92 ff.)

LEBAS, J. B. A. *L'Obélisque de Luxor, Histoire de sa translation à Paris,* etc. (with 15 plates), Paris, 1839.

LEGRAIN, G. " Sur un fragment d'obélisque " (*Recueil,* 1901, Vol. XXIII, page 195).

L'HÔTE, N. *Notice sur les obélisques Égyptiens,* Paris, 1836.

LENOIR, A. *De l'obélisque de Louqsor,* Paris, 1834.

LEPSIUS, R. *Denkmäler,* Bd. III.

LONG, G. *The Egyptian Antiquities in the British Museum,* London, 1846.

MARUCCHI, O. *Gli obelischi Egiziani di Roma,* Rome, 1898.

MERRIAM, A. C. *The Greek and Latin inscriptions on the obelisk-crab,* etc., New York, 1883.

MOLDENKE, C. E. *The New York Obelisk*, New York, 1891.

MOSKONAS, D. *Deux mots sur les Obélisques Égyptiens*, Alexandria, 1877.

PARKER, J. H. *The Archaeology of Rome*, Chapter IV or Part IV. *The Egyptian Obelisks*, Oxford, 1876.

PELLEGRINI, A. *L'Obelisco Mediceo*, Rome, 1900.

PLINY. *Natural History*, Bk. XXXVI, 14.

ROSELLINI. *Monumenti Storici*, Pisa, 1832–44.

SALVOLINI, F. *Traduction des inscriptions sculptées sur l'obélisque Égyptien de Paris*, Paris, 1837.

SETHE, K. URKUNDEN, II, III, Leipzig, 1906 f.

SPON, J., and WHEELER, G. *Voyage d'Italie*, Lyon, 1578.

STUART, V. *Nile Gleanings*, London, 1879.

TOMLINSON, G. "On the Flaminian Obelisk" (*Trans. R. Soc. Lit.*, London, 1843, pages 176 ff.)

UNGARELLI, L. M. *Interpretatio Obeliscorum urbis ad Gregorium XVI Pont. Max.*, Rome, 1842, fol.

WILKINSON, J. G. *The Ancient Egyptians*, ed. Birch, London, 1878, 3 vols.

WILSON, ERASMUS. *Cleopatra's Needle and Egyptian Obelisks*, London, 1877.

ZABAGLIA, N. . . . *descrizione del trasporto dell' Obelisco Vaticano*, Rome, 1743.

ZOEGA, G. *De origine et usu obeliscorum*, Rome, 1797.

INDEX

In the Oriental proper names, diacritical marks are omitted. Thus "ȧ" is printed as "a," "ḥ," as "h," "ḍ" as "d," and "ṭ" as "t." Long vowels are marked with a line, *e.g.* "ā" (in Egyptian words), and with a circumflex, *e.g.* "â," "ê," "î," "û" (in Arabic words).

A CATALOG OF SELECTED

DOVER BOOKS

IN ALL FIELDS OF INTEREST

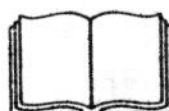

A CATALOG OF SELECTED DOVER BOOKS IN ALL FIELDS OF INTEREST

ILLUSTRATED DICTIONARY OF HISTORIC ARCHITECTURE, edited by Cyril M. Harris. Extraordinary compendium of clear, concise definitions for over 5,000 important architectural terms complemented by over 2,000 line drawings. Covers full spectrum of architecture from ancient ruins to 20th-century Modernism. Preface. 592pp. 7½ × 9⅜. 24444-X Pa. $15.95

THE NIGHT BEFORE CHRISTMAS, Clement Moore. Full text, and woodcuts from original 1848 book. Also critical, historical material. 19 illustrations. 40pp. 4⅝ × 6. 22797-9 Pa. $2.50

THE LESSON OF JAPANESE ARCHITECTURE: 165 Photographs, Jiro Harada. Memorable gallery of 165 photographs taken in the 1930's of exquisite Japanese homes of the well-to-do and historic buildings. 13 line diagrams. 192pp. 8⅜ × 11¼. 24778-3 Pa. $8.95

THE AUTOBIOGRAPHY OF CHARLES DARWIN AND SELECTED LETTERS, edited by Francis Darwin. The fascinating life of eccentric genius composed of an intimate memoir by Darwin (intended for his children); commentary by his son, Francis; hundreds of fragments from notebooks, journals, papers; and letters to and from Lyell, Hooker, Huxley, Wallace and Henslow. xi + 365pp. 5⅜ × 8. 20479-0 Pa. $6.95

WONDERS OF THE SKY: Observing Rainbows, Comets, Eclipses, the Stars and Other Phenomena, Fred Schaaf. Charming, easy-to-read poetic guide to all manner of celestial events visible to the naked eye. Mock suns, glories, Belt of Venus, more. Illustrated. 299pp. 5¼ × 8¼. 24402-4 Pa. $7.95

BURNHAM'S CELESTIAL HANDBOOK, Robert Burnham, Jr. Thorough guide to the stars beyond our solar system. Exhaustive treatment. Alphabetical by constellation: Andromeda to Cetus in Vol. 1; Chamaeleon to Orion in Vol. 2; and Pavo to Vulpecula in Vol. 3. Hundreds of illustrations. Index in Vol. 3. 2,000pp. 6⅛ × 9¼. 23567-X, 23568-8, 23673-0 Pa., Three-vol. set $38.85

STAR NAMES: Their Lore and Meaning, Richard Hinckley Allen. Fascinating history of names various cultures have given to constellations and literary and folkloristic uses that have been made of stars. Indexes to subjects. Arabic and Greek names. Biblical references. Bibliography. 563pp. 5⅜ × 8½. 21079-0 Pa. $7.95

THIRTY YEARS THAT SHOOK PHYSICS: The Story of Quantum Theory, George Gamow. Lucid, accessible introduction to influential theory of energy and matter. Careful explanations of Dirac's anti-particles, Bohr's model of the atom, much more. 12 plates. Numerous drawings. 240pp. 5⅜ × 8½. 24895-X Pa. $5.95

CHINESE DOMESTIC FURNITURE IN PHOTOGRAPHS AND MEASURED DRAWINGS, Gustav Ecke. A rare volume, now affordably priced for antique collectors, furniture buffs and art historians. Detailed review of styles ranging from early Shang to late Ming. Unabridged republication. 161 black-and-white drawings, photos. Total of 224pp. 8⅜ × 11¼. (Available in U.S. only) 25171-3 Pa. $12.95

VINCENT VAN GOGH: A Biography, Julius Meier-Graefe. Dynamic, penetrating study of artist's life, relationship with brother, Theo, painting techniques, travels, more. Readable, engrossing. 160pp. 5⅜ × 8½. (Available in U.S. only) 25253-1 Pa. $3.95

HOW TO WRITE, Gertrude Stein. Gertrude Stein claimed anyone could understand her unconventional writing—here are clues to help. Fascinating improvisations, language experiments, explanations illuminate Stein's craft and the art of writing. Total of 414pp. 4⅜ × 6⅜. 23144-5 Pa. $5.95

ADVENTURES AT SEA IN THE GREAT AGE OF SAIL: Five Firsthand Narratives, edited by Elliot Snow. Rare true accounts of exploration, whaling, shipwreck, fierce natives, trade, shipboard life, more. 33 illustrations. Introduction. 353pp. 5⅜ × 8½. 25177-2 Pa. $7.95

THE HERBAL OR GENERAL HISTORY OF PLANTS, John Gerard. Classic descriptions of about 2,850 plants—with over 2,700 illustrations—includes Latin and English names, physical descriptions, varieties, time and place of growth, more. 2,706 illustrations. xlv + 1,678pp. 8½ × 12¼. 23147-X Cloth. $75.00

DOROTHY AND THE WIZARD IN OZ, L. Frank Baum. Dorothy and the Wizard visit the center of the Earth, where people are vegetables, glass houses grow and Oz characters reappear. Classic sequel to *Wizard of Oz*. 256pp. 5⅜ × 8. 24714-7 Pa. $4.95

SONGS OF EXPERIENCE: Facsimile Reproduction with 26 Plates in Full Color, William Blake. This facsimile of Blake's original "Illuminated Book" reproduces 26 full-color plates from a rare 1826 edition. Includes "The Tyger," "London," "Holy Thursday," and other immortal poems. 26 color plates. Printed text of poems. 48pp. 5¼ × 7. 24636-1 Pa. $3.50

SONGS OF INNOCENCE, William Blake. The first and most popular of Blake's famous "Illuminated Books," in a facsimile edition reproducing all 31 brightly colored plates. Additional printed text of each poem. 64pp. 5¼ × 7. 22764-2 Pa. $3.50

PRECIOUS STONES, Max Bauer. Classic, thorough study of diamonds, rubies, emeralds, garnets, etc.: physical character, occurrence, properties, use, similar topics. 20 plates, 8 in color. 94 figures. 659pp. 6⅛ × 9¼. 21910-0, 21911-9 Pa., Two-vol. set $15.90

ENCYCLOPEDIA OF VICTORIAN NEEDLEWORK, S. F. A. Caulfeild and Blanche Saward. Full, precise descriptions of stitches, techniques for dozens of needlecrafts—most exhaustive reference of its kind. Over 800 figures. Total of 679pp. 8⅛ × 11. Two volumes. Vol. 1 22800-2 Pa. $11.95
Vol. 2 22801-0 Pa. $11.95

THE MARVELOUS LAND OF OZ, L. Frank Baum. Second Oz book, the Scarecrow and Tin Woodman are back with hero named Tip, Oz magic. 136 illustrations. 287pp. 5⅜ × 8½. 20692-0 Pa. $5.95

WILD FOWL DECOYS, Joel Barber. Basic book on the subject, by foremost authority and collector. Reveals history of decoy making and rigging, place in American culture, different kinds of decoys, how to make them, and how to use them. 140 plates. 156pp. 7⅞ × 10¾. 20011-6 Pa. $8.95

HISTORY OF LACE, Mrs. Bury Palliser. Definitive, profusely illustrated chronicle of lace from earliest times to late 19th century. Laces of Italy, Greece, England, France, Belgium, etc. Landmark of needlework scholarship. 266 illustrations. 672pp. 6⅛ × 9¼. 24742-2 Pa. $14.95

ILLUSTRATED GUIDE TO SHAKER FURNITURE, Robert Meader. All furniture and appurtenances, with much on unknown local styles. 235 photos. 146pp. 9 × 12. 22819-3 Pa. $7.95

WHALE SHIPS AND WHALING: A Pictorial Survey, George Francis Dow. Over 200 vintage engravings, drawings, photographs of barks, brigs, cutters, other vessels. Also harpoons, lances, whaling guns, many other artifacts. Comprehensive text by foremost authority. 207 black-and-white illustrations. 288pp. 6 × 9. 24808-9 Pa. $8.95

THE BERTRAMS, Anthony Trollope. Powerful portrayal of blind self-will and thwarted ambition includes one of Trollope's most heartrending love stories. 497pp. 5⅜ × 8½. 25119-5 Pa. $9.95

ADVENTURES WITH A HAND LENS, Richard Headstrom. Clearly written guide to observing and studying flowers and grasses, fish scales, moth and insect wings, egg cases, buds, feathers, seeds, leaf scars, moss, molds, ferns, common crystals, etc.—all with an ordinary, inexpensive magnifying glass. 209 exact line drawings aid in your discoveries. 220pp. 5⅜ × 8½. 23330-8 Pa. $4.95

RODIN ON ART AND ARTISTS, Auguste Rodin. Great sculptor's candid, wide-ranging comments on meaning of art; great artists; relation of sculpture to poetry, painting, music; philosophy of life, more. 76 superb black-and-white illustrations of Rodin's sculpture, drawings and prints. 119pp. 8⅝ × 11¼. 24487-3 Pa. $6.95

FIFTY CLASSIC FRENCH FILMS, 1912–1982: A Pictorial Record, Anthony Slide. Memorable stills from Grand Illusion, Beauty and the Beast, Hiroshima, Mon Amour, many more. Credits, plot synopses, reviews, etc. 160pp. 8¼ × 11. 25256-6 Pa. $11.95

THE PRINCIPLES OF PSYCHOLOGY, William James. Famous long course complete, unabridged. Stream of thought, time perception, memory, experimental methods; great work decades ahead of its time. 94 figures. 1,391pp. 5⅜ × 8½. 20381-6, 20382-4 Pa., Two-vol. set $23.90

BODIES IN A BOOKSHOP, R. T. Campbell. Challenging mystery of blackmail and murder with ingenious plot and superbly drawn characters. In the best tradition of British suspense fiction. 192pp. 5⅜ × 8½. 24720-1 Pa. $3.95

CALLAS: PORTRAIT OF A PRIMA DONNA, George Jellinek. Renowned commentator on the musical scene chronicles incredible career and life of the most controversial, fascinating, influential operatic personality of our time. 64 black-and-white photographs. 416pp. 5⅜ × 8¼. 25047-4 Pa. $8.95

GEOMETRY, RELATIVITY AND THE FOURTH DIMENSION, Rudolph Rucker. Exposition of fourth dimension, concepts of relativity as Flatland characters continue adventures. Popular, easily followed yet accurate, profound. 141 illustrations. 133pp. 5⅜ × 8½. 23400-2 Pa. $3.95

HOUSEHOLD STORIES BY THE BROTHERS GRIMM, with pictures by Walter Crane. 53 classic stories—Rumpelstiltskin, Rapunzel, Hansel and Gretel, the Fisherman and his Wife, Snow White, Tom Thumb, Sleeping Beauty, Cinderella, and so much more—lavishly illustrated with original 19th century drawings. 114 illustrations. x + 269pp. 5⅜ × 8½. 21080-4 Pa. $4.95

SUNDIALS, Albert Waugh. Far and away the best, most thorough coverage of ideas, mathematics concerned, types, construction, adjusting anywhere. Over 100 illustrations. 230pp. 5⅜ × 8½. 22947-5 Pa. $4.95

PICTURE HISTORY OF THE NORMANDIE: With 190 Illustrations, Frank O. Braynard. Full story of legendary French ocean liner: Art Deco interiors, design innovations, furnishings, celebrities, maiden voyage, tragic fire, much more. Extensive text. 144pp. 8⅞ × 11¾. 25257-4 Pa. $9.95

THE FIRST AMERICAN COOKBOOK: A Facsimile of "American Cookery," 1796, Amelia Simmons. Facsimile of the first American-written cookbook published in the United States contains authentic recipes for colonial favorites—pumpkin pudding, winter squash pudding, spruce beer, Indian slapjacks, and more. Introductory Essay and Glossary of colonial cooking terms. 80pp. 5⅜ × 8½. 24710-4 Pa. $3.50

101 PUZZLES IN THOUGHT AND LOGIC, C. R. Wylie, Jr. Solve murders and robberies, find out which fishermen are liars, how a blind man could possibly identify a color—purely by your own reasoning! 107pp. 5⅜ × 8½. 20367-0 Pa. $2.50

THE BOOK OF WORLD-FAMOUS MUSIC—CLASSICAL, POPULAR AND FOLK, James J. Fuld. Revised and enlarged republication of landmark work in musico-bibliography. Full information about nearly 1,000 songs and compositions including first lines of music and lyrics. New supplement. Index. 800pp. 5⅜ × 8¼. 24857-7 Pa. $14.95

ANTHROPOLOGY AND MODERN LIFE, Franz Boas. Great anthropologist's classic treatise on race and culture. Introduction by Ruth Bunzel. Only inexpensive paperback edition. 255pp. 5⅜ × 8½. 25245-0 Pa. $5.95

THE TALE OF PETER RABBIT, Beatrix Potter. The inimitable Peter's terrifying adventure in Mr. McGregor's garden, with all 27 wonderful, full-color Potter illustrations. 55pp. 4¼ × 5½. (Available in U.S. only) 22827-4 Pa. $1.75

THREE PROPHETIC SCIENCE FICTION NOVELS, H. G. Wells. *When the Sleeper Wakes, A Story of the Days to Come* and *The Time Machine* (full version). 335pp. 5⅜ × 8½. (Available in U.S. only) 20605-X Pa. $6.95

APICIUS COOKERY AND DINING IN IMPERIAL ROME, edited and translated by Joseph Dommers Vehling. Oldest known cookbook in existence offers readers a clear picture of what foods Romans ate, how they prepared them, etc. 49 illustrations. 301pp. 6⅛ × 9¼. 23563-7 Pa. $7.95

SHAKESPEARE LEXICON AND QUOTATION DICTIONARY, Alexander Schmidt. Full definitions, locations, shades of meaning of every word in plays and poems. More than 50,000 exact quotations. 1,485pp. 6½ × 9¼. 22726-X, 22727-8 Pa., Two-vol. set $29.90

THE WORLD'S GREAT SPEECHES, edited by Lewis Copeland and Lawrence W. Lamm. Vast collection of 278 speeches from Greeks to 1970. Powerful and effective models; unique look at history. 842pp. 5⅜ × 8½. 20468-5 Pa. $11.95

THE BLUE FAIRY BOOK, Andrew Lang. The first, most famous collection, with many familiar tales: Little Red Riding Hood, Aladdin and the Wonderful Lamp, Puss in Boots, Sleeping Beauty, Hansel and Gretel, Rumpelstiltskin; 37 in all. 138 illustrations. 390pp. 5⅜ × 8½. 21437-0 Pa. $6.95

THE STORY OF THE CHAMPIONS OF THE ROUND TABLE, Howard Pyle. Sir Launcelot, Sir Tristram and Sir Percival in spirited adventures of love and triumph retold in Pyle's inimitable style. 50 drawings, 31 full-page. xviii + 329pp. 6½ × 9¼. 21883-X Pa. $6.95

AUDUBON AND HIS JOURNALS, Maria Audubon. Unmatched two-volume portrait of the great artist, naturalist and author contains his journals, an excellent biography by his granddaughter, expert annotations by the noted ornithologist, Dr. Elliott Coues, and 37 superb illustrations. Total of 1,200pp. 5⅜ × 8.
Vol. I 25143-8 Pa. $8.95
Vol. II 25144-6 Pa. $8.95

GREAT DINOSAUR HUNTERS AND THEIR DISCOVERIES, Edwin H. Colbert. Fascinating, lavishly illustrated chronicle of dinosaur research, 1820's to 1960. Achievements of Cope, Marsh, Brown, Buckland, Mantell, Huxley, many others. 384pp. 5¼ × 8¼. 24701-5 Pa. $7.95

THE TASTEMAKERS, Russell Lynes. Informal, illustrated social history of American taste 1850's–1950's. First popularized categories Highbrow, Lowbrow, Middlebrow. 129 illustrations. New (1979) afterword. 384pp. 6 × 9.
23993-4 Pa. $8.95

DOUBLE CROSS PURPOSES, Ronald A. Knox. A treasure hunt in the Scottish Highlands, an old map, unidentified corpse, surprise discoveries keep reader guessing in this cleverly intricate tale of financial skullduggery. 2 black-and-white maps. 320pp. 5⅜ × 8½. (Available in U.S. only) 25032-6 Pa. $5.95

AUTHENTIC VICTORIAN DECORATION AND ORNAMENTATION IN FULL COLOR: 46 Plates from "Studies in Design," Christopher Dresser. Superb full-color lithographs reproduced from rare original portfolio of a major Victorian designer. 48pp. 9¼ × 12¼. 25083-0 Pa. $7.95

PRIMITIVE ART, Franz Boas. Remains the best text ever prepared on subject, thoroughly discussing Indian, African, Asian, Australian, and, especially, Northern American primitive art. Over 950 illustrations show ceramics, masks, totem poles, weapons, textiles, paintings, much more. 376pp. 5⅜ × 8. 20025-6 Pa. $6.95

SIDELIGHTS ON RELATIVITY, Albert Einstein. Unabridged republication of two lectures delivered by the great physicist in 1920–21. *Ether and Relativity* and *Geometry and Experience*. Elegant ideas in non-mathematical form, accessible to intelligent layman. vi + 56pp. 5⅜ × 8½. 24511-X Pa. $2.95

THE WIT AND HUMOR OF OSCAR WILDE, edited by Alvin Redman. More than 1,000 ripostes, paradoxes, wisecracks: Work is the curse of the drinking classes, I can resist everything except temptation, etc. 258pp. 5⅜ × 8½. 20602-5 Pa. $4.50

ADVENTURES WITH A MICROSCOPE, Richard Headstrom. 59 adventures with clothing fibers, protozoa, ferns and lichens, roots and leaves, much more. 142 illustrations. 232pp. 5⅜ × 8½. 23471-1 Pa. $3.95

PLANTS OF THE BIBLE, Harold N. Moldenke and Alma L. Moldenke. Standard reference to all 230 plants mentioned in Scriptures. Latin name, biblical reference, uses, modern identity, much more. Unsurpassed encyclopedic resource for scholars, botanists, nature lovers, students of Bible. Bibliography. Indexes. 123 black-and-white illustrations. 384pp. 6 × 9. 25069-5 Pa. $8.95

FAMOUS AMERICAN WOMEN: A Biographical Dictionary from Colonial Times to the Present, Robert McHenry, ed. From Pocahontas to Rosa Parks, 1,035 distinguished American women documented in separate biographical entries. Accurate, up-to-date data, numerous categories, spans 400 years. Indices. 493pp. 6½ × 9¼. 24523-3 Pa. $9.95

THE FABULOUS INTERIORS OF THE GREAT OCEAN LINERS IN HISTORIC PHOTOGRAPHS, William H. Miller, Jr. Some 200 superb photographs capture exquisite interiors of world's great "floating palaces"—1890's to 1980's: *Titanic, Ile de France, Queen Elizabeth, United States, Europa,* more. Approx. 200 black-and-white photographs. Captions. Text. Introduction. 160pp. 8⅞ × 11¾. 24756-2 Pa. $9.95

THE GREAT LUXURY LINERS, 1927–1954: A Photographic Record, William H. Miller, Jr. Nostalgic tribute to heyday of ocean liners. 186 photos of Ile de France, Normandie, Leviathan, Queen Elizabeth, United States, many others. Interior and exterior views. Introduction. Captions. 160pp. 9 × 12. 24056-8 Pa. $10.95

A NATURAL HISTORY OF THE DUCKS, John Charles Phillips. Great landmark of ornithology offers complete detailed coverage of nearly 200 species and subspecies of ducks: gadwall, sheldrake, merganser, pintail, many more. 74 full-color plates, 102 black-and-white. Bibliography. Total of 1,920pp. 8⅝ × 11¼. 25141-1, 25142-X Cloth. Two-vol. set $100.00

THE SEAWEED HANDBOOK: An Illustrated Guide to Seaweeds from North Carolina to Canada, Thomas F. Lee. Concise reference covers 78 species. Scientific and common names, habitat, distribution, more. Finding keys for easy identification. 224pp. 5⅜ × 8½. 25215-9 Pa. $5.95

THE TEN BOOKS OF ARCHITECTURE: The 1755 Leoni Edition, Leon Battista Alberti. Rare classic helped introduce the glories of ancient architecture to the Renaissance. 68 black-and-white plates. 336pp. 8⅜ × 11¼. 25239-6 Pa. $14.95

MISS MACKENZIE, Anthony Trollope. Minor masterpieces by Victorian master unmasks many truths about life in 19th-century England. First inexpensive edition in years. 392pp. 5⅜ × 8½. 25201-9 Pa. $7.95

THE RIME OF THE ANCIENT MARINER, Gustave Doré, Samuel Taylor Coleridge. Dramatic engravings considered by many to be his greatest work. The terrifying space of the open sea, the storms and whirlpools of an unknown ocean, the ice of Antarctica, more—all rendered in a powerful, chilling manner. Full text. 38 plates. 77pp. 9¼ × 12. 22305-1 Pa. $4.95

THE EXPEDITIONS OF ZEBULON MONTGOMERY PIKE, Zebulon Montgomery Pike. Fascinating first-hand accounts (1805–6) of exploration of Mississippi River, Indian wars, capture by Spanish dragoons, much more. 1,088pp. 5⅜ × 8½. 25254-X, 25255-8 Pa. Two-vol. set $23.90

DEGAS: An Intimate Portrait, Ambroise Vollard. Charming, anecdotal memoir by famous art dealer of one of the greatest 19th-century French painters. 14 black-and-white illustrations. Introduction by Harold L. Van Doren. 96pp. 5⅜ × 8½.
25131-4 Pa. $3.95

PERSONAL NARRATIVE OF A PILGRIMAGE TO ALMANDINAH AND MECCAH, Richard Burton. Great travel classic by remarkably colorful personality. Burton, disguised as a Moroccan, visited sacred shrines of Islam, narrowly escaping death. 47 illustrations. 959pp. 5⅜ × 8½. 21217-3, 21218-1 Pa., Two-vol. set $19.90

PHRASE AND WORD ORIGINS, A. H. Holt. Entertaining, reliable, modern study of more than 1,200 colorful words, phrases, origins and histories. Much unexpected information. 254pp. 5⅜ × 8½. 20758-7 Pa. $5.95

THE RED THUMB MARK, R. Austin Freeman. In this first Dr. Thorndyke case, the great scientific detective draws fascinating conclusions from the nature of a single fingerprint. Exciting story, authentic science. 320pp. 5⅜ × 8½. (Available in U.S. only) 25210-8 Pa. $5.95

AN EGYPTIAN HIEROGLYPHIC DICTIONARY, E. A. Wallis Budge. Monumental work containing about 25,000 words or terms that occur in texts ranging from 3000 B.C. to 600 A.D. Each entry consists of a transliteration of the word, the word in hieroglyphs, and the meaning in English. 1,314pp. 6⅞ × 10.
23615-3, 23616-1 Pa., Two-vol. set $31.90

THE COMPLEAT STRATEGYST: Being a Primer on the Theory of Games of Strategy, J. D. Williams. Highly entertaining classic describes, with many illustrated examples, how to select best strategies in conflict situations. Prefaces. Appendices. xvi + 268pp. 5⅜ × 8½. 25101-2 Pa. $5.95

THE ROAD TO OZ, L. Frank Baum. Dorothy meets the Shaggy Man, little Button-Bright and the Rainbow's beautiful daughter in this delightful trip to the magical Land of Oz. 272pp. 5⅜ × 8. 25208-6 Pa. $4.95

POINT AND LINE TO PLANE, Wassily Kandinsky. Seminal exposition of role of point, line, other elements in non-objective painting. Essential to understanding 20th-century art. 127 illustrations. 192pp. 6½ × 9¼. 23808-3 Pa. $4.95

LADY ANNA, Anthony Trollope. Moving chronicle of Countess Lovel's bitter struggle to win for herself and daughter Anna their rightful rank and fortune—perhaps at cost of sanity itself. 384pp. 5⅜ × 8½. 24669-8 Pa. $8.95

EGYPTIAN MAGIC, E. A. Wallis Budge. Sums up all that is known about magic in Ancient Egypt: the role of magic in controlling the gods, powerful amulets that warded off evil spirits, scarabs of immortality, use of wax images, formulas and spells, the secret name, much more. 253pp. 5⅜ × 8½. 22681-6 Pa. $4.50

THE DANCE OF SIVA, Ananda Coomaraswamy. Preeminent authority unfolds the vast metaphysic of India: the revelation of her art, conception of the universe, social organization, etc. 27 reproductions of art masterpieces. 192pp. 5⅜ × 8½.
24817-8 Pa. $5.95

CHRISTMAS CUSTOMS AND TRADITIONS, Clement A. Miles. Origin, evolution, significance of religious, secular practices. Caroling, gifts, yule logs, much more. Full, scholarly yet fascinating; non-sectarian. 400pp. 5⅜ × 8½.
23354-5 Pa. $6.50

THE HUMAN FIGURE IN MOTION, Eadweard Muybridge. More than 4,500 stopped-action photos, in action series, showing undraped men, women, children jumping, lying down, throwing, sitting, wrestling, carrying, etc. 390pp. 7⅞ × 10⅝.
20204-6 Cloth. $21.95

THE MAN WHO WAS THURSDAY, Gilbert Keith Chesterton. Witty, fast-paced novel about a club of anarchists in turn-of-the-century London. Brilliant social, religious, philosophical speculations. 128pp. 5⅜ × 8½. 25121-7 Pa. $3.95

A CEZANNE SKETCHBOOK: Figures, Portraits, Landscapes and Still Lifes, Paul Cezanne. Great artist experiments with tonal effects, light, mass, other qualities in over 100 drawings. A revealing view of developing master painter, precursor of Cubism. 102 black-and-white illustrations. 144pp. 8¾ × 6⅜. 24790-2 Pa. $5.95

AN ENCYCLOPEDIA OF BATTLES: Accounts of Over 1,560 Battles from 1479 B.C. to the Present, David Eggenberger. Presents essential details of every major battle in recorded history, from the first battle of Megiddo in 1479 B.C. to Grenada in 1984. List of Battle Maps. New Appendix covering the years 1967–1984. Index. 99 illustrations. 544pp. 6½ × 9¼. 24913-1 Pa. $14.95

AN ETYMOLOGICAL DICTIONARY OF MODERN ENGLISH, Ernest Weekley. Richest, fullest work, by foremost British lexicographer. Detailed word histories. Inexhaustible. Total of 856pp. 6½ × 9¼.
21873-2, 21874-0 Pa., Two-vol. set $17.00

WEBSTER'S AMERICAN MILITARY BIOGRAPHIES, edited by Robert McHenry. Over 1,000 figures who shaped 3 centuries of American military history. Detailed biographies of Nathan Hale, Douglas MacArthur, Mary Hallaren, others. Chronologies of engagements, more. Introduction. Addenda. 1,033 entries in alphabetical order. xi + 548pp. 6½ × 9¼. (Available in U.S. only)
24758-9 Pa. $11.95

LIFE IN ANCIENT EGYPT, Adolf Erman. Detailed older account, with much not in more recent books: domestic life, religion, magic, medicine, commerce, and whatever else needed for complete picture. Many illustrations. 597pp. 5⅜ × 8½.
22632-8 Pa. $8.95

HISTORIC COSTUME IN PICTURES, Braun & Schneider. Over 1,450 costumed figures shown, covering a wide variety of peoples: kings, emperors, nobles, priests, servants, soldiers, scholars, townsfolk, peasants, merchants, courtiers, cavaliers, and more. 256pp. 8⅜ × 11¼. 23150-X Pa. $8.95

THE NOTEBOOKS OF LEONARDO DA VINCI, edited by J. P. Richter. Extracts from manuscripts reveal great genius; on painting, sculpture, anatomy, sciences, geography, etc. Both Italian and English. 186 ms. pages reproduced, plus 500 additional drawings, including studies for *Last Supper, Sforza* monument, etc. 860pp. 7⅞ × 10¾. (Available in U.S. only) 22572-0, 22573-9 Pa., Two-vol. set $29.90

SIR HARRY HOTSPUR OF HUMBLETHWAITE, Anthony Trollope. Incisive, unconventional psychological study of a conflict between a wealthy baronet, his idealistic daughter, and their scapegrace cousin. The 1870 novel in its first inexpensive edition in years. 250pp. 5⅜ × 8½. 24953-0 Pa. $5.95

LASERS AND HOLOGRAPHY, Winston E. Kock. Sound introduction to burgeoning field, expanded (1981) for second edition. Wave patterns, coherence, lasers, diffraction, zone plates, properties of holograms, recent advances. 84 illustrations. 160pp. 5⅜ × 8¼. (Except in United Kingdom) 24041-X Pa. $3.50

INTRODUCTION TO ARTIFICIAL INTELLIGENCE: SECOND, ENLARGED EDITION, Philip C. Jackson, Jr. Comprehensive survey of artificial intelligence—the study of how machines (computers) can be made to act intelligently. Includes introductory and advanced material. Extensive notes updating the main text. 132 black-and-white illustrations. 512pp. 5⅜ × 8½. 24864-X Pa. $8.95

HISTORY OF INDIAN AND INDONESIAN ART, Ananda K. Coomaraswamy. Over 400 illustrations illuminate classic study of Indian art from earliest Harappa finds to early 20th century. Provides philosophical, religious and social insights. 304pp. 6⅝ × 9⅝. 25005-9 Pa. $8.95

THE GOLEM, Gustav Meyrink. Most famous supernatural novel in modern European literature, set in Ghetto of Old Prague around 1890. Compelling story of mystical experiences, strange transformations, profound terror. 13 black-and-white illustrations. 224pp. 5⅜ × 8½. (Available in U.S. only) 25025-3 Pa. $6.95

ARMADALE, Wilkie Collins. Third great mystery novel by the author of *The Woman in White* and *The Moonstone*. Original magazine version with 40 illustrations. 597pp. 5⅜ × 8½. 23429-0 Pa. $9.95

PICTORIAL ENCYCLOPEDIA OF HISTORIC ARCHITECTURAL PLANS, DETAILS AND ELEMENTS: With 1,880 Line Drawings of Arches, Domes, Doorways, Facades, Gables, Windows, etc., John Theodore Haneman. Sourcebook of inspiration for architects, designers, others. Bibliography. Captions. 141pp. 9 × 12. 24605-1 Pa. $6.95

BENCHLEY LOST AND FOUND, Robert Benchley. Finest humor from early 30's, about pet peeves, child psychologists, post office and others. Mostly unavailable elsewhere. 73 illustrations by Peter Arno and others. 183pp. 5⅜ × 8½. 22410-4 Pa. $3.95

ERTÉ GRAPHICS, Erté. Collection of striking color graphics: *Seasons, Alphabet, Numerals, Aces* and *Precious Stones*. 50 plates, including 4 on covers. 48pp. 9⅜ × 12¼. 23580-7 Pa. $6.95

THE JOURNAL OF HENRY D. THOREAU, edited by Bradford Torrey, F. H. Allen. Complete reprinting of 14 volumes, 1837–61, over two million words; the sourcebooks for *Walden*, etc. Definitive. All original sketches, plus 75 photographs. 1,804pp. 8½ × 12¼. 20312-3, 20313-1 Cloth., Two-vol. set $80.00

CASTLES: THEIR CONSTRUCTION AND HISTORY, Sidney Toy. Traces castle development from ancient roots. Nearly 200 photographs and drawings illustrate moats, keeps, baileys, many other features. Caernarvon, Dover Castles, Hadrian's Wall, Tower of London, dozens more. 256pp. 5⅜ × 8¼. 24898-4 Pa. $5.95